Edinburgh Textbooks in Applied Linguistics
Series Editors: Alan Davies and Keith Mitchell

Materials Evaluation and Design for Language Teaching

D1434878

Ian McGrath

Edinburgh University Press

To Natasha,
with my thanks for her unfailing support.

© Ian McGrath, 2002

Edinburgh University Press Ltd
22 George Square, Edinburgh

Reprinted 2005

Typeset in Garamond
by Pioneer Associates, Perthshire, and
printed and bound in Great Britain by
MPG Books Ltd, Bodmin

A CIP record for this book is available from
the British Library

ISBN 0 7486 1330 7 (paperback)

The right of Ian McGrath
to be identified as author of this work
has been asserted in accordance with
the Copyright, Designs and Patents Act 1988.

Contents

Edinburgh Textbooks in Applied Linguistics

Titles in the series include:

An Introduction to Applied Linguistics
From Practice to Theory
by Alan Davies

Teaching Literature in a Second Language
by Brian Parkinson & Helen Reid Thomas

Materials Evaluation and Design for Language Teaching
by Ian McGrath

Series Editors' Preface

This new series of single-author volumes published by Edinburgh University Press takes a contemporary view of applied linguistics. The intention is to make provision for the wide range of interests in contemporary applied linguistics which are provided for at the Master's level.

The expansion of Master's postgraduate courses in recent years has had two effects:

1. What began almost half a century ago as a wholly cross-disciplinary subject has found a measure of coherence so that now most training courses in Applied Linguistics have similar core content.
2. At the same time the range of specialisms has grown, as in any developing discipline. Training courses (and professional needs) vary in the extent to which these specialisms are included and taught.

Some volumes in the series will address the first development noted above, while the others will explore the second. It is hoped that the series as a whole will provide students beginning postgraduate courses in Applied Linguistics, as well as language teachers and other professionals wishing to become acquainted with the subject, with a sufficient introduction for them to develop their own thinking in applied linguistics and to build further into specialist areas of their own choosing.

The view taken of applied linguistics in the Edinburgh Textbooks in Applied Linguistics Series is that of a theorising approach to practical experience in the language professions, notably, but not exclusively, those concerned with language learning and teaching. It is concerned with the problems, the processes, the mechanisms and the purposes of language in use.

Like any other applied discipline, applied linguistics draws on theories from related disciplines with which it explores the professional experience of its practitioners and which in turn are themselves illuminated by that experience. This two-way relationship between theory and practice is what we mean by a theorising discipline.

The volumes in the series are all premised on this view of Applied

Linguistics as a theorising discipline which is developing its own coherence. At the same time, in order to present as complete a contemporary view of applied linguistics as possible other approaches will occasionally be expressed.

Each volume presents its author's own view of the state of the art in his or her topic. Volumes will be similar in length and in format, and, as is usual in a textbook series, each will contain exercise material for use in class or in private study.

Alan Davies
W. Keith Mitchell

Acknowledgements

Over the years, I have been lucky in my teachers, in my professional colleagues, in my co-authors, in my editors, and in my students (among them language teachers following Master's programmes in Edinburgh, Nottingham and Hong Kong). Some are named in the text. Others know who they are, and, with a small number of exceptions, it would be invidious to single out individuals. This is, however, a suitable opportunity to thank Philip Prowse for inviting me to become a co-writer on a coursebook series, for what I learned from that and subsequent collaborations, and for his friendship over the last twenty years. I am grateful to Alan Davies and Keith Mitchell, editors of the series in which the present book appears, for their belief in this project and their patience during an extended gestation period. And I owe a particular debt of thanks to Andy Morrall for his help with the Internet section of Chapter 6. Such deficiencies as remain in that chapter and elsewhere are, of course, my own.

This is also an appropriate place to thank the publishers who responded to my request for sample copies of materials by generously supplying the books (and many more) on which I have drawn for examples. Addison Wesley Longman, Macmillan/Heinemann, Oxford – my sincere thanks.

Grateful acknowledgement is made to the following sources for permission to reproduce material previously published elsewhere. Every effort has been made to trace the copyright holders, but if any have been inadvertently overlooked, the publisher will be pleased to make the necessary arrangements at the first opportunity.

Fig. I: Brumfit and Rossner, 'The "decision pyramid" and teacher training for ELT', in *ELT Journal* Vol. 36, No. 4 (1982) by permission of Oxford University Press.

Table 2.1 and App. 2.3: Littlejohn (1998) 'The analysis of language teaching materials: inside the Trojan horse', in Tomlinson (ed.) (1998) *Materials Development in Language Teaching* by permission of Cambridge University Press.

Figs 4.1, 4.7, 9.8 and App. 2.4E: Cunningsworth (1995) *Choosing Your*

Coursebook, Macmillan Heinemann. Reprinted by permission of Macmillan Oxford.

Fig. 4.2: Swan and Walter (1984) *Cambridge English Coursebook I* by permission of Cambridge University Press.

Fig. 4.3: Ur (1996) *A Course in Language Teaching* by permission of Cambridge University Press.

Task 4.8: Prodromou (1990) 'A mixed ability lesson', in *Practical English Teaching*, 10.3 © Mary Glasgow Magazines/Scholastic, pp. 28–9.

Table 5.1 and App. 5.1: Acklam (1994) 'The role of the coursebook', in *Practical English Teaching*, 14.3 © Mary Glasgow Magazines/Scholastic, pp. 12 and 14.

Fig. 5.1: Naunton (1996) *Think First Certificate*, © Longman Group UK Limited/Addison Wesley Longman 1996, reprinted by permission of Pearson Education Limited.

Figs 5.2, 9.6, 9.7 and App. 5.2: Jolly and Bolitho (1998) 'A framework for materials writing', in Tomlinson (ed.) 1998, *Materials Development in Language Teaching* by permission of Cambridge University Press.

Fig. 7.1: McGrath (1992) 'The ideas grid', in *Practical English Teaching*, 12.4 © Mary Glasgow Magazines/Scholastic, pp. 13–14.

Fig. 7.4: Scott et al, 'Using a "standard exercise" in teaching reading comprehension', in *ELT Journal* Vol. 38, No. 2 (1984) by permission of Oxford University Press.

Fig. 7.5 and App. 7.5: Axbey (1989) 'Standard exercises in self-access learning' by permission of the author.

Fig. 7.6: Hutchinson and Waters (1987) *English for Specific Purposes: A Learning-centred Approach* by permission of Cambridge University Press.

Extract pp. 172–3: Assinder, 'Peer teaching, peer learning: one model', in *ELT Journal* Vol. 45, No. 3 (1991) by permission of Oxford University Press.

Fig. 9.2: Ellis (1998) 'The evaluation of communicative tasks' in Tomlinson (ed.) (1998) *Materials Development in Language Teaching* by permission of Cambridge University Press.

Fig. 9.4 and App. 3.3C: Spencer and Vaughan (1999) *Team Player 4*, Macmillan Heinemann. Reprinted by permission of Macmillan Oxford.

App. 2.1: catalogue excerpts reproduced by permission of Cambridge University Press, Macmillan Heinemann and Pearson.

App. 2.4A: Tucker (1975) 'Evaluating beginning textbooks', in *English Teaching Forum* by permission of the publishers.

App. 2.4B: Williams, 'Developing criteria for textbook evaluation', in *ELT Journal* Vol. 37, No. 3 (1983) by permission of Oxford University Press.

App. 2.4C: Sheldon, 'Evaluating ELT textbooks and materials', in *ELT Journal* Vol. 42, No. 4 (1988) by permission of Oxford University Press.

Apps 3.3A, 5.3D, E and G: Gershon and Mares (1995) *On Line (Workbook)*, Macmillan Heinemann. Reprinted by permission of Macmillan Oxford.

App. 3.3B: Etherton et al. (1997) *Easy English 1B* by permission of Oxford

University Press (China) Ltd.

Apps 3.3D, 4.1A and 9B: Helgesen et al. (1999) *English Firsthand 1* by permission of Longman Asia ELT.

Apps 3.3F and 4.1B: Cunningham and Moor, 1998, *Cutting Edge Intermediate*, © Addison Wesley Longman Ltd 1999, reprinted by permission of Pearson Education Limited.

Apps 4.1D, 5.3K and N: Etherton and Kingston (1999) *Oxford Certificate English 4* by permission of Oxford University Press (China) Ltd.

App. 4.1E: Kniveton and Llanas (1995) *Kid's Club 4 (Activity Book)*, Macmillan Heinemann. Reprinted by permission of Macmillan Oxford.

App. 4.1F: Etherton and Kingston (1999) *Oxford Certificate English 5* by permission of Oxford University Press (China) Ltd.

Apps 5.3C, J and L: McGrath and Prowse (1993), *Intermediate Grammar Helpline* by permission of the authors.

Apps 5.3F and M: Greenall (1997) *Reward Elementary*, Macmillan Heinemann. Reprinted by permission of Macmillan Oxford.

Apps 5.3H and I: Ellis and Gaies (1999) *Impact Grammar* by permission of Longman Asia ELT.

App. 5.4A: Mauer and Schonberg (1999) *True Colours*, reprinted by permission of Pearson Education, Inc., White Plains, New York

Apps 5.4C, G and J: McGrath and Prowse (1987) *Extensions* by permission of the authors.

Apps 5.4D and 6.1A: Taylor et al. (1994) *Reflections* by permission of the authors.

Apps 5.4E, F and 9A: Prowse and McGrath (1984) *Advances* by permission of the authors.

App. 6.1B: Day and Yamanaka (1996) *Impact Issues* by permission of Longman Asia ELT.

App. 7.2: Walker, 'Individualising reading' in *ELT Journal* Vol. 41, No. 1 (1987) by permission of Oxford University Press.

Apps 7.3, 7.6A and B: *Self-Access* by Susan Sheerin, © Oxford University Press 1989. Reproduced by permission of Oxford University Press.

App. 7.4: Kissinger (1990) 'Universal worksheets for using with satellite television' by permission of the author.

Apps 8.1A, B, C: *Learner-based Teaching* by Colin Campbell and Hanna Kryszewska, © Oxford University Press 1992. Reproduced by permission of Oxford University Press.

App. 8.1D: Deller (1990) *Lessons from the Learner*, © Longman Group UK Limited 1990, reprinted by permission of Pearson Education Limited.

Introduction

MATERIALS EVALUATION AND DESIGN AS APPLIED LINGUISTIC ACTIVITIES

Those with a responsibility for the development and administration of language-learning programmes in either educational or workplace settings will need little persuading that materials evaluation and design, along with, for example, syllabus design, learner assessment and the study of classroom processes, are centrally important applied-linguistic activities.

The effects of work on materials has also been recognised within the academic community. Johnson (1989a), for instance, writing of three phases in the development of applied linguistics, describes the second phase as one in which work on needs analysis, the syllabus, materials design, the roles of teacher and learner and classroom interaction brought the language curriculum 'more closely into line with our new and broader understanding of communicative competence and the processes of language acquisition and use' (p. xi). Acceptance of the appropriateness of materials as a field of serious study, from the perspective of evaluation, design or research, is reflected in book-length publications (e.g. Madsen and Bowen 1978, Dubin and Olshtain 1986, Dendrinos 1992, McDonough and Shaw 1993, and the collection edited by Sheldon 1987a), some of which explicitly mention students among their target audience. (See also the sections on materials in Jordan 1983 and Johnson 1989b.) Related indicators are the increasing inclusion of materials evaluation and design as a field of study within Master's programmes and the trickle of students pursuing doctoral research (e.g. Littlejohn 1992, Hutchinson 1996).

Writing in 1982 and concerned to make the point that materials writing is not in itself an appropriate goal for pre-service training, Brumfit and Rossner commented parenthetically: 'Materials construction (which does not, of course, require specialized training) . . .' (p. 129). If this was ever true, it is certainly not the case now. Byrd (1995a: 6) notes that 'materials writing and publication has become a professional track within the professional field of teaching ESL'. Byrd's comment comes from her introduction to a collection of papers (Byrd 1995b) written by members of the Materials Writers Special Interest Section within TESOL, the American-based international association of teachers of English to speakers of other languages; a further collection (Tomlinson 1998a) has been produced by the British-based international Materials Development Association (MATSDA), which also publishes a regular journal.

THE IMPLICATIONS FOR TEACHER EDUCATION

To say that materials evaluation and design are applied-linguistic activities is to make two further claims: that on the one hand they are oriented towards practical outcomes (some might say 'the solution of problems') that necessitate relevant experience and specialist knowledge/skill, and on the other that this specialist knowledge/skill is something that is possessed by applied linguists (rather than any other group of experts). So does this mean that to evaluate or design materials language teachers have to be applied linguists (in the sense that they have successfully completed a suitably broad and rigorous programme) and that if they are not we cannot expect them to be capable of carrying out either of these functions?

A functional separation between classroom teachers and others whose work has an impact on language learning may be a helpful way of thinking about the implications for education and training (see Figure I, below); however, there is a danger that if applied too narrowly such differentiation has the effect of disempowering those at the lowest level.

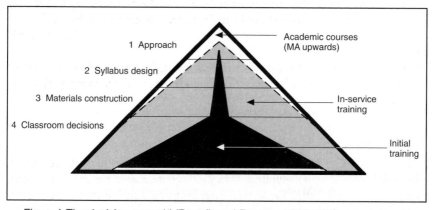

Figure I The decision pyramid (Brumfit and Rossner 1982: 230)

In describing their pyramid model, Brumfit and Rossner (1982) are at pains to point out that the decisions made at higher levels must take account of lower level decision-making and that in taking informed decisions at the class-room level teachers need to mediate between higher level decisions and actual conditions. Seen in this light, the teacher is not simply someone who executes higher level decisions but someone who considers if (and if so, how) these decisions can be implemented in the light of classroom realities. Thus, to refer to the right-hand side of the diagram, an appropriate objective for an in-service programme (and this need not be at Master's level) would be to enable classroom teachers to construct their own materials if this seemed desirable.

One of the implications of this view is that teacher education programmes must prepare teachers, psychologically as well as theoretically and practically, for this role, a role which involves evaluation as well as creativity. A second consideration, made explicit in the model, is the need to distinguish in a principled way between pre-service and in-service education. These concerns are given a personal dimension in the following quotation from a teacher with several years' experience:

> In Chinese, 'study' means 'read the textbooks'. From the first day I went to school, I had to bring my textbooks. Throughout my school years, I learned with textbooks. It was not until I entered the College of Education that I was told not to use textbooks, and I had to design and produce my own teaching materials during teaching practice. Since becoming a teacher I have mixed feelings towards the textbook. Sometimes I hate it and sometimes I love my inevitable teaching partner. This seems unlikely to be a perfect marriage; however, I cannot ask for a divorce. Every day I have to strive to bridge the gap, to 'satisfy the demands of the textbook, but in ways that will be satisfying to those who learn from it' (Stevick 1972). Is this totally due to the quality of textbooks? Is there something I have long neglected? Is there something I can do to help resolve the dilemma?
>
> (Yuen 1997)

The early experiences, the powerful central metaphor of a teacher 'married' to a textbook and the questions raised will no doubt strike a chord with many teachers.

Pre-service teacher education

It is not uncommon on initial training courses such as the one referred to above for trainees to be encouraged to produce their own materials, and there are good reasons for this. Views about teaching and learning change, textbooks change in tune with these, and teachers must be able to respond flexibly to such changes. Thus, there is value in trainees learning to analyse learners' needs and set appropriate objectives and then going on to plan lessons and develop materials to meet those needs *if suitable materials are not available*. However, if this means that there is little opportunity to practise working with existing textbooks that are potentially suitable or that the use of textbooks is actually discouraged, then the emphasis of such courses is misguided. As Yuen points out in the above quotation, for most language teachers working within formal school systems, the textbook is for a variety of reasons an 'inevitable teaching partner', the basis for everyday teaching, and 'the visible heart of any... programme' (Sheldon 1988: 237), hence the term *course*book. Given institutional and external constraints, there is little prospect that this situation will change. To recognise this is to acknowledge the need for a rather different orientation in teacher education courses from that indicated above. What is important is that teachers should see the coursebook not as *the course* but as an aid to fulfilling the aims and objectives which they have themselves formulated. The implication for initial training courses is obvious: trainees need to develop the capacity to evaluate existing materials in relation to the teaching–learning context and their teaching purposes (Cunningsworth 1979, Brumfit and Rossner 1982, Hutchinson and Waters 1987), and there is further evidence from teacher informants (see e.g. Henrichsen 1983) that this is a *want* as well as a need. Guidance in materials design (principally in the form of adaptation and supplementation) could then be logically related to the perceived inadequacy of existing materials in relation to course objectives and/or learner needs.

In-service teacher education

One of the advantages that experienced teachers have over their inexperienced colleagues is that the former's experience consists in part of being able to predict how learners will cope with and respond to certain types of published material. Thus, when experienced teachers teach using a coursebook that they know well, they will have a sense of what to use and what not to use, what to adapt and where to supplement. In many cases less adaptation and supplementation would be necessary if the textbook had been selected more carefully. It seems logical therefore that one of the most important foci for in-service education should be guidance in the selection of course materials. Even where this lies outside the control of individual teachers, there may be opportunities for them to contribute to selection decisions on an individual or group basis, either by presenting a case for the abandonment of ineffective materials or for the adoption of one set of potentially suitable materials rather than another. If, as is often said, knowledge is power, then wider awareness of materials-evaluation procedures and an understanding of the concepts that typically underpin evaluation criteria might encourage those who have been silent to speak. Teachers themselves are also likely to appreciate guidance in materials design in a broad sense (adaptation, supplementation, the development of stand-alone materials); as indicated above, this would flow naturally from dissatisfaction with existing materials.

The suggestion made here, then, is that the more teachers know, understand and can do, the more capable they will be of carrying out the mediating function referred to earlier, especially in relation to materials. This does not mean that language teachers have to be applied linguists in the sense that they have followed a Master's degree, but it does mean that they need to possess the confidence and at least basic competences to (1) make informed decisions about the choice and use of materials and (2) develop materials when existing materials are found to be inadequate.

THIS BOOK

The aims of the book

In line with the above thoughts on teachers' needs, I set out to write a 'How to' book. As normally used, this phrase is applied – sometimes disparagingly – to practical guides. My intention was to write a book that would be seen as practical by teachers but would also exemplify *a way of thinking* (about materials, about the teacher's responsibility, about the ways in which learners can contribute) that would give a secondary meaning to the 'How to' label. I can remember saying, as a student towards the end of an MSc in Applied Linguistics (in Edinburgh): 'I've learned a lot from this course, but I think the most important thing I've learned is how to think critically.' In one sense, this book springs from that insight (reflected in the frequent recurrence of the words 'systematically' and 'principles'). However, it derives more directly from the experience over a good many years since then of teaching elective courses in materials evaluation and design as components of Master's courses in Applied Linguistics and English Language Teaching and of running workshops on materials design as part of specialist courses in the UK and overseas. The elective courses and workshops are always well subscribed. This not only points to the value that teachers attach to materials, but also to their wish for guidance in choosing materials, adapting these and preparing their own. The book is an attempt to meet that need in a different form.

The structure of the book

Since this is a volume within a series on applied linguistics, the assumption has been made that the primary readership will be teachers with some experience of teaching. This assumption has influenced both the structure and the content of the book. The linear development of Chapters 2–6, from the selection of a coursebook to materials adaptation and then supplementation, is based on experience of working with practising teachers, but takes little for granted in terms of prior training; subsequent chapters, on topics such as systematising the design process, involving learners in materials design and in-use and post-use evaluation of materials, will obviously be of most relevance to experienced teachers. The final chapter, which brings together a selection of special topics (e.g. materials and culture, materials and syllabus, materials and research), has been included for those with an interest in *studying* materials. The many tasks sprinkled through the book are intended to guide and stimulate reflection, critical thinking and learning through doing.

Using the book

I imagine some using the book as a 'set text', reading prescribed sections in their own time and discussing these and working through tasks in class. The symbol K next to a Task signifies that a Key or Commentary can be found on pp. 288–94. Some I see in libraries, using the book as a resource for assignments or their own research. Others, who are not following a course but are keen to do better the things they do every day, may search the book for guidance and inspiration. Within the latter group there may be little clusters of practising teachers with common needs (such as how to select materials in a more systematic way), who will choose to use specific sections of the book as a basis for discussion or coordinated activity.

What this implies is that there is no one way to use the book. Although it has been planned in such a way that it can be used as a set text, it is not in itself a course. The lecturer who decides to adopt it will – as I will myself – use it like any coursebook, as a resource, selecting, adapting and supplementing according to time constraints, course-participant factors and insight into what is relevant in that context. Lecturers working in pre-service contexts with trainees who are engaged in teaching practice may even wish to stand the book on its head, as it were, working through Chapters 4–6 first and dealing with the content of Chapters 1–3 (a prospective rather than an actual need) only just before trainees graduate.

The hope

My hope is that what I have written will be of value to all teachers with an interest in this topic, irrespective of their experience, level of training and their present circumstances (e.g. studying, teaching or combining the two). My particular hope is that it will embolden readers to take at least one step beyond where they stand at present: that, for instance, those who currently carry out only impressionistic materials evaluation will do this more systematically; that those who evaluate systematically at the point of selection will continue that process by evaluating systematically materials in use; that those who have in the past made only minimal changes to the materials they use will develop the confidence to make more substantial changes when these are called for. These are, of course, progressive steps away from textbook-dependence and towards teacher autonomy. But I also hope that those who have thus far taken on themselves all the responsibility for materials evaluation and development will be encouraged to involve learners and colleagues and that institutions will be prepared to facilitate cooperative initiatives. All stand to benefit from this cooperation.

Ian McGrath
Hong Kong

Chapter 1

A systematic approach to materials evaluation

What are materials? – attitudes to coursebooks: metaphors; who needs published materials?; arguments for and against coursebook-based teaching – teachers as materials evaluators – inputs to evaluation – materials evaluation as a cyclical process – the structure of this volume

1 WHAT ARE MATERIALS?

The 'materials' in the title of this book are not *any* materials for learning and teaching languages. In a broad sense, materials could include 'realia' (real objects such as a pencil, a chair or a bag) and representations (such as a drawing or photograph of a person, house or scene). Materials of these kinds can, of course, be exploited effectively for language learning and advice on their use can be found in books that deal specifically with the use of visual aids. The focus here, however, is primarily on *text* materials. Such materials include those that have been either specifically designed for language learning and teaching (e.g. textbooks, worksheets, computer software); authentic materials (e.g. off-air recordings, newspaper articles) that have been specially selected and exploited for teaching purposes by the classroom teacher; teacher-written materials; and learner-generated materials.

In many situations the expectation is that teaching will be based on a single textbook, although other materials may be used at the teacher's discretion. The term 'coursebook' will be used to refer to a textbook on which a course is based.

2 ATTITUDES TO COURSEBOOKS

2.1 Metaphors

Lakoff and Johnson's (1980) fascinating *Metaphors We Live By* testifies to the power of metaphors in everyday life. Metaphors can also offer a useful insight into the way teachers perceive coursebooks (see the quotation from Yuen (1997) in the Introduction to this book).

Task 1.1

Here are a number of metaphors suggested by teachers from very different contexts:

A coursebook is . . .

a recipe	a springboard	a straitjacket	a supermarket
a holy book	a compass	a survival kit	a crutch

1. What does each of the metaphors mean? In what sense can a coursebook be said to be a 'recipe', for example?

2. Which of the metaphors can you identify with most closely?

3. What would be your own metaphor for a coursebook?

Two opposing themes are apparent in the metaphors listed above: that of *control* and that of *choice*, with that of *support* being somewhere between the two. The choice by an individual of a control metaphor, say, rather than a choice metaphor will almost certainly be influenced by the context in which that individual works, but it also has important implications for the way in which a textbook is used. In this respect, one metaphor, that of the coursebook as holy book, is particularly worrying for its undertones of transferred responsibility and undue veneration for the authority of the printed word. Richards (1998: 131), who warns against the 'reification' (or 'unjustifiable attribution of qualities of excellence, authority and validity') of textbooks, comments:

> Teachers in some parts of the world . . . tend to assume that any item included in a textbook must be an important learning item for students, and that explanations (e.g. of grammar rules or idioms) and cultural information provided by the author are true and should not be questioned; they assume they do not have the authority or knowledge to adapt the textbook. They likewise believe that activities found in a textbook are superior to ones that they could devise themselves. (ibid.)

Since the possibility of conflict exists between a teacher's way of thinking about a coursebook and that of his or her learners – for instance, learners may 'reify' the textbook and the teacher see it merely as a springboard – there is value as well as interest in teachers seeking to uncover learners' attitudes. We come back to this point in Chapters 2 and 3.

2.2 Who needs published materials?

Coursebook use tends to spread along a continuum, from those who in a sense 'teach the book' either because that is what they are (or think they are) required to do, to those who never use a coursebook because they disdain to do so or are unable to find something suitable. Occupying the space between the two extremes are teachers who might be said to base their teaching on a book or a number of books and those who only make use of a book for limited and specific purposes.

Since it is generally held to be desirable for teachers to make informed decisions when a choice is possible, it seems appropriate at this point to review the arguments for and against coursebook-based teaching. Before we do this, however, it is worth making the point that although the principal users of textbooks are teachers and learners, others also have a vested interest. Those in positions of authority, from officials in a Ministry of Education, say, down to the Head of Department in an individual school, will wish to ensure that there is some degree of standardisation and continuity in relation to what is taught, and a set textbook is one way of ensuring this, others being official syllabuses, an inspectorial system and public examinations. In many countries, there will be a textbook committee within the Ministry whose function is to approve books for use within the school system. Seen in this light, 'the book', as it is often known, is an instrument of control within systems that emphasise accountability and the *status quo*. Textbooks can also be used by those in positions of authority to facilitate curricular change. When this is the case, the book serves both as an instrument of change and a means of supporting teachers during such a period, a view that has been persuasively argued by Hutchinson and Torres (1994). Parents may also have an interest. Those who are in a position to help their children, either directly or by employing a private tutor to provide remedial help, will find it easier to do so if they can see what the child is supposed to know or be able to do and have something concrete against which to measure his or her progress. Training officers in companies employing teachers of languages for specific purposes (LSP) may have similar reasons for preferring a book to the use of a combination of photocopied and teacher-produced materials. It is perhaps a little ironic to refer also to the vested interests of textbook writers, publishers and even governments (for whom linguistic spread is associated with the spread of influence), but the financial motives of these groups does have an effect on the way in which textbooks are produced and marketed and ultimately on teaching and learning. Low (1987) has observed that those occupying different roles in relation to the language-learning process will adopt different evaluative perspectives, illustrating this with reference to ten different roles. Apart from the roles referred to or implied above, these include the teacher trainer and the educational researcher.

2.3 Arguments for and against coursebook-based teaching

There has been vigorous debate concerning the desirability of basing teaching on coursebooks, with a number of well-known figures coming out against this. Brumfit (1979: 30) claims that although textbooks can help teachers, 'many of them don't', and that 'even the best textbooks take away initiative from teachers by implying that there is somewhere an "expert" who can solve problems' for the teacher and individual students (see also Richards (1993, 1998 and Task 1.2, below) on teacher dependence and the de-skilling effect of coursebooks). The answer, Brumfit suggests, lies in 'resource packs, sets of materials with advice to teachers on how to adapt and modify the contents' (Brumfit 1979: 30). This idea is developed in a well-known paper by Allwright (1981), who demonstrates convincingly by reference to goals, content, method and guidance that 'the management of language learning is far too complex to be satisfactorily catered for by a pre-packaged set of decisions embodied in teaching materials' (Allwright 1981: 9). The alternative, he argues, lies in the provision of *learning* materials which, in the form of a 'learners' guide to language learning' and 'ideas books' and 'rationale books' for teachers, and supported by learner training and an appropriate focus within teacher training, would allow for the cooperative management of learning by learners and teachers. An equally well-known riposte, by O'Neill (1982), presents a number of counterarguments (see below), which are largely reiterated in O'Neill (1993). Although there is general agreement that global coursebooks can never meet local needs (or, to put it in a more extreme form, that every classroom is unique – see e.g. Davison 1976, Williams 1983, Cunningsworth 1995, Maley 1998), other commentators have tended to take the same view as O'Neill (see e.g. Cunningsworth 1979, Hutchinson and Torres 1994). In essence, their view is that a coursebook is a convenient aid.

Some of the most frequently voiced arguments that have been made for coursebooks in relation to the needs of learners and teachers are summarised below. The summaries draw on Grant (1987), O'Neill (1982, 1993), Hutchinson and Torres (1994), and Ur (1996).

Why teachers and learners need a coursebook

1. A coursebook is a map. It shows where one is going and where one has been.
2. It provides language samples.
3. It offers variety.

Why learners need a coursebook

4. It defines what is to be learned and what will be tested.
5. It reinforces what the teacher has done and makes revision and preparation possible. It thus offers support for learning outside class.

Why teachers need a coursebook

6. It provides a structure for teaching.

7. It saves time. To prepare materials from scratch for every lesson would be impossible.
8. It offers linguistic, cultural and methodological support.
9. It is easy to keep track of what you have done and to tell others where you have reached (e.g. when reporting to the Head of Department or briefing a substitute teacher).

One point which is sometimes made by teachers is that if a coursebook represents a new approach to language teaching, which is illustrated and clearly explained in the teacher's book, then this can be a useful form of professional development (Nunan 1991, Edge and Wharton 1998). When these explanations include advice on how to conduct particular types of activity that are not specific to the book in question (e.g. organisation and management of small group work or role play, correction of spoken errors), teacher's books provide on-the-job training for inexperienced teachers (Richards 1998). Teachers working in contexts in which access for learners to 'real' spoken or written materials is difficult also attach particular value to coursebooks that include these (the 'samples' referred to in point 2, above, might, after all, be simply the specially-written texts found in traditional textbooks).

Task 1.2

It has been argued that if teaching decisions are based largely on the textbook and the teacher's book, this has the effect of de-skilling a teacher (Richards 1993, 1998, citing Apple and Jungck 1991; Shannon 1987). The argument is as follows: if the person doing the teaching cedes to the textbook writer responsibility for planning what happens, he or she gradually loses the capacity to exercise the planning function, i.e. 'lack of use leads to loss' (Apple and Jungck 1991: 230, cited in Richards 1998: 132). As a result, 'the teacher's role is trivialized and marginalized to that of little more than a technician' (Richards 1998: 132).

1. Do you agree?
2. Do you see any other dangers if a teacher follows the textbook too closely?

How one reacts to this argument will probably depend on interpretations of the words 'largely' and 'based'. Richards' (1998) brief review of literature on textbook use, which extends to the use of textbooks in areas other than English language teaching, suggests that experienced teachers are selective in what they use and therefore that pedagogic reasoning skills do not atrophy over time.

The view taken in this book is that where a suitable coursebook is available coursebook-based teaching makes sense. However, teachers must use their judgement in deciding which parts of the book to use and how to use them.

3 TEACHERS AS MATERIALS EVALUATORS

The selection of a textbook for use in a particular context may be determined by any one of a number of different individuals or groups other than the teacher who will ultimately use it: a Ministry of Education (which may have commissioned a single textbook series for nationwide use), a state board (in America), a school principal, a Head of Department, a Director of Studies (in a private language school), or a group of teachers within the institution concerned. Yet even where teachers have no direct control over textbook selection, it is important that they are able to adopt a critical stance in relation to the material they are expected to use. This implies an awareness of learner needs and contextual constraints and the willingness and capacity in the light of this awareness to make decisions concerning the selection from the textbook of what is appropriate, and the extension/exploitation, adaptation and supplementation of this as necessary. These aspects of materials evaluation by teachers are dealt with in Chapters 4–6. In the remainder of this chapter and in Chapters 2 and 3, the main focus is on the process of initial textbook selection.

The decision to use one textbook rather than another cannot be taken lightly. Since the textbook tends to be the main teaching–learning aid, in school systems at least, it influences what teachers teach and what and to some extent how learners learn. For institutions and often individuals, textbooks are a financial investment. For teachers they require an important investment of time. Having taken the trouble to familiarise themselves with a new coursebook and its accompanying teacher's book, cassettes, workbook and so on, and plan lessons based on these, teachers will normally be very reluctant to change books the following year, even if they were allowed to do so.

These considerations notwithstanding, textbooks are only too often chosen in an arbitrary fashion. How many of us have rued the decisions made by others! How many of us have been so impressed by a conference talk or author demonstration, by a persuasive bookseller or publisher's representative, or by an author's or publisher's reputation, that we have ourselves made a rash choice! As Grant (1987) points out, we may even be deluded by the surface appearance of a book: 'Most of us have had the experience of publishers' representatives calling round and dazzling us with their new books. Many of these books are beautifully presented, with jazzy covers and attractive artwork which distracts the eye and dulls the brain' (p. 119). Over twenty years ago, Brumfit (1979: 30), referring to EFL textbooks, commented that 'masses of rubbish is skilfully marketed'. Since there has been no slowing down in the production of language teaching materials, and since some of this is presumably still 'rubbish', it is clearly important that teachers and others who select textbooks for a specific context at least are able to distinguish between what is likely to be more and less suitable.

Task 1.3

Here are some reasons why the wrong choice of coursebook has made life difficult for teachers.

> *Local cultural taboos meant that I had to leave out whole units.*

> *It was too difficult. So I had a choice between working through everything very slowly and not finishing the book or skipping bits.*

> *The students couldn't imagine themselves taking planes to Britain, booking into hotels, all that stuff. It was just too unreal.*

Sheldon (1987b: 3) lists a number of other problems:

> Grammatical explanations in some ELT textbooks (as opposed to reference grammars) often take too much terminological and linguistic knowledge for granted. Some ancillary workbooks force students to adopt microscopic handwriting, and are not meant to be worked in at all. Many books have a density of text or diagram which is disconcerting to the hapless learner trying to find his/her way round.

1. What difficulties have you experienced in working with coursebooks?
2. Did you choose the coursebook? If not, do you know how the decision was taken? If so, would you say the selection procedure was systematic?

4 INPUTS TO EVALUATION

The most secure basis for deciding which textbook to select is to try out the materials with the students (or the kinds of students) for whom they are intended (Harmer 1991, Cunningsworth 1995). This is particularly desirable where large-scale or long-term adoptions are involved. Where two or more coursebook series are being considered, it may be possible to organise a short-term comparative trial.

An alternative to trialling within an institution is to obtain information from other users. The local bookseller or publisher's representative should know if a coursebook is being used by other similar institutions. Careful questioning of teachers who have used the materials – or, better still, an opportunity to observe the materials in use – may give strong indications as to the potential suitability of the material. Indeed, it would be preferable to attempt to obtain feedback of this kind before taking the decision to embark on the kind of trialling suggested above.

If neither feedback from other users nor prior trialling is possible, we are left with 'armchair evaluation'. Although this may appear to be a substitute for user-based evaluation, the two are not mutually exclusive. As Figure 1.1 (overleaf) indicates, where user-based evaluation is possible (whether in the form of other-feedback or evidence from use within the institution), this should ideally be guided by prior armchair evaluation. In many situations, feedback from others is not available and trialling is not feasible. In such cases, armchair evaluation assumes particular importance.

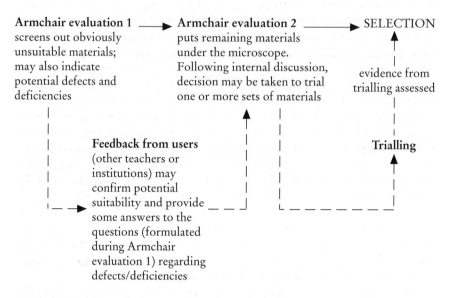

Figure 1.1 A framework for materials evaluation for selection

5 MATERIALS EVALUATION AS A CYCLICAL PROCESS

There are two dimensions to a systematic approach to materials evaluation, for which the terms macro and micro seem appropriate. The *macro* dimension consists of a series of stages (the approach, in a broad sense); the *micro* dimension is what occurs within each stage (the steps or set of techniques employed). We have already identified a series of such steps leading up to selection (see Figure 1.1, above) and subsequent chapters take a closer look at the armchair evaluation phases in this. Formal evaluation very often stops at the point of selection. In stressing the importance of two further stages within the macro dimension, this section argues for a cyclical approach to materials evaluation.

As noted in the previous section, so much can depend on making the right decision about materials that it pays (in terms of money and time) to be as rigorous as possible when evaluating. The emphasis in much that has been written on materials evaluation is therefore rightly on what we might call **pre-use evaluation** in relation to coursebook selection.

Once the decision has been taken, however, the evaluation process should not be at an end. As Nunan (1991: 211) points out in reference to the pre-use evaluation of materials, 'while we can exercise professional judgement in answering questions such as, "does the introduction, practice and recycling of new linguistic items seem to be shallow/steep enough for your students?", ultimately, such questions can only be settled with reference to their actual use'. In fact, the planning of every lesson based on a coursebook will involve evaluation, as we shall see in Chapter 4, and notes made following each lesson on the suitability or otherwise of the materials represent an invaluable form of continuing, **in-use evaluation**. Where several teachers are using the same materials, periodic meetings focusing on such questions as *What worked well? What difficulties did learners have?* and *What forms of additional help might be needed?* can be useful, both as a way of checking the generalisability of individual experiences and brainstorming ways of adapting and supplementing the material. Such meetings might have to be combined with observation, however, in order to satisfy Allwright's (1981: 5–6) demand that 'the use of the textbook . . . be monitored to permit evaluation of its use and effectiveness'. Apart from its contribution to the evaluation of the effectiveness of materials, observation of materials in use has additional benefits: it can, for instance, afford general insights into how teachers use materials (Torres 1993, Richards and Mahoney 1996), and therefore suggest directions both for materials development and professional development activities.

At the end of the course, most teachers and students will want to close the book with a sigh of relief and forget about it. Nevertheless, it is worth spending a little time on end-of-course or **post-use evaluation**. At this stage, it should be possible to assess in a more comprehensive way the effects of using the materials, for instance by considering short-term effects (such as motivation) or long-term effects (measured by retention or application of learning) (Tomlinson 1999).

Ellis (1998), who suggests that the same procedure is followed as was used for selection, acknowledges that this is rarely done, citing as reasons teachers' feeling that after using a coursebook they know what 'works' and the perception of post-use evaluation as a 'daunting' task for which not only time but expertise are needed. Teachers the world over seem to be under increasing pressure and at the end of a term, semester or year, who can blame them if they fail to close the circle? And yet there may be useful lessons to be learned, insights that can feed into subsequent teaching using the same materials and/or to the process or criteria by which they were selected.

Students can also be involved in post-use evaluation. They may have experience of using other materials and therefore are able to make comparisons; even if they have not, they can still express a view on the suitability of the materials they have used. Like in-use evaluation, post-use evaluation is most reliable when it draws on the experiences of several teachers and several groups of learners.

We return to in-use and post-use evaluation in Chapter 9.

6 THE STRUCTURE OF THIS VOLUME

This chapter has introduced a way of thinking about materials (attitudes to them, the role they play) and their evaluation (the importance of careful evaluation and a three-stage approach to this). Subsequent chapters offer guidance at the level of both principle and practice in dealing *systematically* with such tasks as materials evaluation for selection, materials evaluation for lesson planning and the processes of adaptation, supplementation and the preparation of 'stand-alone' materials. Although the emphasis within the book as a whole thus shifts progressively from evaluation to design, evaluative criteria remain an important dimension, and evaluation is again the focus of the penultimate chapter. In the quotation below, Stevick (1972) offers a few crumbs of encouragement to would-be authors, but he also makes the point that the evaluative criteria we use in judging the work of others should be our guide when we design our own materials.

> More than courses in French, Spanish, German, or English, a course in a seldom-taught language is likely to be the brain child of one author, conceived in desperation, brought forth in obscurity, and destined to be despised and rejected by all other men. Sometimes rejection is inevitable, but often it is the result of hasty, or unperceptive, or unappreciative examination of the existing book . . . guidelines for evaluation may be applied to the efforts of others, but also to one's own handiwork both before and after it is completed.
>
> (Stevick 1972: 102)

This is the underlying principle on which this volume has been designed: the more we can develop our perceptiveness (linguistic, psychological and pedagogic) and our capacity for discrimination and context-sensitivity in relation to materials evaluation, the more likely it is that these qualities will also shine through and be appreciated in the materials we produce.

Chapter 2

Choosing a coursebook 1:
from analysis to first-glance evaluation

Taking stock of the situation: context analysis and survey of learner needs
– textbook analysis – methods of analysis and evaluation: the impressionistic
method; the checklist method; the in-depth method – first-glance evaluation
– criteria for evaluation: from general to specific; applying the criteria

In Chapter 1, we distinguished three main stages in evaluation, which we
termed pre-use, in-use and post-use evaluation. In this chapter and the next,
we take a closer look at the first of these stages: the evaluation of materials,
and particularly coursebooks, with adoption in mind.

1 TAKING STOCK OF THE SITUATION

Let us begin by considering what we might need to know in order to select
materials for a particular context.

Task 2.1

Imagine yourself in one of these positions:

A. You have just been appointed Head of the English Department in a new
   secondary school. In order to ensure that books are available when the term
   begins, they need to be ordered now. It's your decision what to order. Other
   staff have not yet been appointed, but since in your country secondary
   school teachers must be graduates with a teacher training certificate, you
   can probably take certain things for granted.

B. This is your first year as Director of Studies of a UK language school which
   runs intensive summer courses for teenagers and young adults. The school
   takes on extra staff (who are usually quite young and relatively inexperienced) to teach on these courses. It is your responsibility to decide which
   books will be used.

C. You've just been offered a new job in an institution where teachers are free
   to choose the books they teach with. The question is: which book to choose?

1. What kinds of information would you need in order to make a decision? Think in *general* terms (e.g. information about the *learners*).

2. Would the people in the other roles need other kinds of information?

3. Keep your own role in mind and look through the extracts from publishers' catalogues in Appendix 2.1. Which of the books described would you seriously consider? Which features of the description influenced your decision? What other *specific* information would you need in order to decide which, if any, would be most suitable? Use as a starting point the general categories you came up with in answer to question 1 above.

Deciding which of a number of published textbooks is 'best' cannot, of course, be answered in the abstract. But if we ask instead, 'Which would be the most suitable?' we still need some terms of reference before we can venture an answer: suitable for what purpose, for whom, in what situation, and judged by what criteria?

Teachers selecting a textbook or other published materials for use in a familiar teaching situation will be well aware of the multiplicity of factors in that situation which will need to be taken into account (even if, for one reason or another, these cannot fully determine the ultimate selection). However, those who are selecting materials for a new course, for a new type of student or for an unfamiliar teaching context will need to carry out some form of context analysis and/or survey of needs in order to ensure that they too are fully aware of the contextual and learner factors that need to be considered. For both groups, but particularly for the second group, it is worth drawing up a list of these factors before proceeding to the next stage involving the examination of potential materials. This list will constitute the fixed element (the variable element being the materials under consideration) in what has been described as a matching process (Hutchinson and Waters 1987). It should be emphasised, however, that the list is fixed only in the sense that it defines a particular teaching–learning context at a particular point in time, and that while 'matching' may be a convenient way of referring to what goes on, the term undoubtedly belies the complexity of the process.

1.1 Context analysis and survey of learner needs

The point has been made by Cunningsworth (1979: 31) that 'course materials are not intrinsically good or bad – rather they are more or less effective in helping students to reach particular goals in specific situations'. Although we might wish to take issue with the first part of this statement (materials can surely be both ineffective *and* intrinsically bad), the second part – with its implication that evaluation needs to be learner- and context-related – seems uncontroversial. Surprisingly, the importance of a prior analysis of contextual and learner factors is not acknowledged in some discussions of materials evaluation and selection. This section looks in turn at the micro context (characteristics of the learner group and the teacher(s) who will use the material, the programme and the institution) and the macro (external) context.

The following summary of the **learner factors** that need to be considered in materials selection draws on Daoud and Celce-Murcia (1979), Matthews (1991), Harmer (1991), McDonough and Shaw (1993), and Cunningsworth (1995).

1. age range
2. proficiency level in the target language (and homogeneity within the learner group)
3. first language (all the same?)
4. academic and educational level
5. socio-cultural background
6. occupation (if relevant)
7. reasons for studying the target language (if applicable)
8. attitudes to learning (including attitudes to the language, its speakers, the teacher, the institution)
9. previous language-learning experience (of the target language and any other languages)
10. language-learning aptitude
11. general expectations (of the course/textbook/teacher/own role)
12. specific wants
13. preferred learning styles
14. sex distribution (single sex? If mixed, what proportion of M/F)
15. interests (insofar as these are generalisable)

Many of these are briefly discussed in McDonough and Shaw (1993: 8–9); see also Matthews (1991).

It is also possible in many situations to identify **learners' needs** in relation to the target language. In a context where there is a defined syllabus and/or a public examination (which itself defines what needs to be known), the syllabus/exam will be the starting point for a profile of needs. Some possible categories in such a profile are listed below. These are based in part on Bruder (1978), Daoud and Celce-Murcia (1979), and Harmer (1991).

1. dialect (e.g. British versus American English)
2. language-skill emphasis
3. contexts and situations of use, which may require different levels of formality or different registers
4. subskills
5. notions
6. functions
7. language-system (grammar, vocabulary, phonology) emphasis

8. language forms (e.g. structures, vocabulary items, features of stress or intonation)
9. whether language systems will be used productively, receptively or both
10. attention given to mechanics (handwriting, spelling, punctuation)

Procedures for needs analysis would include syllabus analysis, analysis of past examination papers, diagnostic tests and other analyses of student performance (e.g. scrutiny of previous written work, classroom observation), feedback from other teachers, student questionnaires, interviews and group discussion. The most detailed approach to needs analysis can be found in Munby (1978), but see Brindley (1989) for a broader view of learner needs which includes needs in the learning situation.

Although Harmer (1991) appears to suggest that a teacher who is armed with a description of the learners and their needs, and who has thought through the implications of this information for the kind of material required, is in a position to proceed to the evaluation stage, other writers have recognised the need for a broader approach to data-gathering.

There are **teacher factors** to be considered, for instance (Bruder 1978, Cunningsworth 1995). These would include:

1. language competence (as target language users and analysts but also as speakers of the learners' first language)
2. familiarity with the target language culture (and that of the learners, where this is homogeneous)
3. methodological competence and awareness (including ability to adapt coursebook, and prepare supplementary material)
4. experience of teaching the kind of learner for whom the materials are being selected
5. attitude to teaching and to learners
6. time available for preparation
7. beliefs about teaching–learning, preferred teaching style, preferred method

The respective needs in relation to textbooks of teachers who are native and non-native speakers of the target language and of inexperienced and experienced teachers are discussed by Ariew (1982) and summarised by Skierso (1991). See also Masuhara (1998), who argues that teachers' needs and wants should be taken much more seriously than they have been. The fact that teachers are the mediators between published material and learners, and can choose to work with its intentions or undermine them, is a good reason for not only listening to what they have to say if they choose to voice their views but actively researching those views.

Information will also be needed on the **institution(s)** and the **specific programme** for which the material is intended. This would include:

1. level within the educational system (e.g. kindergarten, primary, secondary, tertiary)
2. public sector (state) versus private
3. role of the target language (e.g. English-medium versus English as curriculum subject)
4. time available for the study of the target language (per week/per academic year)
5. timetable (whether the language is typically taught in single or double lessons or after lunch/at the end of the day)
6. class size
7. physical environment (e.g. classroom size, flexibility of seating, acoustics)
8. additional resources available (e.g. cassette recorder, video recorder, overhead projector, photocopier, computers)
9. aims of the programme
10. syllabus
11. form of evaluation
12. decision-making mechanisms and freedom given to teachers

See McDonough and Shaw (1993: 9–10) for a brief discussion of institutional factors. Skierso (1991), which contains a useful overview of learner, teacher and institutional factors, also includes examples of pro-formas on which such information can be summarised.

The institution exists within the larger educational system and, indeed, within an *overall socio-political system* in which social, cultural, religious, economic and political issues can all have an influence (British Council 1980, Malamah-Thomas 1987). This argues for a more macro level of analysis which takes account of such factors as the following:

1. aims of education (which may influence, for instance, curriculum content, the nature of the public examination system, teaching methods and roles of teacher and learner)
2. language policy and the role of the target language within the country (which may have widespread effects, including economic support for language learning; learner and teacher access to speakers of the target language and authentic materials; attitudes to language learning; target language competence as a requirement for access to tertiary education; the use of the target language in tertiary-level instruction; and in the case of English, say, the preference for British or American English)
3. aims of language education (usually stated in a national syllabus)
4. cultural and religious considerations

Task 2.2

1. Now go back to your answers to Task 2.1. Can you add anything to the lists you have just looked at?

2. In the list of macro-level factors immediately above this task, an indication has been given of how specific factors might affect the micro level (institution, classroom, teachers, learners). Go through this or one of the previous lists and consider how each factor might affect, directly or indirectly, *the selection of materials*.

3. Imagine you have been asked to advise on the selection of a coursebook for one class in your own teaching situation. Draw up a chart for the analysis of contextual and learner factors and complete it for that class.

4. Appendix 2.2 contains examples of structured interview prompts used to elicit learners' and teachers' attitudes to and expectations of textbooks. The resulting information served as one input to the design of an instrument for coursebook evaluation. If you were also planning to design your own instrument, would you try to obtain information about learner and teacher likes and wants? If so, what procedure would you adopt (e.g. interview, questionnaire, group discussion) and what questions would you ask?

2   TEXTBOOK ANALYSIS

When the object of the exercise is to evaluate, it is tempting to jump straight into evaluation. In the previous section, it was suggested that context analysis and needs analysis are a necessary step before evaluation can take place. This section deals with an equally important pre-evaluation stage: textbook analysis.

The distinction between analysis and evaluation is an important one (Littlejohn 1998, Tomlinson 1999). At its most basic level, analysis is a process which leads to an objective, verifiable *description*. Evaluation, as the word suggests, involves the *making of judgements*. When we compare a description of a textbook with a description of a context in order to establish in a preliminary way whether that textbook might be suitable for that context we are evaluating. If time is short – as it usually is – we might decide to skip analysis or try to combine it with evaluation. If we do, we take a risk because the two processes, though logically related, are different. In its simplest form, analysis seeks to discover what is there (Littlejohn 1998), whereas evaluation is more concerned to discover whether *what one is looking for* is there – and, if it is, to put a value on it. In evaluating, we look selectively, and in looking selectively we may miss the unusual or the innovative.

The purpose of textbook analysis, then, is to provide a description, but this description can be at different levels of sophistication. Beyond the most basic level, the concern is to understand what assumptions and beliefs lie beneath the surface and what effects can be anticipated; analysis involves inference and deduction. The process thus becomes progressively more subjective but also more illuminating (Littlejohn 1998), as can be seen in Table 2.1, below.

Table 2.1 Textbook analysis at three levels (based on Littlejohn 1998: 195–202)

Level	Focus of analysis	Examples of features to be considered
1	'what is there'	publication date; intended users; type of material; classroom time required; intended context of use; physical aspects, such as durability, components, use of colour; the way the material is divided up across components; how the student's book is organised, and how learners and teachers are helped to find their way around
2	'what is required of users'	tasks: what the learner has to do; whether their focus will be on form, meaning or both; what cognitive operations will be required; what form of classroom organisation will be involved (e.g. individual work, whole class); what medium will be involved; who will be the source of language or information
3	'what is implied'	selection and sequencing of content (syllabus) and tasks; distribution of information across teacher and student components; reconsideration of information collected at levels 1 and 2

The analysis at level 1 could be carried out by looking at what the materials say about themselves (on the back cover, in the introduction), at the information provided in a publisher's catalogue, and by looking quickly through the materials.

Table 2.2 (overleaf) contains a first draft of a checklist that might be used for a level 1 analysis of a coursebook.

Task 2.3

1. What would you want to add to or change in the checklist? Remember, the aim is simply to *describe* the material in a preliminary way.

2. Try out the checklist (with any changes that you have made to it) to analyse *two* sets of materials. Make a note of the time it took you to do this.

3. Did the checklist bring out the key differences between these materials or would you now want to make any (further) changes to it?

Table 2.2: Towards a level 1 materials analysis checklist

Components/support for teacher
What do the materials consist of in addition to the student's book?

- teacher's book
- tests (may also be in student's book, sometimes 'disguised' as 'Review')
- workbook (may also be integrated with student's book)
- cassettes (may be available as CD, packaged with student's book)
- video
- pictorial materials (e.g. flashcards, wallcharts)
- CD-ROM
- other

Date of publication
When were the materials published?
Are all the components available?

Cost
What does the student's book cost?
What do the other items cost?

Target learners
What kinds of learners is the material intended for?
- age
- level
- interests

Target teaching context
What kind of teaching situation is it intended for?
- type of course (e.g. general English, exam-oriented)
- total time available
- lesson length
- syllabus
- self-study

As you will have noticed, the questions require little more than a tick or a short answer and, at least as it stands, the whole checklist should have taken you very little time to administer. Appendix 2.3 contains a section of a more elaborate schedule in which the details of a level 1 analysis are recorded.

Following level 1 analysis, the logical next step would seem to be finer grained analysis, as implied in Littlejohn's three-level approach. However, an alternative would be to move straight to a form of preliminary evaluation (see the section on 'First-glance evaluation' somewhat later in this chapter), returning to analysis later. This might even be a necessary economy when a number of coursebook packages are being considered for possible adoption.

At level 2, the analyst would need to carry out a more careful examination of extracts from the materials (student's book, teacher's book and ideally other components, if these exist) in order to arrive at a sense of what is envisaged. Littlejohn (1998) comments: 'It is precisely in the nature of classroom tasks that materials designers' assumptions about the best route to language learning become clear, and in consequence, teacher and learner roles become defined' (p. 200).

Such detailed analysis also serves a further purpose:

> It is also through an analysis of tasks that we can most effectively test out the various claims made for materials. If, for example, the materials claim to be 'learner-centred' yet we find that by far most of the tasks involve the learners in 'responding' and in working with content supplied by the materials, there would appear to be a serious mismatch. Similarly, if the materials claim to promote cognitive work and problem-solving, but we find that this forms a very small part of the 'mental operations' required and that the rest of the tasks involve simple 'repetition', then we would have reason to doubt the accuracy of the claim. (ibid.)

The analyses carried out at levels 1 and 2 feed in to the third level of analysis, where the focus is on drawing conclusions regarding such questions as the aims of the materials (the underlying aims may, of course, differ from the stated aims), the anticipated roles of teacher and learners, and the rationale for the selection and ordering of content and tasks. The overall outcome should be that the analyst can reach a general understanding of the philosophy underlying the materials.

3 METHODS OF ANALYSIS AND EVALUATION

Three basic methods can be discerned in the literature on textbook evaluation. For convenience, these will be referred to as *the impressionistic method*, *the checklist method*, and *the in-depth method*. As we shall see, however, certain proposals cut across these categories and for this reason the terms are not entirely satisfactory.

3.1 The impressionistic method

Impressionistic analysis is concerned to obtain a general impression of the material. As Cunningworth's (1995: 1) term 'impressionistic overview' suggests, one form of this is wide-ranging but relatively superficial. In the case of global textbooks (i.e. textbooks intended for the international market), such an overview typically involves glancing at the publisher's 'blurb' (i.e. the brief description of the book on the back cover), and at the contents page (for an indication of the syllabus-type and coverage), and then skimming through the book looking at organisation, topics, layout and visuals. This kind of overview, which equates roughly to Littlejohn's analysis level 1, is of course inadequate if it constitutes the sole basis for textbook evaluation and selection.

It is also possible to gain an impression of a book by looking rather more carefully at representative features, such as the design of a unit or lesson, or more specific features, such as the treatment of particular language elements (Cunningsworth 1995: 2) or – through analysis of exercises, for instance – the author's view of learning (Hutchinson 1987). Johnson (1986: 55) suggests a combined approach which starts with the kind of 'guided browsing' described above but is followed by both analysis of a single unit and examination of the treatment of the language skills across the book as a whole. It will be clear from these examples that the distinction between 'impressionistic' and 'in-depth' methods is not as neat as it might be.

The reality is that techniques of impressionistic evaluation cover a wide spectrum, from Lee (1975), who enumerates those features in textbooks of which he approves and disapproves, to Stevick (1972), who sets out a characteristically thought-provoking scheme. Stevick's proposal involves three 'qualities' (strength, lightness and transparency), three 'dimensions' (linguistic, social and topical) and four essential 'components' of lessons (opportunities for language use, sample of language, exploration of vocabulary and exploration of phonological, orthographic or grammatical form). While the three qualities of strength (essentially, pay-off for the learner), lightness (e.g. learnability, lesson length) and transparency (e.g. clarity of organisation and presentation) are assessed impressionistically, by browsing, the dimensions and components lend themselves to much more systematic evaluation, a socio-topical matrix being suggested for this purpose.

3.2 The checklist method

Like the impressionistic method, the checklist method is not a watertight category. However, in that it contrasts *system* (and therefore ostensible *objectivity*) with *impression* (and implicitly *subjectivity*), it seems appropriate to deal with it separately.

In its most literal sense, a checklist consists of a list of items which is 'referred to for comparison, identification or verification' (*Collins English Dictionary* 1992), the items being 'checked off' (or ticked) once their presence has been confirmed. Shopping lists and packing lists are checklists in this sense. The *use* of checklists for specific evaluation purposes is discussed later in this chapter and in the next. Here we deal briefly with their advantages and limitations.

Compared to the most obvious alternatives, impressionistic evaluation involving dipping into a book and in-depth evaluation based on close analysis of features or sections, the checklist has at least four advantages:

1. It is *systematic*, ensuring that all elements that are deemed to be important are considered.

2. It is *cost effective*, permitting a good deal of information to be recorded in a relatively short space of time.
3. The information is recorded in a *convenient* format, allowing for easy comparison between competing sets of material.
4. It is *explicit*, and, provided the categories are well understood by all involved in the evaluation (see Chambers 1997), offers a common framework for decision-making.

The systematicity of the checklist method is well brought out by Skierso (1991: 440, citing Tucker 1978):

A textbook evaluation checklist should consist of a comprehensive set of criteria based on the basic linguistic, psychological, and pedagogical principles underlying modern methods of language learning. These criteria 'should be exhaustive enough to insure assessment of all characteristics of the textbook. And they should be discrete enough to focus attention on one characteristic at a time or on a single group of related characteristics' (Tucker 1978, p. 219).

However, the method also has its potential limitations. For instance, the systematicity (or inclusivity) referred to above is only a strength if the criteria or categories of which a checklist is composed are relevant to the specific context in which it is to be used. An 'off-the-shelf' checklist is likely to need tailoring to suit a particular context, and this can involve a good deal more than simply deleting checklist items which are inapplicable. Moreover, as Williams (1983) has noted, a checklist cannot be a static phenomenon. The categories in all materials evaluation checklists, like those in other forms of apparently objective evaluation instrument or observation schedule, are as much a reflection of the time at which they were conceived and of the beliefs of their designer as are published materials themselves.

Task 2.4

In Appendix 2.4, you will see two complete checklists (A and C) and extracts from a number of others.

1. Look at the criteria in extracts A and E. What differences do you notice?

2. Which of these differences seem to you to be a reflection of the time at which the checklist was conceived?

3.3 The in-depth method

In-depth techniques go beneath the publisher's and author's claims to look at, for instance, the kind of language description, underlying assumptions about learning or values on which the materials are based or, in a broader sense, whether the materials seem likely to live up to the claims that are being made for them (see levels 2 and 3 in Table 2.1, above). As indicated in an earlier section, specific procedures recommended include a focus on specific features (Cunningsworth 1995), close analysis of one or more extracts (Hutchinson 1987), or thorough examination of two units using predetermined questions (Johnson 1986).

While such techniques have the virtue of ensuring that the selection process is a more considered affair, they may also have certain disadvantages:

1. *Representativeness of samples*: the samples (e.g. exercises, lessons, units) selected for analysis may not be representative of the book as a whole, and this may therefore distort any judgement.
2. *Partiality*: because in-depth analysis is normally narrowly focused (being based either on a particular section of the material or one or more threads running through it), it gives only a partial insight into what the material offers.
3. *Time and expertise required*: some proposals for in-depth evaluation would involve a good deal of time; others require expert knowledge (e.g. of language description) that is not available. Though it can be argued that the time spent on evaluation is well spent if a potentially unsuitable textbook is rejected, there may be more economical ways of arriving at this decision.

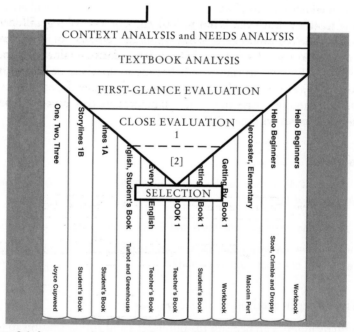

Figure 2.1 An approach to materials evaluation for adoption

This section has suggested that used in isolation each of these methods has its limitations as well as its specific uses. This argues for an integrated approach in which evaluative purpose dictates the method selected at any one time. Such an approach would involve at least two stages. The first of these, here referred to as **first-glance evaluation**, serves to eliminate from further consideration any obviously unsuitable materials. As Figure 2.1 on page 28 indicates, two further stages, involving close evaluation, may be needed before a final selection can be made.

4 FIRST-GLANCE EVALUATION

Faced with the need to choose a new coursebook, we are tempted to make economies. And this might have the fairly obvious consequence that we make a decision that we subsequently regret. An earlier section of this chapter has suggested that evaluation ought to be preceded by analysis, but three-level analysis of the kind recommended by Littlejohn (1998) is not always feasible. Picture this. Spread out on the table are six piles of material. Each pile contains a student's book and what Grant (1987) has called 'add-ons' – a teacher's book, cassettes, a workbook, and possibly other ancillary materials. If what is at issue is the adoption of a multi-level course (i.e. a series), there may be several students' books, teachers' books, and so on. And instead of six sets of material there might be eight or ten. It would take hours to go carefully through even one or two piles.

The alternative, however, is not to look through everything with precisely the same degree of care, but to make an initial selection of those materials which pass the test of what we will call **first-glance evaluation**, and then submit these to closer examination. When the materials to be selected will be used by more than one teacher it is obviously desirable if all those who will be affected have an opportunity to participate in this process. The steps involved are shown in Figure 2.2:

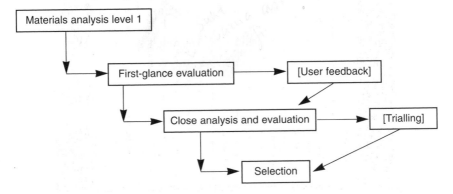

Figure 2.2 From analysis to selection

It is clear from the suggestions made along similar lines by other writers that it is not always easy to draw a clear line between first-glance evaluation and close evaluation. Grant's CATALYST test for 'initial evaluation' (Grant 1987: 119), for example, comprises 'the eight criteria by which we can decide whether a textbook is suitable for our classroom' (ibid.). The criteria are laid out in the form of the acronym CATALYST – the textbook, like a chemical catalyst, being seen as something which brings about change:

C Communicative?
A Aims?
T Teachability?
A Available add-ons?
L Level?
Y Your impression?
S Student interest?
T Tried and tested?
(ibid.)

Leaving aside the question of contrivance, Grant's list contains two criteria that would be difficult to apply without close examination of the materials: *Communicative?* (glossed on p. 119 as 'Is the textbook communicative? Will the students be able to use the language to communicate as a result of using the book?) and *Teachability?* ('Does the course seem teachable? Does it seem reasonably easy to use, well organised, easy to find your way around? (ibid.)).

A similar point can be made about McDonough and Shaw's (1993) much more extensive set of prompts. Adopting a more structured approach, McDonough and Shaw (1993: 66–77) distinguish between 'external' and 'internal' evaluation, using the terms almost literally. External evaluation, which constitutes a form of initial evaluation, is based on what can be gleaned from the cover of a book, including the back cover, where the publisher's blurb is typically found, the introduction and the table of contents. Materials which pass this test are then subjected to internal evaluation, that is, careful scrutiny of the lesson materials.

External evaluation, as discussed by McDonough and Shaw (1993: 66–77) should yield information on the following:

- intended audience
- proficiency level
- context of use (i.e. general English vs ESP)
- organisation of teaching material (time taken to cover units/lessons)
- the views of the author(s) on language and methodology and the relationship between language, the learning process and the learner.

Other aspects of the materials that can be established at this stage are as follows:

- whether materials are designed as a main course or as supplement to a main course
- whether the teacher's book is in print/available locally
- what kinds of visuals are included and what use is made of these
- whether layout and presentation are clear
- whether there is any cultural bias or cultural specificity
- whether there is any bias in relation to the presentation of minority groups and/or women, and whether a particular society is presented in a balanced way
- whether audio/video components are essential
- whether there are tests and, if so, the suitability of these.

(based on McDonough and Shaw 1993: 66–74)

While this seems a more principled approach to preliminary analysis and evaluation than that proposed by Grant, it also makes demands on a scale that is perhaps out of proportion to the purpose. First-glance evaluation should be a matter of establishing whether there is a rough match between learning context and needs on the one hand and materials on the other; anything beyond that is best incorporated within a more detailed analysis. In McDonough and Shaw's list, criteria relating to the views of the author(s), the use made of visuals and bias, for instance, all seem to belong more appropriately to a more systematic or in-depth evaluation; and even within the external/internal framework advocated by these authors the latter two categories fall on the wrong side of the line.

5 CRITERIA FOR EVALUATION

One of the key problems facing the designer of an evaluation instrument, as the above discussion illustrates, is the specification of criteria. Here we consider one aspect of that problem, the appropriateness of criteria to the evaluative purpose. A second aspect, the transparency of criteria, is discussed in Chapter 3.

Much of the discussion on materials evaluation is posited on the assumption that the evaluator has in mind fairly well defined end-users (learners, teacher(s)) and context. As a result, discussions of evaluation criteria tend to be context-related. Important though this emphasis is, it is helpful to make a distinction, following Ur (1996), between *general* criteria (i.e. the essential features of any good teaching–learning material) and *specific* (or context-related) criteria.

Task 2.5

Ur (1996: 184) lists as examples of general criteria: 'clear layout and print' and 'provides periodic review or test sections', examples of specific criteria being 'attractive and colourful illustrations' (which may be particularly relevant for younger learners) and 'vocabulary and texts relevant to topic' (if the materials are intended for students of science or technology).

What other examples of general criteria can you think of? Limit yourself to characteristics which you feel to be essential and not simply desirable.

Tomlinson (1999: 11–12) takes the definition of specific criteria a step further, suggesting four categories of specific criteria:

1. *Media-specific* criteria: i.e. those which relate to the particular medium used. In reference to audio-recorded material, for instance, one might consider the audibility of the recording.
2. *Content-specific* criteria: i.e. those which relate to the nature of the material, such as the choice of topics, situations or language in a business English book or the texts included and skills covered in a book focusing on the development of reading skills.
3. *Age-specific* criteria: i.e. the suitability of the material (e.g. visuals, cognitive challenge) for the age-group for which it is intended.
4. *Local criteria*: i.e. the appropriateness of the material for the particular environment in which it is to be used.

If a group of teachers were faced with the task of drawing up a list of criteria to evaluate material of a particular kind, they would almost certainly come up with both general criteria and specific criteria in each of the categories suggested by Tomlinson, especially the last. The value of such a categorisation may therefore not be that it reminds us to consider each of the specific categories but that it prompts us to draw up sets of criteria to ensure that each relevant category is systematically considered.

Clarifying for ourselves the distinction between general criteria and specific criteria on the one hand and essential and desirable characteristics on the other can serve two purposes. The general/specific distinction leads to the identification of a set of 'core' criteria which can be applied irrespective of evaluation method in any situation; the essential/desirable distinction establishes a principled basis for rejection (if essential features are lacking, the material should almost certainly be rejected, however many desirable features it contains). As we shall see in subsequent sections, both processes have direct applications in the construction and use of checklists.

5.1 From general to specific

One way of thinking about general criteria is as headings or ways of summarising sets of more specific criteria. However, whereas the general criteria should be seen as essential, the specific criteria can only be determined on the basis of individual circumstances. Table 2.3 on page 33 sets out a possible basic set of such criteria.

The relationship between this and the draft checklist intended for level 1 analysis (Table 2.2, above) will be obvious. Descriptive information (e.g. the cost of the materials to students or institution, the availability of tests and assumptions about the teaching time needed) recorded at the analysis stage now serves to answer evaluative questions framed with a particular context in mind.

Table 2.3 Example of a checklist for first-glance evaluation

Practical considerations	
all components available?	Y/N
affordable?	Y/N
multi-level (i.e. series)?	Y/N
Support for teaching and learning	
additional components:	
– teacher's book?	Y/N
– tests?	Y/N
– cassettes?	Y/N
suitable for self-study?	Y/N
Context-relevance	
suitable for course:	
– length of course?	Y/N
– aims of course?	Y/N
– syllabus?	Y/N
– exam?	Y/N
suitable for learners:	
– age?	Y/N
– level?	Y/N
– cultural background?	Y/N
suitable for teachers	Y/N
required resources (e.g. cassette recorder) available?	Y/N
evidence of suitability (e.g. piloted in local context?)	Y/N
Likely appeal to learners	
layout	Y/N
visuals	Y/N
topics	Y/N
suitable over medium term (i.e. unlikely to date)?	Y/N

Task 2.6

In the sample checklist above (see Table 2.3), the specific criteria within each area have been selected so that they can be assessed without lengthy examination of the material. Provided that the evaluator has the necessary information (i.e. context, needs and level 1 analyses have been carried out) and samples of the material are to hand, the whole process need take no more than 10 minutes. (Remember that the purpose at this stage is simply to filter out obviously unsuitable materials, not to make a final choice.)

1. Do you think the YES/NO format of the checklist is appropriate?
2. If a particular set of materials 'failed' on one of the *specific* criteria, do you think it should be automatically discarded? If so, how would you justify this? If not, what conditions would you set for material to meet the general criteria?
3. How appropriate are the specific criteria for your own teaching situation? Would you want to delete certain items? Add any items? (You might like to look back at Table 2.2.)
4. Once you have reached a decision on questions 1–3, read the 'Commentary' below. This offers a rationale for the specific criteria included in the checklist. Additional criteria that may be considered important in particular situations are italicised.
5. Now think of a context for which you might wish to select materials and the various features of that context. Decide whether to use the checklists for first-level analysis and first-glance evaluation included in this chapter (Tables 2.2 and 2.3 respectively) or your own versions of these. Try out the checklists on materials you have not seen before. Keep a note of the time you took to do this and any problems you had – these might indicate criteria that require revision.

5.2 Commentary

5.2.1 Practical considerations

In the sample checklist, only three items are included under this heading. Two of these are linked by the notion of availability. Although the guaranteed continuing availability of books may pose problems only in some countries, in relation to new publications the availability of specific components (teacher's book or cassettes, for example) is of concern to everyone, and the smooth progression of students from one level to another is often dependent on the existence of further books within the same series. *Publisher reliability* may therefore be an issue. Where there is a problem with only one level within a series, it is relevant to ask whether the new choice can be *easily integrated* with other books in use. Where courses consist of multiple components *cost* is an important consideration, and *durability* (especially where books form part of an institution's store or are handed on from student to student) can also be a factor.

5.2.2 Support for teaching and learning

The minimum requirement in terms of published materials is a student's book. This may or may not contain progress tests. From a teacher's point of view, life is easier if it does, although some teachers with the time and confidence might prefer to write their own. (Note that one of the textbook packages described in Appendix 2.1 contains 'customizable' tests.) Similarly, the provision of a teacher's book, cassette recordings, and a student's workbook or photocopiable worksheets containing additional exercises all reduce pressure on the teacher. Learners should also be able to use the material for self-directed study. Reference sections containing, for instance, grammar explanations and examples, verb lists, and word lists showing pronunciation (and, in the case of single-language editions, translations) and advice on how to learn can all support students' out-of-class learning. Additional categories under this heading might include (1) *format of teacher's book* (there is convenience in a teacher's book which combines learner materials – interleaved or in reduced format – and teacher's notes) (2) *print size* (young learners find it easier to deal with a larger print size), and – in well-resourced contexts – such add-ons as (3) *video* or *CD-ROM*. Teachers in some contexts might also welcome materials that convey (4) *information about life and institutions in the English-speaking world*.

Some evaluators may feel that criteria listed under this heading are desirable rather than essential. My own view is that while teachers can cope if they have to operate with just a student's book, especially if they see this as a resource rather than the course, and while learners do learn from materials that are less than comprehensive in the support they offer, there is every reason to reject such materials if something better is available; and normally something better will be available.

5.2.3 Context relevance

From a pedagogic perspective, this is the most important of the priority areas. There needs to be a reasonably good fit between the material, the learners (age, level, cultural background – including sophistication) and the constraints under which teaching takes place (length of course, course aims, official syllabus, public examinations). If not, the teacher will face a good deal of extra work (selecting what is appropriate, cutting out or adapting what is not, and supplementing as necessary), and perhaps pressure to justify the choice of the original material – and the decision not to use certain sections – to learners and others. We can all do without these kinds of pressure. Some evaluators might therefore wish to ascertain whether *the authors* have first-hand professional knowledge of the context (country, institutional type, teaching environment, learner-type) for which the materials are being considered.

For some years now there has been a tendency for coursebooks produced in Europe and North America to contain integrated listening materials (i.e. cassette recordings, with listening tasks in the student's book). This makes certain assumptions: that the cassettes will be available, that the teacher has access to a recorder (and, ideally, an extension lead), that the acoustics in the classroom will be satisfactory, and that there is a reliable electricity supply. Where any of these conditions cannot be met, it is worth checking whether the listening component is independent of other components. The same applies to video components.

As suggested in Chapter 1, it is also worth trying to discover whether the materials have been piloted or previously used in circumstances similar to those for which they are being assessed and if so with what effect. This will give a clue to whether the material can be easily used by the teachers concerned. The publisher's representative or local bookshop should be able to supply information on piloting and institutions where the materials have been used.

5.2.4 Likely appeal to learners

The relationship between motivation and learning hardly needs stating. It is logical therefore that we consider the likely appeal to students of the appearance of the materials (clarity of layout, visuals) and their content (choice of topics). Since materials once selected may be used for several years, it is important that they do not date too quickly. This can be a problem with, for instance, news items, texts about celebrities and photographs showing people's clothes and hairstyles. The *date of publication* is one indication of topicality. As far as likely appeal is concerned, the most reliable way of ensuring that this priority is taken seriously is to ask learners (either those for whom the material is needed or a comparable group) for their views on the various sets of materials from which the choice is to be made. (But beware: like teachers, learners may be attracted/distracted by the cover of a book, its title or its convenient size.)

5.3 Applying the criteria

Deciding how strictly to enforce the specific criteria is a matter of judgement related to individual circumstances. If a criterion is not important for a particular context, it should not be included in first-glance evaluation (or any evaluation for that matter); nevertheless, certain items may be more important in one context than another. With this in mind, it is conceivable that a set of materials be judged unsatisfactory in respect of one specific criterion, yet still be felt to merit closer examination. However, any argument among evaluators about whether materials which fail to meet several specific criteria should pass this preliminary test may well point to a problem with the criteria themselves: either the criteria are not sufficiently transparent (and are therefore being interpreted in different ways) or the features to which they refer are not really essential.

The issue of how strictly to enforce criteria is also relevant at the higher level of general criteria. In the flowchart below the general evaluative criteria (headings) from Table 2.3 have been prioritised as part of a procedure for first-glance evaluation. As will be clear, the implication is that if the material under consideration does not meet the first of these criteria (which could be further specified as in Table 2.3) it is immediately discarded.

Task 2.7

Look through Figure 2.3 and answer the questions on page 38. Gather information (on supply, availability of components and levels, cost, and piloting or previous use) and samples from bookshop or publisher's representative.

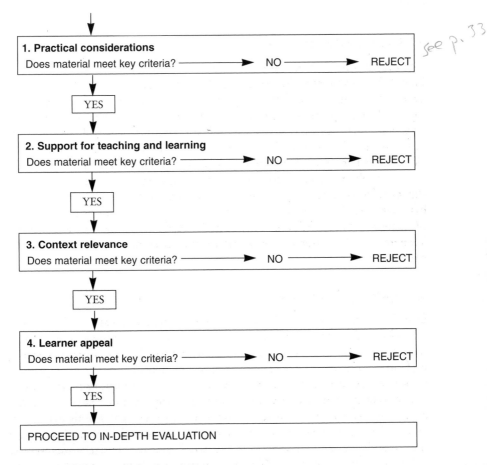

See p. 33

Figure 2.3 A procedure for first-glance evaluation

1. Do you agree that first-glance evaluation should be based on these four general criteria – and only these?
2. Do you think it is possible to prioritise general criteria? If so, why do you think these criteria were ordered in this way? Do you agree with the order adopted in the flowchart?
3. Should material that is unsatisfactory in just one of these categories be automatically rejected?
4. If you disagree with the approach suggested in the flowchart or any of its features, how would you approach first-glance evaluation?

In deciding on a procedure for first-glance evaluation, a key consideration is economy. The intention is to eliminate any obviously unsuitable materials without spending any more time on these than is absolutely necessary. First-glance evaluation is meant to function as a broad filter. To defer a decision about materials that 'fail' on one of these general categories (or any alternative categories that you might prefer) is simply to make more work for another day. The same can be said for less decisive ways of judging the material: to use a numbered or descriptive scale rather than *Yes/No* is a hindrance rather than a help to decision-making. For this whole process to be valid, however, the general categories must be accepted as essential by (and ideally suggested by) all those involved in the evaluation.

The reasons for the order adopted in the flowchart are as follows: (1) practicality: if materials are not affordable there is no point in considering them any further; this criterion can also be evaluated quickly and any obviously unsuitable materials rejected without further ado; (2) materials must facilitate the work of a teacher; again, a criterion that can be evaluated quickly; (3) resourceful teachers can compensate for some weaknesses, but if the materials fail on too many items of the relevance test, then they have to go; note that more judgement is involved at this stage than the two previous stages (4) and last but not least, the learner test – which requires experience or empathy or the elicitation of learners' opinions, and is therefore more demanding. Though differences in circumstances will mean that individual evaluators or institutions might attach different levels of importance to these four general categories – and perhaps for this reason therefore order them differently, there can be little doubt that all should figure in first-glance evaluation.

6 SUMMARY

This chapter has outlined the first steps in a systematic approach to armchair evaluation for materials selection. Step 1 involves a form of stocktaking: the consideration of relevant contextual factors and, if any aspect of the context is unfamiliar, the gathering of information. This is followed by analysis of the materials. The methods used for this purpose have been here characterised as impressionistic, checklist and in-depth. As this characterisation implies, analysis can take place on a number of levels. The resulting description is then compared with the needs identified in the target situation to establish the potential suitability of the materials. This might be an extremely lengthy process if several sets of materials are being considered. The concept of first-glance evaluation, when a specially-designed checklist is used to eliminate from further consideration any obviously unsuitable materials, has therefore been proposed to reduce the time required at the evaluation stage. Chapter 3 suggests how the final decision might be reached.

Choosing a coursebook 2: close evaluation

Close evaluation using a checklist: approaches to checklist design; determining general categories; determining specific criteria; determining format; piloting and revising checklists; group evaluation; making the final decision – in-depth analysis

Because the choice of a coursebook can have such an important impact on learners and teachers, the decision-making process needs to be careful and systematic. What has been described in Chapters 1 and 2 is a procedure by which the choice can be narrowed down. During a preliminary armchair evaluation stage (first-glance evaluation), the most unsuitable materials are weeded out. If user reports are available on any of the remaining materials, this might permit more of these to be eliminated from further consideration. The remaining materials would be examined in more detail during a second armchair evaluation stage (close evaluation). Trialling, if this were possible, would be a final check on the suitability of materials provisionally selected.

If user reports are unavailable and trialling is impossible, then close evaluation takes on even more importance. In this chapter, two methods of close evaluation will be discussed. A checklist will again be proposed as the most effective way of gathering comparable data systematically; but the contribution of in-depth analysis, as a supplement to a checklist, will also be considered.

1 CLOSE EVALUATION USING A CHECKLIST

1.1 Approaches to checklist design

For the evaluator who wishes to carry out a close evaluation using a checklist, there are probably three basic options, each of which might be combined with one or more of the others. These are set out in Task 3.1, below.

Task 3.1

What do you see as the pros and cons of each of these options?

A. *Borrow and adapt*: Look at all the checklists available, published or otherwise.

Choose the one that looks most suitable. Make any modifications to content or format that seem necessary.

B. *Originate*: Brainstorm ideas for a checklist (content and format).

C. *Research*: Find out what end-users (teachers and learners) consider to be important.

We will return to this question towards the end of the chapter.

The following is a list of possible steps in the design of a checklist for close evaluation of materials.

Step 1 Decide general categories within which specific criteria will be organised.
Step 2 Decide specific criteria within each category.
Step 3 Decide ordering of general categories and specific criteria.
Step 4 Decide format of prompts and responses.

Not everyone would go about this in the same way. For instance, Tomlinson (1999) states that he finds it helpful first to generate specific criteria by brainstorming beliefs about the principles on which the material should be based, and then to sort these criteria into categories. In thinking about materials he will teach himself, he notes, he draws on his own beliefs about language learning; if he were evaluating course materials for use in another country, he would take into account what he knows about the norms in that country.

Task 3.2, below, encourages you to do some preliminary thinking about categories, criteria and format for close evaluation. The design process as a whole is then discussed in more detail.

Grant (1987) states:

The perfect textbook does not exist, but the best book available for you and your students certainly does. Such a book should satisfy three conditions:

- It should suit the needs, interests and abilities of your students
- It should suit *you*. (The best book in the world won't work in your classroom if you have good reasons for disliking it.)
- The textbook must meet the needs of official public teaching syllabuses or examinations.

(Grant 1987: 118)

The three conditions are then amplified in the form of three checklists, each containing ten questions.

Task 3.2

Imagine that, like Grant, you decide to devise your own checklist in order to assess the suitability of a book for your own use with a class of students you know well in a situation where there is an official syllabus and/or where students will take a public examination at the end of the year.

1. Draft four items in each of the following categories (twelve items in all):

   A. suitability for students
   B. suitability for teacher
   C. suitability for situation

   You will need to think about whether the items should be in the form of questions or statements, and what kind of response would be appropriate.

2. Appendix 3.1 contains extracts from Grant's three-part questionnaire. Compare the items you have devised with those of Grant; how similar are they? Do you think all Grant's questions are appropriate to the categories in which they appear? What further questions might you want to ask in each of these categories?

3. What do you think about the format of Grant's questionnaire (e.g. number of questions (ten per section); ordering of questions within sections – insofar as it is possible to judge this from the extracts; response format; scoring system)?

1.2 Commentary

While the rationale for Grant's decision to prepare a three-part (three-category) checklist and the categories selected is clear from the quotation above, it is less clear why there should be ten questions in each part (What is magic about the number ten?) or, indeed, why there should be the same number of questions in each part. This requirement may lead either to the exclusion of important questions (or the 'sideways movement' of these to another category) or the inclusion of trivial questions, just to make up the number. This way of giving equal weighting to the three categories may look neat; it can also be argued that the evaluator is able to reach a balanced judgement. However, the approach is based on two false premises: that the individual items within each category are equal in importance, and that the categories are themselves equally important. The weighing of factors involved in textbook selection is actually a much more complex process than this suggests. There is, in fact, no logical reason why a checklist should have any specific number of questions or, if it consists of sections, why these should be of equal size. A similar criticism might be made of the regular response format. While this also looks neat, it is difficult to conceive of a situation in which 'Partly' would be an appropriate response to a question about 'the right length', or indeed to many of the other questions. Moreover, certain questions have two or more foci. One might wish to answer 'Yes' to 'Does it achieve an acceptable balance between the relevant language skills?', for example, and 'No' to the second part of this question (which focuses on opportunities for integrated skills practice). Responding will also be a problem if a question seems inapplicable. If the real answer to the penultimate question regarding the relationship between the book and the syllabus ('If it does more than the syllabus requires, is the result an improvement?') happened to be 'Actually, it doesn't do more', this can hardly be answered 'No' because this would be an invalid criticism. However, if we were to include 'not applicable' as a category, how would we score it? One answer might be to ignore questions that are not applicable when it comes to scoring and instead calculate the ratio between the total score and the remaining number of questions.

It will be clear from this commentary that designing a checklist is no easy matter. It therefore helps to take things step by step.

1.3 Determining general categories

The first step is to determine evaluation criteria and, as with first-glance evaluation, to group these into categories. Context analysis, learner needs analysis, and your own beliefs about teaching and learning should have indicated what features of textbooks are most important for you (or the teachers who will use the materials) and for the potential learners. If you have carried out a first-glance evaluation, as recommended in Chapter 2, you will have already assessed certain of these features in a preliminary way. However, it also makes sense to consult checklists devised by others to make sure that nothing important has been overlooked.

Numerous checklists have been designed for the systematic evaluation of coursebooks, some of the best-known published examples being Tucker (1975), Haycraft (1978), Daoud and Celce-Murcia (1979), Cunningsworth (1979, 1984), Williams (1983), Sheldon (1988), Harmer (1991), Skierso (1991) and Ur (1996). Of these, by far the most detailed is Skierso. What is clear from examination of these checklists and other sources is that while checklists may vary considerably in their scope, form, detailed criteria and the terms used to describe criteria, there is a degree of consensus concerning the broad areas of focus. Most of the checklists surveyed make reference to the following:

- **design**: includes both layout of material on the page and overall clarity of organisation
- **language content**: coverage of linguistic items and language skills
- **subject matter**: topics
- **practical considerations** (referred to as 'general' or 'technical' in some checklists): this category includes availability, durability and price.

Task 3.3

1. Would all of these categories be relevant for the context in which you work/ have worked most recently and the type of material you would probably wish to evaluate?

2. Are there any other categories which you feel should be included?

3. Appendix 3.2 summarises the main features of a number of checklists. Look at the 'main categories' column. Are there any additional categories here that you would consider including?

1.4 Determining specific criteria

The process of generating and grouping criteria is not simply a matter of (1) decide general categories of criteria (2) decide specific criteria – or vice versa. The reality is rather messier. Brainstorming usually throws up specific criteria alongside general categories, and general categories suggest specific criteria. This sorting process is important, however, because once a tentative decision has been reached concerning general categories, the comprehensiveness and relevance of the specific criteria listed under these can more easily be assessed. Again, published checklists are helpful as sources of ideas. Apart from the general sources already listed (extracts from some of which are included in Appendix 2.4), more specific checklists also exist: see, e.g., Cunningsworth (1987) on conversational skills in coursebooks, Gairns and Redman (1986, Ch. 11) on vocabulary in coursebooks and Hedge (1988) on writing tasks. Cunningsworth (1995) contains checklists covering a variety of aspects. On teacher's books, see Coleman (1985) and Cunningsworth and Kusel (1991) as well as Skierso (1991).

Other writers have adopted evaluative perspectives which are not primarily linguistic. These include Risager (1990), Prodromou (1992a), and Alptekin (1993) on culture in coursebooks; Hewings (1991) on culturally-influenced perceptions of illustrations; and Porreca (1984), Sunderland (1992) and the section on materials in Sunderland (1994) on gender stereotypes. Survey reviews of the type found in *ELT Journal*, such as those on learner training by Sinclair and Ellis (1992) and Lake (1997), also include explicit statements of the criteria on which the comparative reviews are based. Although these concerns may also be reflected in more general evaluative frameworks (see, e.g., sexism in Matthews (1991) or learner training in Ur (1996)), such papers offer useful background reading for anyone contemplating checklist design.

1.4.1 Transparency of criteria

One problem with many checklists is that they tend to take for granted understanding of certain concepts which may be unfamiliar to or only partially understood by potential teacher-users.

Task 3.4

1. Look through the extracts on p. 45 from published checklists. Which terms might not be understood by teachers in your teaching context?

2. How would you explain these terms or rephrase them so that they were clearer?

- appropriate sequencing of grammatical patterns
- adequacy of drill model and pattern displays (i.e. clarity of instructions for learner)

(Tucker 1975)

- sentence length reasonable for students of that level
- vocabulary load (number of new words in each lesson) reasonable

(Daoud and Celce-Murcia 1979)

- based on a contrastive analysis of English and L1 sound systems
- gives practice in controlled composition in the early stages

(Williams 1983)

- spiral approach
- enough communicative activities

(Grant 1987)

- attention to grammatical accuracy
- balance of language skills (enough attention to reading and writing)

(Matthews 1991)

- enough roughly tuned input
- practice of individual skills integrated into practice of other skills

(Harmer 1991)

- plenty of authentic language
- encourages learners to develop their own learning strategies

(Ur 1996)

The best way to check whether criteria work in the way they were intended is to try them out, to see how transparent they really are. The next task focuses on the concept of communicativeness, but it will probably also involve you in considering allied concepts such as authenticity and integration.

Task 3.5 K

One of the criteria in Grant (1987) is 'enough communicative activities'.

1. Look at the extracts in Appendix 3.3 from a variety of published materials. Which of the tasks are more/less 'communicative'?

2. Do you think all activities can be or should be communicative?

This is not the place for a detailed discussion of the principles of communicative language teaching. However, most theorists and practitioners would probably agree on the following.

In communicative language teaching:

- there is attention to meaning and use as well as language form
- purposeful communication between learners is encouraged (and information-gap and opinion-gap tasks are one way of providing for this)
- the classroom is seen as a place where learners rehearse (by doing authentic tasks on authentic texts) for real-world target language use
- learners should have opportunities to express their own meanings in their own words
- the term 'communicative' does not only apply to speaking activities

See also 'Tasks: Key and Commentaries' at the back of the book.

The task above is not meant to imply that communicativeness is something that teachers should necessarily be looking for in a coursebook, or that each and every text or task should be communicative. In relation to this and any other criterion, context-sensitivity is important. Moreover, while we must keep faith with our beliefs in the sense that we do not surrender to the requirements and constraints of the situation in which we find ourselves, compromise will often be necessary between the desirable and the possible. Rossner (1988), whose paper on 'Materials for communicative language teaching and learning' includes an analysis of extracts from a number of randomly selected coursebooks, supplementary materials and resource books, comments shrewdly:

> Interestingly, teachers have themselves used terms like *communicative* less and less frequently over the last five years. This may be because they view as unfortunate the implications of the communicative movement; namely, that what went before or what goes on outside it was or is not 'communicative'; that only work that can be classified as *communicative* in Breen and Candlin's (1980) sense of the term is useful; or because they find the demands implicit in full adoption of the approach impossible to meet. Rather, teachers have become accustomed to seeing teaching/learning as a process in which the focus must shift along a continuum.
>
> (Rossner 1988: 141)

Whether it is true that teachers use the term 'communicative' less than they did (and Rossner is referring to the period from the early 1980s) may depend on the circles in which one moves. What is certain is that the pendulum-swing that was evident in the 1970s has now been corrected, and teachers are in general more aware of the need to locate their teaching at points along a form-focused/communication-focused continuum that suit their learners' needs. (See e.g. Harmer (1991) and Littlewood (1981) for discussion of non-communicative/communicative activities and pseudo-communicative/communicative activities.)

1.4.2 Dated criteria

As the last two tasks will have demonstrated, it is important to ensure that checklist criteria are transparent to those who will use them. A second problem with published checklists, as noted in the last chapter, is that they date almost as fast as materials. We expect materials to reflect new insights into language description, theories of learning and teaching and changes in society. These changes should also be reflected in the content of checklists. If we are using a checklist designed by someone else or using someone else's checklist as the basis for our own design, we need to be able to 'see through' the categories to the assumptions that underlie them. Where they appear to be out of date or do not match our own beliefs, we need to make the necessary changes.

Task 3.6

1. Go back to the extracts in Task 3.4. Which of the criteria in those extracts reflect views on language, learning or teaching that differ from your own?

2. What modifications would you make to these items or what alternative items would you include to reflect your own views?

3. For each of the categories you listed in Task 3.3, formulate a number of specific criteria.

   Example:

   category: LANGUAGE CONTENT
   specific criteria: • authenticity of language samples
                      • opportunities for real communication

4. Ask other people to comment on your criteria.

1.4.3 Assumptions

Littlejohn (1998) argues that another potential problem with criteria is that they may be based on implicit assumptions about what '"desirable" materials should look like' (p. 191). His critique of specific criteria in the checklists of Williams (1983), Dougill (1987), and Harmer (1991) is worth quoting in full:

Thus we have features listed such as an 'up-to-date methodology of L2 teaching' (Williams, *ibid*: 252) and questions such as 'Is it foolproof (i.e. sufficiently methodical to guide the inexperienced teacher through a lesson)' (Dougill, *ibid*: 32) and 'Is the language used in the materials realistic' (Harmer, *ibid*: 282). Each of these areas, however, will be debatable – being 'up to date' is not in itself a good thing; 'foolproof' materials will reflect particular views of the role of the teacher and ideas about the best route to teacher development; 'real-life English' may lead to an emphasis on authenticity at the expense of pedagogic good sense; and so on. There are further problems, too, in establishing whether the materials are indeed 'foolproof' or 'up to date'. How can the teacher-analyst know, other than by making impressionistic, unguided judgements?

(Littlejohn 1998: 191–2)

Littlejohn's comments are also based on beliefs and assumptions. One is the belief that materials analysis should be separate from and precede materials evaluation (see the summary of his ideas in Chapter 2). A second is that any judgement should be based on evidence. A third, much more dubious, is that materials evaluation (as opposed to materials analysis) can be a value-free undertaking. The reality is that evaluation *is* value laden, and this will be less of a problem if evaluators (1) look critically at the criteria formulated by others; (2) are aware of their own values; and (3), in specifying criteria for use by others, investigate and take the values of the ultimate users into account.

1.5 Determining format

A materials evaluation checklist has to fulfil a number of potentially conflicting functions:

1. provide comprehensive information of the sort that will facilitate evaluation
2. and comparison
3. while making as few demands on the evaluator as possible (e.g. be easily understandable; easy/quick to complete)
4. lead to the selection of materials which are appropriate for the context (in the fullest sense, including suitability for the teachers who will use them)
5. but also contribute to the *advancement* of learning and teaching in that context.

As will be clear, there is likely to be a tension between breadth and depth, between informativity and economy, between the needs of the evaluator and the needs of the checklist designer – if these are different people, and between the forces of conservatism and innovation. Though this last issue (point 5) poses a number of difficulties that can probably only be tackled in the context of a wider developmental process, the other requirements can be largely met through instruments and procedures that minimise the chance of decisions being taken on the basis of individual subjective judgement. Up to this point, we have concentrated on the selection and formulation of criteria. We now turn to issues of format.

1.5.1 Information

It is probably useful to include at the top of the checklist a section summarising basic information about the book under consideration (see Appendix 2.4 for ideas). This may well have formed part of level 1 analysis and first-glance evaluation.

1.5.2 Item format and response

Thereafter, the basic decision to be made is between open-ended questions on the one hand and on the other statements or prompts, the response to which is a tick or a score. Open-ended questions have their advocates, on the grounds that they require more of an investment on the part of the evaluator and are therefore more likely to be answered thoughtfully. However, a checklist in which statements or questions are combined with a numerical response can probably be completed more quickly and the responses (of different evaluators or the same evaluator regarding different books) compared more easily. A basically closed format of this kind can also incorporate space for a comment (see, e.g., the extracts from Sheldon 1988 or Harmer 1991 in Appendix 2.4) which explains and amplifies the response. The additional information generated in this way can be of value if a comparison is made between the views of different evaluators on specific criteria. Thinking more holistically, and drawing on his own practice, Tomlinson (1999) records that he completes a statement for each item, summarises the positive and negative comments relating to each category, and writes a final summary highlighting the key positive and negative findings. For a rather different approach in which the evaluator simply uses plus, minus or zero to determine the degree of match between the material and the learners and teachers for whom material is being selected, see Bruder (1978).

1.5.3 Sequencing of categories and specific criteria within these

At some point during considerations of layout, it will be necessary to think about the ordering of items and categories. User convenience and logical interrelationships need to be taken into account, but this is essentially a matter of judgement. The sequencing of criteria within a category may, however, lead to the realisation that certain criteria overlap.

1.5.4 Rating, weighting, scoring

Some checklists (e.g. Tucker 1975, Daoud and Celce-Murcia 1979, Williams 1983, Sheldon 1988, and Skierso 1991) include a *rating* scale. Although a Yes/No answer format may be appropriate for certain types of question (e.g. those concerning the presence or absence of a particular feature), a rating scale permits qualitative judgements to be made (i.e. a response to the questions *How much? How well?*). Rating scales typically contain three to five points. The inclusion of five points appears to allow for finer judgements, but there is a strong argument for a four-point scale (rather than three or five), which makes it impossible for the evaluator to choose the non-committal central point.

Hutchinson and Waters (1987: 105) warn: 'Note that the highest number of points does not necessarily indicate the most suitable materials, since the points may be concentrated in one area.' They therefore advise: 'Look for the widest spread of desired features and concentrations in the areas you consider most important' (ibid.). An alternative approach is to give prominence to specific features by allocating them a higher *weighting* on a designated scale (e.g. 1–3) (Daoud and Celce-Murcia 1979, Williams 1983). This also permits a checklist which has been developed elsewhere to be fine-tuned to the requirements of a particular context. Ur (1996), who – like Tucker (1975) – rather confusingly uses the term 'rating' for what others have called 'weighting', proposes a five-point weighting scale using ticks, question marks and crosses rather than numbers. She has this suggestion to make about deciding weightings:

> In deciding on the rating [*sic*] for each item, it might help to ask yourself: if this quality were missing, would I therefore not use this book? If so, then you obviously think the quality essential or very important. If, however, the quality is desirable, but its absence would not necessarily stop you using the book if all the other criteria were fulfilled, then perhaps a single tick [indicating 'fairly important'] may be enough.
>
> (Ur 1996: 185)

In similar vein, Skierso (1991) suggests a three-point scale to indicate 'absolutely essential' (A), 'beneficial, preferred' (B), and 'not applicable' (N), or 4, 2 and 0 if a numerical scale is preferred. Appendix 2.4 contains an extract from Williams' checklist, which uses both rating and weighting scales.

If the evaluation is to involve several people, the coordinator of the evaluation can determine how to weight each criterion on the scale or this can be discussed (Skierso 1991, Chambers 1997) – a potentially valuable form of professional debate in itself.

The great advantage of quantifying responses in this way is that once the 'score' for each criterion has been calculated by multiplying rating and weighting scales – R(ating) x W(eighting) = score – and the scores subtotalled and totalled, it is a simple matter to make comparisons between competing sets of materials both globally and in relation to specific criteria or sets of criteria. Table 3.1 on the next page shows an extract from such a comparison. While it would be unwise to assume that this kind of scoring system is somehow more objective than a purely impressionistic judgement, a clear difference between scores *is* a strong indication that the materials with the higher overall score are likely to be more suitable. Equally important, however, is the fact that the scores also indicate, in a more specific way than an impressionistic judgement and in a clearer way than a verbal response to an open question, which features of the materials are weak and would need supplementation if that particular set of materials were selected.

An example might be helpful at this point. Let us suppose that an institution is looking for a new series of books to replace the ones they have been using. Let us also suppose that this evaluation is taking place in a context where cost and durability are relatively important for learners and convenience a consideration for teachers. Table 3.1 shows an extract from a partially completed checklist in which these factors have been differentially weighted on a scale of 1–3 (where 3 = very important) and two competing textbook series (A and B) rated using a scale of 1–4 (where 4 indicates an extremely positive judgement). From the scores awarded thus far, we can see that the evaluator considers Book A is somewhat cheaper than Book B, but that the higher cost of Book B is more than offset by its superior durability.

Table 3.1 Extract from a weighted rating scale for the comparative evaluation of textbooks

		BOOK A		BOOK B	
CRITERIA	*W*	*R*	*W x R*	*R*	*W x R*
Practical considerations					
cost	2	3	6	2	4
durability (cover/binding/paper quality	2	1	2	3	6
size of student's book	1				
T's book includes S's book materials	2				
multi-level (and number of levels)	3				
		Subtotal		Subtotal	

W = predetermined weighting (1–3), R = rating (1–4)

1.6 Piloting and revising checklists

Like questionnaires, an evaluation checklist should ideally be piloted. This applies even if it is to be used only by its designer. A realistic trial would involve the designer (or preferably someone else) using the checklist to evaluate, for example, one coursebook which he or she has used and another with which he or she is unfamiliar. In relation to the known book, this should give a rough indication of whether the checklist captures known strengths and weaknesses – in other words, whether it accords with experience; the unknown book may turn out to have features which are not picked up by the checklist. Evaluating either book may reveal that there are problems with the criteria themselves: that a particular criterion is too wide, for example; that two criteria can be conflated into one; or that a single criterion has a dual focus. Following such a trial, the checklist can be revised and offered to other colleagues for individual or group evaluation. This may indicate that further revisions are needed; it may also reveal unexpected differences of opinion within the group of evaluators – differences that can only be resolved through discussion. This whole process is best thought of as exploratory. As Hutchinson and Waters (1987) suggest: 'You should use the materials evaluation process as a means of questioning and developing your own ideas as to what is required' (p. 97).

1.7 Group evaluation

On the basis that two or more heads are better than one, Daoud and Celce-Murcia (1979) suggest that each set of materials under consideration be assessed by three experienced teachers. Group evaluation has obvious advantages. The vested interests of all concerned make it likely that any decision will be based on consensus, and the discussion of the pros and cons that precede that decision ensure that the materials will be thoroughly examined from a variety of perspectives. The responsibility for such decisions is also shared. Chambers (1997) describes a process in which a group of teachers worked together to establish the features that they would find desirable, weighted these, and then went on to apply the criteria to distinguish between two coursebooks. At a more specific level, Tucker (1975) suggests an ingenious graphic system in which individual judgements based on the same checklist – and their deviation from an ideal – can be compared.

The obvious problem in group evaluation, even if this takes the form described above, is that anyone who has not been involved in the design of the checklist will need some time and help to get 'inside' the categories and the evaluation system. Where evaluation is organised in such a way that the materials to be evaluated are shared out and individuals take responsibility for evaluating one or two books it is even more important that everyone interprets and applies the criteria in the same way. Before group evaluation based on an existing set of criteria takes place for the first time it is therefore essential that the checklist designer or coordinator takes everyone through the criteria and allows opportunities for clarification or rephrasing of anything that is unclear. It is also useful to include an element of 'practice' in such a briefing session by looking at a book with which everyone is familiar and checking that all would make similar judgements about its key features. A similar procedure should be followed whenever anyone new has to be inducted.

1.8 Making the final decision

The discussion thus far has perhaps given the impression that if textbook evaluation is carried out carefully it will inevitably lead to the right result. Ellis (1998) points to the rather uncomfortable fact that it may be difficult to reconcile strengths and weaknesses in the same textbook; and this leads him to quote Sheldon's (1988: 245) observation, 'coursebook evaluation is fundamentally a subjective, rule-of-thumb activity'. Ellis' example (how is one to reconcile a positive rating for authenticity on the grounds that authentic texts are included with a negative rating on the criterion of vocabulary load because an excessive number of new words is introduced?) is perhaps a little mischievous, since the two criteria are in this case inextricably linked, but he nevertheless draws attention to an important issue.

To be taken seriously, materials evaluation has to address the questions of validity and reliability. The development of criteria by consensus, especially if end-users are involved, can perhaps overcome the problem of validity, and careful briefing of evaluators may counter the problem of the reliability of evaluator judgements. One problem remains. However carefully and systematically comparative materials evaluation is conducted, it cannot really resolve the problem of choice between competing textbooks which obtain a similar overall rating yet have very different patterns of strengths and weaknesses. This is a rather different point from that raised by Ellis; it is also more important. Coursebook evaluation, as treated here, is not only the evaluation of individual sets of material against criteria, but also the *comparison* of different sets of material against those criteria. Although this process should reveal the particular strengths and weaknesses of each set of materials considered, the primary aim is to use this information to select the most suitable materials for the context and not – at this stage, at least – to agonise over tensions within a specific set of materials. In fact, the weighting of key criteria (see above) may help the evaluator to distinguish between significant and less significant weaknesses, within and across the materials under consideration. If this tactic fails to indicate that one textbook is more suitable than the other, the final decision has to be made on the basis of instinct, feel or general impression. This may seem a paradoxical abandonment of reason in favour of emotion, and a surrender to the pessimism implicit in Sheldon's position. It is not: on most occasions, reason will be sufficient, and a principled decision will be possible; on others, reason will take us almost to the point of a decision, and whatever decision is finally taken will therefore have been taken largely on rational grounds. There is inevitably a subjective element in textbook selection, but we can seek to minimise this.

Task 3.7

1. Devise your own checklist for close evaluation. This might be for coursebooks, supplementary skills books or practice books of some kind. Bear in

mind that since coursebook packages normally include not just a student's book but various add-ons such as teacher's book, cassettes, and so on, you may need to devise *media-specific* criteria. Before you begin, give some thought to the various options listed in Task 3.1.

2. Try out the checklist on two sets of material, one that you know well and another with which you are unfamiliar. List any problems you had in using the checklist and consider how you would revise it to overcome these problems.

3. If you can persuade one or two colleagues to do the same, using the same books, this would be even more useful.

After you have worked through his task, you might like to reconsider the question posed in Task 3.1.

2 IN-DEPTH ANALYSIS

Recent years have seen the emergence of packages of materials designed, or so we are led to believe, to provide everything the teacher and learner might need and clear instructions for use. 'The extent to which materials now effectively structure classroom time has thus increased considerably' (Littlejohn 1998: 190). Littlejohn may be overstating the case – teachers and learners may deviate from these instructions or choose to disregard the materials altogether – but his argument that we need to look inside the 'Trojan Horse' represented by materials nevertheless has some force.

Checklists are convenient. However, they can encourage rather superficial judgements. Cunningsworth (1995), who is clearly in favour of checklists, also suggests detailed analysis of one or two units and close analysis of the treatment of specific features (his examples being the treatment of the Present Perfect in English with particular reference to meaning and use; the use of articles; intonation; and discourse features, i.e. language above the level of the sentence). This approach is taken further by a number of writers, all of whom share an interest in learning and the learner. In a paper entitled 'What's underneath?: an interactive view of materials evaluation', Hutchinson (1987) argues for and exemplifies a kind of close analysis – in this case of a single extract – that affords an insight into the view of language learning on which the materials are based. Breen and Candlin (1987) propose a two-phase approach involving a detailed series of questions. Phase one is designed to shed light on the following:

(a) the aims and content of the material
(b) what they require learners to do
(c) what they require the teacher to do
(d) their function as a classroom resource

and thereby permit a judgement as to the *usefulness* of the materials. Phase two focuses on the following:

(a) learner needs and interests
(b) learner approaches to language learning
(c) the teaching–learning approach in the teacher's own classroom.

The question-prompts which form the basis for phase one are summarised in Appendix 3.4A and those for phase two are reproduced in Appendix 3.4B; in the original paper, both sets of prompts are glossed. Taken together, the questions constitute a framework for detailed evaluation with reference to learners' needs (questions 1–3 in Appendix 3.4A and questions 19–30 in Appendix 3.4B) and learning style preferences (questions 31–4 in Appendix 3.4B), but also encourage teachers to draw on their own experience of and beliefs about language learning and teaching (questions 7, 9–11 in Appendix 3.4A) and think in concrete terms about the implications of using the materials for their own role (questions 12–15, and perhaps 8, in Appendix 3.4A).

The authors note that the procedure has been extensively used in workshops on materials evaluation, and it seems likely that in such a setting it would lead to rigorous analysis of the materials in question, offer a framework for future evaluation which is both wide-ranging and searching, and, by virtue of the questions in Parts II and III of Appendix 3.4A, contribute in a broader way to individual and institutional professional development (presumably one of the aims of the workshops).

Although there is nothing about the prompts that makes them intrinsically unsuitable for individual use, the demands they make in terms of detailed analysis and effort means that they are likely to be used on an individual basis only by the most dedicated. There may also be an issue concerning the analytical expertise required.

The emphasis in this chapter has been on the design of checklists for close evaluation. The justification for this bias is that a carefully designed checklist will in many situations offer the most economical and at the same time reliable means of reaching a decision concerning the relative suitability of competing textbooks. This is not to deny that other methods may also have a part to play in the evaluative process. In-depth analysis in particular may be used as an alternative to a checklist or in conjunction with a checklist. In institutions where staff are divided as to the value of methods of analysis, both methods might be used in parallel by different evaluators and the results compared. In-depth analysis can also be used, as acknowledged above, in cases where checklist-based evaluation has failed to suggest a clear preference.

Task 3.8

1. Suppose you had carried out an evaluation of two sets of materials using a checklist and this had failed to indicate sufficiently clearly which set of

materials would be the more suitable for the intended context. Which of the forms of in-depth analysis described in this section would you then use – and why?

2. Where do you stand on the question of checklists versus in-depth evaluation?

3 SUMMARY

Chapter 2 discussed the first of two armchair evaluation stages. This chapter has explored in some detail the second of these stages (close evaluation). Again, *systematic evaluation using a checklist* offers certain advantages over other approaches; however, the checklist needs to be carefully tailored to the needs of learners and the teaching context and the need for periodic updating recognised. For practical purposes, the use of a checklist which utilises rating and weighting scales should prove an adequate indicator as to the relative suitability of the materials and serve to highlight any particular defects or deficiencies. Where any doubt remains and the time and expertise are available, there is value in extending the evaluation process into a third stage, involving one of the techniques of *in-depth analysis*.

Chapter 4

Coursebook-based teaching: adaptation

Course and lesson planning: a course; coursebook-based teaching; syllabus, examination, course and book; evaluation processes in lesson planning; from objectives to lesson structure – selection, rejection and replacement: relevance; processes and principles – adaptation: defining adaptation; the purpose of adaptation – adaptation as addition: extemporisation; extension; exploitation – adaptation as change: a principled approach to adaptation; foci and forms of change; principles motivating change – a lesson-planning task

Chapter 1 put forward a number of reasons why teaching using a textbook may be desirable as well as, for many teachers, necessary. It also made the point that teachers need to exercise judgement concerning the extent to which and the way in which they use books. Coursebook teaching, went the argument, cannot be justified; coursebook-*based* teaching can. This chapter begins by looking at what coursebook-based teaching might mean in practice.

1 COURSE AND LESSON PLANNING

1.1 A course

One very minimal definition of a course might be: 'a planned series of learning events'. This definition distinguishes between a one-off event and a *number* of such events; it suggests that the events will be *linked* in some way; it draws attention to the *planning* involved; and it specifies that one of the intended outcomes is *learning*.

Task 4.1

How would you define 'course' in relation to the language courses that you teach?

1. First consider the highlighted features of the definition (e.g. in what way are the events, or lessons, linked? What kind of planning is involved?).

2. Do you think the definition is adequate? Do you think a course needs to

have explicit aims, for instance? If so, on what should these be based? Should the emphasis actually be on what happens, i.e. on course as experience, rather than on what is planned?

1.2 Coursebook-based teaching

Most people would probably agree that if a course does not have fairly specific aims it may easily become aim*less* – that is, lacking a clear purpose. As noted in Chapter 1, when there is no external structure in the form of an official syllabus or a public examination, teachers may hand over (consciously or unconsciously) responsibility for the formulation of aims to a coursebook – in that they accept unquestioningly the foci, structure, emphases and content of the book.

Teaching a book is very different from basing a course on a book. A book should not be a course in the sense that it determines the totality of learning experiences for those using it. Books are written to be relevant to as large a number of students as possible, which also means as wide a range of teaching –learning contexts as possible. It follows that no one book can be perfect for a particular institution, let alone a particular class within that institution or an individual within a class. This means that at the selection stage (see Chapters 1–3) and again after a book has been selected, teachers need to think carefully about how the book can contribute to the aims of *their* course.

1.3 Syllabus, examination, course and book

A problem facing many teachers is that described by Dubin and Olshtain (1986: 29) as 'non-compatibility' (see Table 4.1, below).

Table 4.1   Non-compatibility of syllabus and coursebook (after Dubin and Olshtain 1986: 29)

OLD	NEW
syllabus	coursebook
coursebook	syllabus

Non-compatibility exists when either a new coursebook has been introduced which is different in its overall aims or skill focus from the official syllabus or when the opposite is the case: a new syllabus has been introduced but a coursebook to go with this is not yet available. There are even worse scenarios, of course, as when the public examinations are incompatible with both syllabus and coursebook.

In any of these situations, long-term planning is essential to reduce the gap between book and syllabus/exam. This also applies when the various elements are compatible, since learners may have their own needs, lacks and wants (Allwright 1982, Hutchinson and Waters 1987).

The first step in such planning – and for obvious reasons (see Chapter 2) this should be ideally taken prior to the selection of a coursebook – is to establish aims for the course (i.e. the whole year if you will be teaching the same class for that long), drawing on what is known of the official syllabus (if any), public exam (if any), learners and institutional resources and constraints. Only when this is done is it appropriate to consider how the coursebook can be utilised; to start from the coursebook would be to accept implicitly the aims of the book. The next stage, however, the preparation of a scheme of work (detailed planning for units of time such as terms, months, or, in the case of an intensive course, weeks), necessitates careful study of the coursebook. This is when decisions are made about the time needed to deal adequately with specific elements in the scheme of work and the implications for the use, non-use or reordering of particular parts of the coursebook (Acklam 1994). As the next section makes clear, a similar set of decisions are also involved at the lesson-planning stage.

Where the teacher is under considerable pressure to teach to a specific (exam-oriented) syllabus using a book specially written for that purpose (and there is apparently perfect compatibility, therefore) it may seem almost irrelevant to think of evaluating the coursebook. This chapter will suggest that evaluation of the coursebook is a necessary aspect of course planning and lesson planning in any situation, including those in which teachers appear to be tightly constrained.

1.4 Evaluation processes in lesson planning

If the first step in course planning is to establish aims for the course, then the first step in lesson planning is to determine the objectives of the lesson. When the lesson is to be based on a coursebook, four evaluative processes are subsequently involved:

1. **Selection** – of coursebook material that will be used unchanged.
2. **Rejection** – complete (e.g. omitting a whole activity or even a whole lesson) or partial (e.g. cutting one or more stages within an activity).
3. **Adding** – in the form of extension or exploitation of the existing material, this can be regarded as *adaptation*; where new materials are introduced, this will be termed *supplementation* (the focus of the next chapter).
4. **Changing** – i.e. more radical forms of adaptation, such as modifications to procedure or changes in context/content (*replacement*).

Processes 3 and 4 (adaptation) will normally have a creative as well as an evaluative side.

Although adaptation need not form part of every lesson, the argument underlying the remainder of this chapter, and the next, is that if we are not wholly satisfied with what the coursebook has to offer we have a responsibility to do something about it – and this is the argument for adding to or changing the existing material. The neat categorisation above is not always reflected in planning decisions, of course (e.g. the decision to reject something may necessitate its replacement by something else), and the structure of the subsequent discussion recognises this.

1.5 From objectives to lesson structure

Determining the objectives of a particular lesson is perhaps more complex than it might at first seem. Regardless of whether teaching is based on a coursebook, the decision-making process should involve relating (1) the overall aims of the course to (2) students' present level of knowledge. The question that guides the decision should be: 'Taking account of (1) and (2), and the time available, what should be the focus of this lesson?' rather than 'What comes next in the coursebook?'

The lesson-planning process also requires consideration of the stages that will be necessary to reach the objective(s). In a short but usefully practical article, Hunt, Neher and Banton (1993) describe this second-level planning as 'backwards planning', or 'starting with what we ultimately wish to achieve and identifying all essential stages that will enable this' (p. 19). In this kind of logically rigorous approach, each stage can be justified in terms of its contribution to the next. As Hunt et al. point out, the problem with an unsuccessful lesson can often be traced back to the fact that an essential stage was left out. This kind of retrospective evaluation will be easier if a lesson plan has been prepared which contains details not only of objectives and stages but also the aids to be used (including specific reference to coursebook pages if a book is being used), patterns of interaction (teacher–learner(s) and learner–learner) and estimated timings for each stage.

In practice, decisions about lesson structure will normally go hand in hand with reflection on method and materials. Here the questions will be: 'By what means can I help learners to develop in the desired directions, and how, if at all, will these materials assist the learners and me in that task?' From this perspective, materials are seen as a potential resource, a support for teaching and learning, rather than what is to be taught and learned.

2 SELECTION, REJECTION AND REPLACEMENT

2.1 Relevance

Once we have established what we feel to be appropriate objectives for the lesson, we are in a position to take a closer, more critical look at the materials.

At this point we should be able to distinguish between those materials which seem directly relevant and can be used unchanged, and those which are totally irrelevant (e.g. because inappropriate to these objectives or to the learners we are teaching). Examples of the latter would be pronunciation practice on minimal pairs which includes non-problematic contrasts and language functions unlikely to be required by learners outside an English-speaking environment (McDonough and Shaw 1993).

Some materials may be relevant, but pressure of time makes it impossible to include them in the lesson. In this case, we need to decide what can most usefully be done in class and what can be set for homework. Time-consuming written exercises can, for instance, be started in class to give students a feel for what is required and then finished for homework.

What is likely – and this will depend on the care with which the coursebook was originally selected – is that much of the material falls somewhere between the extremes of totally relevant and totally irrelevant (i.e. though it can be used, some adaptation will be necessary).

2.2 Processes and principles

Teachers experienced in making the kinds of decisions discussed in this chapter will tend to reply on their instincts in selecting, rejecting, replacing and adapting. Other teachers may find helpful the decision paths suggested by Grant (1987: 17) or Cunningsworth (1984, 1995; see Figure 4.1 on p. 62).

Figure 4.1 suggests a systematic path through the processes of materials evaluation in relation to lesson activities. According to the logic of the diagram, a teacher would first consider the suitability of the *objective* of the activity; then the *method* would be considered, and finally the *content* and/or *topic*. A 'No' answer at any point would prompt a particular decision: to omit or replace, and so on.

Task 4.2

1. Does the proposed sequence – consider objective, method, content/topic – correspond to your own approach to the evaluation of material at the lesson-planning stage?

2. Where the objective of the material is in your judgement unsuitable, what might be the arguments for using the materials for other purposes rather than simply omitting (rejecting) it altogether?

3. Where the objective is suitable but the method is inappropriate, what might be the arguments for changing the method rather than replacing the activity?

4. In your view, should any other factors have a bearing on your decision to use, omit, replace or change coursebook material?

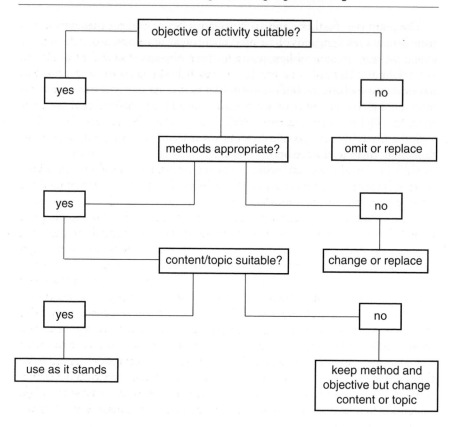

Figure 4.1 Evaluating lesson activities (Cunningsworth 1995)

Haycraft (1978) has suggested that one factor that should influence the extent to which teaching is based on a coursebook is that of learner level: beginners have predictably similar needs, which can be met by a coursebook; however, clear differences start to emerge at intermediate level, he states, differences which cannot adequately be catered for by a single book, and at advanced level even more differentiation is needed. While this constitutes an argument for less dependence on coursebooks at higher levels and seems to strengthen the case for greater selectivity, the frequent rejection of activities or exercises and the omission of whole lessons needs to take learner reaction into account, especially if they have paid for the book themselves: 'If the book is so bad, why was it selected in the first place?' (Harmer 1998: 111). In those contexts where printed works carry great authority, learners may lose confidence in the teacher. Large-scale cutting, however good one's intentions, can be a high-risk strategy; it therefore makes sense to minimise the risk of a reaction by explaining to learners why one does not intend to spend class time on these sections of the book, or to involve them in such decisions (Acklam 1994).

There are two further dangers in rejecting lessons or part-lessons: one is that there is a resulting loss of coherence within or across lessons and the other is that subsidiary items of language which are embedded in the materials and potentially relevant are not covered. The teacher who is aware of these potential problems will try to build in coherence or coverage by other means: for instance, by creating links between those parts of the material that are to be used; by suggesting that learners look through the rejected material in their own time; and by incorporating into future activities useful items of language that might otherwise have been neglected.

If the original material really is irrelevant, then – the above problems apart – there can be no justification for using it. There will, however, be times when important learning points are carried by material which is inappropriate for other reasons (e.g. learners' age, interests, cultural background, prior knowledge). A partial solution to these problems – partial because the replacement materials will never fulfil exactly the same purposes as the original – is to replace the material which has been omitted with other materials which are more appropriate (Grant 1987, Harmer 1998). Examples (based on Tice 1991) are the replacement – in a course for teenage boys – of a text on a day in the life of, say, a famous British person or a fictional character by a day in the life of, say, a local sporting hero or the replacement of a general text about crime or disasters by a recent account of a specific local event (crime/disaster). Similarly, Block (1991) suggests that textbook materials for the practice of 'used to', which typically take the form of contrasting (earlier/later) facts about a person or town that students cannot identify with, might be replaced by details of the life of an entertainer or politician known to the learners or a map of the learners' own town.

In these and any other examples of replacement, care is needed. In our efforts to find alternative material which captures the interest of our learners, it is only too easy to lose sight of the original learning purpose. We return to this point under 'Adaptation', below.

3 ADAPTATION

The importance of adaptation as a process and of teachers' competence in managing that process has been widely recognised. Although they may not always be in a position to select the materials they use, teachers do decide, consciously or instinctively, how much of those materials will be used, and how much of what is used will be modified.

3.1 Defining adaptation

Definitions of adaptation can be unhelpfully broad. Madsen and Bowen (1978) claim that 'Every teacher is in a very real sense an adapter of the material he uses' (p. vii), employing 'one or more of a number of techniques:

supplementing, editing, expanding, personalizing, simplifying, modernizing, localizing, or modifying cultural/situational content' (p. ix); Ellis, M. (1986: 47) mentions the processes of 'retaining, rejecting, re-ordering and modification'; and Tomlinson (1998b: xi) refers to 'reducing, adding, omitting, modifying and supplementing'. In this chapter, as indicated above, two main categories of adaptation will be discussed: adaptation as addition (in a restricted sense) and adaptation as change.

3.2 The purpose of adaptation

The two most frequently cited purposes for adaptation are as follows:

1. to make the material more suitable for the circumstances in which it is being used, i.e. to mould it to the needs and interests of learners, the teacher's own capabilities and such constraints as time, or, as McDonough and Shaw (1993: 85) put it: 'to maximize the appropriacy of teaching materials in context, by changing some of the internal characteristics of a coursebook to better suit our particular circumstances';
2. to compensate for any intrinsic deficiencies in the material, such as linguistic inaccuracies, out-of-datedness, lack of authenticity (Madsen and Bowen 1978) or lack of variety (Tice 1991).

We could take McDonough and Shaw's definition of purpose a little further. Maximising the appropriacy of teaching materials (by, e.g., modifying them in such a way that they seem more relevant to learners' interests and needs) is important because it can stimulate motivation, and increased motivation is in turn likely to lead to a classroom atmosphere more conducive to learning. In point of fact, when we make changes to a coursebook 'to better suit our particular purposes', what we are really trying to do is to improve the effectiveness of the learning experience. In the next sections, we look at specific techniques for achieving this.

4   ADAPTATION AS ADDITION

4.1 Extemporisation

It is probably important to point out that adaptation need not involve a teacher in a great deal of extra work. In fact, the most natural form of adaptation is *extemporisation*, that is, a spontaneous response on the part of the teacher to a problem or an opportunity (Madsen and Bowen 1978, McDonough and Shaw 1993). This might take such forms as the substitution in a coursebook example of the familiar (e.g. items of fruit or vegetables) for the unfamiliar; the paraphrase of a coursebook instruction or explanation that has not been understood; or reference to previously taught items (structures, vocabulary, phonemes, functions) when teaching new items. Extemporisation, which is by its very nature predominantly oral (though it might include blackboard drawing or writing), is closely allied to *exploitation* (see below); the latter, however, tends to involve planned and more extended activities.

4.2 Extension

One particular form of adaptation which seems to have been largely ignored in the literature (see, however, McDonough and Shaw 1993: 88–90) is *extension*. This refers to the provision by the teacher of additional material (e.g. further examples of a rule or further items in an exercise) in order to enhance understanding or learning. The main difference between extension and *supplementation* (see below, and Chapter 5) is that extension means 'more of the same'. If the coursebook contains only one short exercise to practise a point which your students find particularly difficult and you devise more items of the same type as the original exercise, this is extension. If you give them another exercise from another source or make up another exercise yourself, this is supplementation. The distinction is not just terminological: when we extend an exercise we can be fairly sure that we are staying true to the design of the original material and will be contributing to the goals that underpin this material; when we supplement, especially when we design our own material, we have to be very vigilant lest we introduce a new learning objective.

4.3 Exploitation

Exploitation is the creative use of what is already there (e.g. text, visual, activity) to serve a purpose which is *additional* to that foreseen by the textbook writer. Thus, a text may be accompanied by a photograph and a battery of questions which are intended to develop comprehension skills and linguistic resources, but a teacher might use any of these for additional purposes: the picture, for instance, as well as illustrating the theme, might also be used to predict content or activate vocabulary; the topic and language of the text might provide the basis for discussion of students' own experiences; and the questions might serve as models for student-devised questions on the same text.

The term 'adaptation' is problematic because it is used with both broad and narrower meanings; what makes 'exploitation' problematic is that this concept is referred to using different terms. McDonough and Shaw (1993), for instance, seem to be thinking of exploitation when they describe 'expansion' as the development of material 'in new directions'. They go on to make two important distinctions between extension and 'expansion'. Whereas extension involves quantitative change, expansion represents a qualitative change (p. 90); in expansion, moreover, the new elements can come before or after the existing material. Thus, the picture referred to in the previous paragraph might also be the focus of a post-reading activity in which students comment on the appropriateness of the picture, and/or suggest other ways in which the theme of the text might be represented, and/or find a picture they prefer and talk or write about it. Again on the terminological issue, Maley's (1998) list of adaptation options (see Chapter 7) includes 'extension', which for him involves lengthening to include an added dimension (note the difference between this and the definition of extension given previously), and 'branching' (i.e. providing one or more alternatives to the original activity or paths through it). Within the categorisation adopted here, both would be forms of exploitation.

Task 4.3

1. If you are currently teaching, choose an exercise or activity from your own coursebook that in your view could be appropriately extended or exploited to better suit the needs of your learners. (If you are not teaching at present, think of a group of learners you have taught recently and choose a suitable activity/exercise from Appendix 4.1.)

2. If you have decided to extend an exercise, write down the additional items. If you have decided to exploit an activity, write down what you would do.

3. If possible, exchange ideas with colleagues.

5 ADAPTATION AS CHANGE

5.1 A principled approach to adaptation

Cunningsworth (1984) suggests three questions that might be asked when one is considering adaptation:

- What does the exercise actually get the learner to do?
- What do I want the learner to do?
- How can I get the exercise to do what I want it to do for the learner?

(Cunningsworth 1984: 66)

To these we should perhaps add a fourth, and logically prior question:

- What is the objective of the activity?

This last question calls for a description of the linguistic intention behind an activity or exercise (e.g. 'to provide practice in the use of past-tense questions' or 'to provide practice in eliciting information about someone's past'). Cunningsworth's first question, on the other hand, is oriented towards effects and is – implicitly, at least – evaluative. It is the recognition that there is a gap between the two, that an activity/exercise does not do what it was intended to or does not do it as effectively or as efficiently or as interestingly as it might, that allows us to justify adaptation.

Task 4.4

Look again through your coursebook or at the extracts in Appendix 4.1 and choose one that you can imagine yourself using. Ask yourself the four questions listed above, starting with the objective of the activity. If you decide that there is no reason to adapt the activity, that's fine. If possible, compare your answers with those of someone else.

5.2 Foci and forms of change

One of the reasons given above for adaptation was to maintain learner interest by varying what might otherwise be a rather repetitive diet. The problem of 'the textbook straitjacket' and some flexible responses to this are described by Tice (1991: 23):

> Many coursebooks adopt a very similar format for each unit and include a rather limited range of exercise types. For example, new language is always presented through a dialogue, comprehension tested through 'wh' questions, grammar practised through gap-fills ... Vary the means of testing comprehension by introducing prediction tasks, nonlinguistic tasks (such as ordering or selecting pictures) or notetaking. You can also set up roleplays and sketches based on the reading and listening texts. Grammar exercises can be adapted; for example, supply the answers to an exercise to half the class, and let them work with a partner who doesn't have the answers. Or, supply the answers to an exercise, some wrong, and then do a sentence auction (in groups, learners bid for correct sentences).

Task 4.5

1. Think about your normal practices. What are *your* reasons for adapting published materials?

2. What kinds of changes do you make?

3. Here is a summary of the suggestions made in the above quotation by Tice. Can you add any further suggestions from your own experience?

	NORMAL	*VARIATION*
PRESENTATION OF NEW LANGUAGE	dialogue	?

LISTENING/READING TEXTS	comprehension tested through *wh-* questions	• prediction tasks • non-linguistic tasks (e.g. ordering or selecting pictures) • note-taking • role plays/ sketches • ?
GRAMMAR PRACTICE	gap-fill exercises	• peer 'tutoring' • sentence auction • ?

The next task asks you to consider rather similar questions but in this case in relation to specific examples.

Task 4.6

1. Would you want to adapt any of the following examples if they appeared in a coursebook you were using? If so, which and why?

2. What changes would you make? Try to be as specific as possible. You might like to write your ideas down to refer to later or for comparison with other people.

Example 1

Change the following sentences as in the example:
Example: This is my book.
        These are our books.

(a) This is my pencil.
(b) That is his bag.
    (etc.)

Example 2

In this activity, which comes from *The Cambridge English Course Book 1* (Swan and Walter 1984), a course for adult beginners, learners listen to a commentary on the results of the third day of the Fantasian National Games and complete the table shown below. The spoken text (see the extract below), a transcript of which appears in the teacher's book only, is delivered 'at a very brisk speed' (Grant 1987: 25). Teachers are recommended to play the tape several times.

'... Over to you, Simon.'

'Thank you, John. Well, it's been a really sensational day here in the National Stadium, with records falling right and left. In the final of the men's 100 metres we had a very fine performance from Arnaldo Higgins, with a time of exactly ten seconds for a national record. You may be interested to know that that corresponds to a speed of just 36 kilometres an hour, so Arnaldo was really travelling...'

5 **Listening for information. Copy the table. Listen to today's results from the Fantasian National Games, and note the times and speeds.**

EVENT	TIME	SPEED
Men's 100m		
Women's marathon		
Women's 100m swimming (freestyle)		
Downhill Alpine skiing		

Figure 4.2 Listening activity (Swan and Walter 1984)

Example 3
Another listening activity:

BOX 8.3.3: LISTENING ACTIVITY 3

Instructions
Listen to the following recorded talk, and then answer the multiple-choice questions below.

The listening text
Crash! was perhaps the most famous pop group of that time. It consisted of three female singers, with no band. They came originally from Manchester, and began singing in local clubs, but their fame soon spread throughout the British Isles and then all over the world. Their hairstyle and clothes were imitated by a whole generation of teenagers, and thousands came to hear them sing, bought recordings of their songs or went to see their films.

The questions
1. Crash! was
   a) notorious   b) well-known   c) unpopular   d) local
2. The group was composed of:
   a) three boys   b) two girls and a boy
   c) two boys and a girl   d) three girls
3. The group was from:
   a) Britain   b) France   c) Brazil   d) Egypt
4. A lot of young people wanted to
   a) sing like them   b) look like them
   c) live in Manchester   d) all of these   © Cambridge University Press 1996

Figure 4.3 Listening activity (Ur 1996)

Example 4

Rewrite these sentences using the correct form of the conditional.

1. If a man with a knife (STOP) me in the street, I (GIVE) him all my money.
2. If a dog (BITE) me, I (HAVE) a rabies injection.
3. If a fly (LAND) on my dinner, I (NOT KILL) it.
   (etc.)

Example 5

A dialogue to practise speaking.

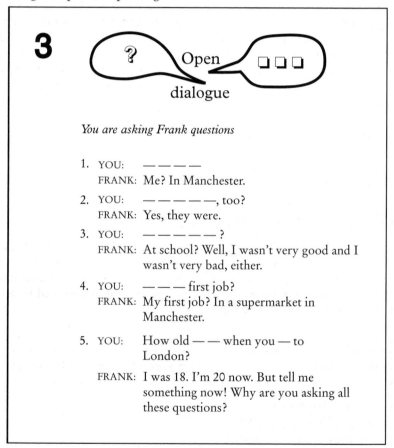

3   ? Open ☐ ☐ ☐
    dialogue

You are asking Frank questions

1. YOU: — — — —
   FRANK: Me? In Manchester.

2. YOU: — — — — —, too?
   FRANK: Yes, they were.

3. YOU: — — — — — ?
   FRANK: At school? Well, I wasn't very good and I
           wasn't very bad, either.

4. YOU: — — — first job?
   FRANK: My first job? In a supermarket in
           Manchester.

5. YOU: How old — — when you — to
           London?

   FRANK: I was 18. I'm 20 now. But tell me
           something now! Why are you asking all
           these questions?

Figure 4.4 Dialogue (O'Neill 1979)

Task 4.7 K

Suggested adaptations, with accompanying brief commentaries, are given below. Consider the adaptations one by one in relation to the ideas you came up with yourself.

1. Do you think that the suggested adaptation is an improvement over the original? Compare it with your own. Which adaptation is better, in your opinion, yours or the one given here? Why?

2. How would you categorise the changes that have been made in the examples below? And in your own adaptations?

Example 1: adapted version (Mosback 1984)

The original, a mechanical transformation exercise practising demonstratives, was probably intended to be done individually in writing or as a teacher-led drill. In the adapted version (see below) this has been turned into a game-like activity for groups of six–eight learners. The group leader, who changes after each 'round', cues other learners' sentences by pointing to an item such as a pencil, some books or a part of the body. A group member who makes a mistake or hesitates for more than a few seconds is 'out'.

Leader (holds up own hands)
P1: Those are your hands.
Leader (points to answerer's books)
These are my books.

Example 2: adapted version (Grant 1987)

Feeling that as it stands this listening activity is 'quite demanding', Grant suggests two changes: (1) splitting the task up into different stages and getting the learners to listen for one category of information at a time, and (2) modifying the table (see adapted version, below). The teacher is recommended to write this up on the board for learners to copy.

Event	Winner	Time	Speed
Men's 100m Women's marathon Women's 100m swimming (freestyle) Downhill Alpine skiing			

Figure 4.5 Adapted table (Grant 1987)

Example 3 (Ur 1996)

Ur's critique of this type of exercise ('lacks most of the common characteristics of real-life listening . . . is based on a dense, obviously written text, and does not give much help with learner problems . . . gives practice in reading as much as in listening' (p. 118)) gives the impression that she would probably reject it rather than trying to adapt it. She does, however, suggest that it could be improved 'to some extent' by (1) going through the questions with students before they listen to the text (to set listening objectives and reduce the need to read while listening), and possibly getting them to predict what the answers might be and (2) encouraging them to listen selectively by concentrating on only one or two questions each time they hear the tape.

Example 4: adapted version (McGrath 1994)

In the version below, this standard exercise format has been adapted in two ways: by creating mini-scenarios to which the student has to give a personal response, and by incorporating an 'open slot' to allow students freedom to respond with their own ideas and in their own words.

What would you do in these situations?
Choose one of these possibilities or
make up your own answer.

Example

What would you do if you saw a child fall into a river?
I'd jump in.

What would you do if . . .

1. a man with a knife stopped you in the street?
   a. scream.
   b. give him all my money
   c. ....

2. a dog bit you?
   a. scream.
   b. have a rabies vaccination.
   c. ....

3. a fly landed on your dinner?
   a. scream.
   b. eat the fly too.
   c. ....

Figure 4.6 Adapted version of a standard exercise format (McGrath 1994: 19)

Example 5: adapted version (Cunningsworth 1995)

Cunningsworth comments on the following features of 'fixed' dialogues of the sort illustrated in Task 4.5: 'The participants . . . are told what to say, and more or less how to say it, giving them little freedom for self-expression. Equally importantly, at certain points it is necessary to look at the answer before formulating the question – exactly the reverse of what happens in reality' (p. 145). You may have also noticed that Frank's habit of echoing the question is a very overt clue to the question needed and that the number and placing of spaces in the text prompt particular ways of formulating these questions. Cunningsworth adds: 'Students need the sort of practice provided by fixed dialogues, but they also need to progress to less predictable models of interaction if they are to function in English independently' (ibid.). His answer, a kind of 'halfway stage between fixed and completely free dialogues' (ibid.), is to recast the dialogue as cue-card prompts (see below). Students are given an indication of what they should say (A is clearly much more explicit than B) but not the exact words; and there is a degree of unpredictability in that neither speaker knows what the other will say next.

Student A	Student B
You are talking to someone that you don't know very well. Begin the conversation with a question. 1. Ask him/her where he/she was born. 2. Ask if his/her parents were born there too. 3. Ask if he/she was good at school. 4. Respond (tell the truth!)	Someone that you don't know very well asks you some questions. 1. Answer the question. 2. Answer the question. 3. Answer the question. Ask if he/she is a student or has a job.

Figure 4.7 Cue cards (Cunningsworth 1995)

5.3 Commentary

McDonough and Shaw's description of the purpose of adaptation quoted above ('to maximize the appropriacy of teaching materials in context, by changing some of the internal characteristics of a coursebook to better suit our particular circumstances') makes it clear that two processes are involved in adaptation: first, the evaluation of materials against contextual criteria (though pedagogic criteria will probably also be involved); and subsequently, the tailoring of the materials to suit these criteria. What are the possible foci of this kind of tailoring and what forms might it take?

The foci would include (1) *language* – the language of explanations, examples, texts, exercises and the language that students are expected to produce; (2) the *contexts and content* to which the language relates; and (3) *procedures and classroom management* – who does what with whom and how this is organised. As the detailed Commentary on this task indicates (see 'Tasks: Keys and Commentaries'), each of these can be illustrated with reference to the above examples.

In a fourth kind of change, *restructuring* (McDonough and Shaw 1993), components are reorganised. This might be motivated by the teacher's prioritisation of learners' needs or it might be an attempt to make the order 'more logical'. Restructuring in relation to a particular activity in order to build in variety or increase the degree of challenge is more of a procedural change (category 3, above). Examples of this would include re-sequencing activities such as cutting up a text and asking students to put it together again, presenting a picture story in jumbled order or creating a groupwork task in which each learner must describe their picture in order that the group can determine the original sequence.

5.4 Principles motivating change

The kinds of changes discussed above (and others not illustrated) are based on a number of principles. These have been described as follows:

- *Localisation*: recognising the need for contextual relevance – 'what may work well in Mexico City may not do so in Edinburgh or in Kuala Lumpur' (McDonough and Shaw 1993: 87).
- *Personalisation*: broadly speaking, 'increasing the relevance of content in relation to learners' interests and their academic, educational or professional needs' (ibid.); more narrowly, drawing on learners' lives and exploiting their knowledge and interests to devise examples and activities which are *about them*.
- *Individualisation*: addressing 'the learning styles both of individuals and of the members of a class working closely together' (McDonough and Shaw 1993: ibid.).
- *Modernisation*: changing any instances of language usage that seem out of date (Madsen and Bowen 1978); this might equally well apply to changes in the time-bound content of material (e.g. prices of goods).
- *Simplification*: procedures designed to make things easier for or more accessible to the learner: e.g. the editing of texts to reduce linguistic or conceptual difficulty, and modifications to tasks. On linguistic simplification, Tomlinson (1998b: xii) comments:

The usual principles of simplification involve reduction in length of the text, shortening of sentences, omission or replacement of difficult words or structures, omission of qualifying clauses and omission of non-essential detail. It is arguable, however, that such simplification might make the words easier to understand but could make it more difficult for the learners to achieve global understanding of a text which is now dense with important information. It might be more profitable to simplify texts by adding examples, by using repetition and paraphrase and by increasing redundant information. In other words, by lengthening rather than shortening a text.

This is a valid point: increased text density could well mean greater processing difficulty. However, one problem with the proposal made here, as with the more traditional approach to simplification, is that it would render authentic text less authentic; a second problem is that it fails to take into account learners' psychological problems with text length.

There are occasions, of course, when we might want to *increase* the level of difficulty of a task, or at least to provide different levels of challenge for students with different levels of confidence or competence (see the adaptation of example 4, above). This was the starting- point for the lesson described below.

6 A LESSON-PLANNING TASK

This chapter finishes almost where it started, with a focus on lesson planning, but with adaptation as a central feature of this.

Task 4.8

The serious message behind Prodromou's (1990) short description of a 'mixed-ability lesson' is that we need to think carefully about our own responsibility in relation to bored or failing students ('No one chooses failure and no one chooses boredom' (p. 28)).

The lesson is based on a questionnaire from an elementary coursebook which, he notes, 'is not particularly suited to the teaching of a mixed-ability class' (ibid.). The questionnaire is reproduced overleaf:

1. What problems do you see with the questionnaire? (Imagine using it with a class in which there is a range of proficiency levels.) Note down your ideas.

2. An earlier section of this chapter drew attention to the importance, when adapting coursebook material, of retaining the original linguistic objective(s). Prodromou's lesson plan includes the following specifications of learners and lesson aims:

> **Level**: elementary
> **Age**: adolescents

	YOU	YOUR PARTNER	SCORE	
			YES	NO
CHECK YOUR DIET				
Yesterday . . .				
1. Did you have more than two pieces of toast for breakfast?			0	1
2. Did you have sugar in your tea or coffee?			0	1
3. Did you drink half a litre of milk?			1	0
4. Did you eat any fruit?			1	0
5. Did you eat any sweets or chocolates?			0	1
6. Did you eat any biscuits or cake?			0	1
7. Did you drink any alcohol?			0	1
CHECK YOUR CONDITION				
Yesterday . . .				
8. Did you go for a run?			1	0
9. Did you do any exercises?			1	0
10. Did you walk or cycle to work/school?			1	0
11. Did you smoke at all?			0	1
CHECK YOUR DAILY ROUTINE				
Yesterday . . .				
12. Did you get up before 8 o'clock?			1	0
13. Did you go to bed before 11 o'clock?			1	0
14. Did you watch TV for more than 2 hours?			0	1
15. Did you sleep with your windows open?			1	0
TOTAL				

Figure 4.8 Questionnaire from Abbs and Freebairn, *Building Strategies*

Previous knowledge: language of health, making suggestions, Simple Present

Aims:

1. to practise talking about the recent past
2. to present and practise the Simple Past with *yes/no* and questions
3. to revise vocabulary of health, for example, *healthy, go for a run, go on a diet, do exercises, keep fit*
4. to revise making questions

Which of these aims underlie the original coursebook material (the questionnaire) and which derive from Prodromou's wish to develop this?

3. Plan a lesson of, say, 45 minutes with the following stages:

Stage 1: revision and introduction to lesson theme (health)
Stage 2: presentation of new material
Stage 3: controlled practice
Stage 4: communication

Remember to take into account the fact that there may be significant differences between learners in terms of their previous knowledge, aptitude, and confidence.

Subsequent steps in the task will allow you to compare your own decisions with those of Prodromou.

4. *Stages 1–2*: Prodromou's own lesson plan makes considerable use of elicitation in Stages 1 and 2 both to activate/pool existing linguistic knowledge and to personalise the practice stages that follow. A key transitional question during the second stage is: 'We want to find out who is fit and healthy; what questions can we ask?' He then describes building up a substitution table for practice of the Past Simple. This incorporates students' answers.

Two of the six questions in the table are given below. Why do you think he has included a *wh-* question? What other questions would you include, and why? Do you have any comment on the layout of the table?

	Question	Yesterday	Answer
1.	Did	you have sugar in your coffee?	
2.			
3.			
4.			
5. What time	did	you get up?	
6.			

On his own questions, Prodromou comments: 'The answers to the *wh-* questions require more than a parroted "yes" or "no", and they thus avoid the practice becoming meaningless. Moreover, I wanted the task which follows this presentation to sound less mechanical than the 15 unvaried *yes/no* questions provided by the textbook' (p. 29).

5. *Stage 3*: During the subsequent controlled-practice stage using the substitution table, he elicits possible answers to the questions and writes them up, and then asks students to practise asking and answering the questions.

How would you go on to exploit the substitution table so that students are not merely engaged in reading aloud?

For Prodromou, the guiding principle is differentiation, but differentiation which takes account of individual confidence as well as proficiency. The less confident are free to repeat the answers on the board; the more confident can give their own (true) answers. After some practice of this kind, he starts to rub out words from the substitution table and students are asked to reconstitute the original questions with less and less guidance. 'Initial practice is done with weaker students, while better students work from an increasingly blank board.'

6. *Stage 4*: The communication stage takes the form of a survey to find out who is the fittest and healthiest person in the class. It is based on a skeleton questionnaire consisting of only minimal prompts (see below). Following a little plenary practice to check that students can use the prompts to generate questions, they are asked first to give their own answers to the questions, then interview other students. Finally, candidates for the title of healthiest student in the class are discussed in groups and by the whole class. This involves students asking each other further questions.

Prodromou's questionnaire and his rationale for this and the way in which it is exploited are reproduced below. Do you have any comments?

Question	You	S1	S2	S3 etc.
1. breakfast				
2. sugar				
3. milk				
4. fruit				
5. go to bed				
6. cake				
7. run				
8. exercise				
9. cycle				
10. get up				
11. ?				
12. ?				

'My questionnaire differs from the one in the textbook in the following ways:
a) The complete *yes/no* questions of the textbook are replaced by cues which allow students to choose either an easy *yes/no* question or a more challenging *wh-* question.
b) I left two questions blank, to allow the early finishers the option of adding their own questions to the questionnaire.

c) The format of the questionnaire in the textbook does not allow for students who have completed the pairwork to go on to work with a third or fourth student. By re-designing the questionnaire on the board I was able to extend the activity into trios and quartets.

d) The original activity ends with the students adding up their own scores. My own ending involves the students in using language to compare results, propose candidates for the 'healthiest person' competition, to argue their case before the class and finally to decide on the 'winner' by asking more questions using the target structures of the lesson.

7. Think back to the discussion earlier in this chapter concerning foci of adaptation (language, procedure, etc.) and principles motivating adaptation (localisation, personalisation, simplification, etc.). What kinds of change has Prodromou made and what principles motivated these changes?

(Text by L. Prodromou first published in *Practical English Teaching*, 1990. © Mary Glasgow Magazines/Scholastic).

6.1 More examples of adaptation

For further published examples of adaptation, see, for example, Cunningsworth, (1984,1995); Grant (1987) – a rich source of ideas; Harmer (1998: 113–14), Madsen and Bowen (1978); Mosback (1984); Nunan (1991: 219–23); Richards (1985: Ch. 14); Ur (1996: 115–18).

7 SUMMARY

In this chapter two linked assumptions were made: (1) that no textbook will be perfect for a specific teaching–learning situation – and the book should therefore not be regarded as the course; (2) that a conscientious teacher whose teaching is by necessity or choice based on a textbook will want to do something to compensate for the lack of match between course aims and learner needs on the one hand and what the textbook provides on the other. In relation to (2), one possibility is to *adapt* the material, by adding to it or changing it in such a way that it better meets the needs of the situation and the individual learners, and various forms of adaptation have been described and exemplified. A second possibility is for the teacher to *supplement* the material. This is the focus of the next chapter.

Chapter 5

Supplementation: designing worksheets

The argument for supplementation – identifying gaps in a coursebook – forms of supplementation: supplementation using published material; devising one's own material – the process of supplementary materials design: syllabus driven or concept driven? – designing worksheets: the function of worksheets; general issues in worksheet design; computerised worksheets – designing your own worksheet exercises: designing grammar exercises; designing vocabulary exercises

1 THE ARGUMENT FOR SUPPLEMENTATION

To judge by their claims (see Appendix 2.1 for examples), most modern coursebooks offer everything their target users need (and which publisher would give competitors an advantage by openly admitting to deficiencies?). They provide 'coverage', often using authentic texts, of the 'skills' of listening, speaking, reading and writing, and tasks that offer opportunities to practise integrating these; they include a range of grammatical structures, now normally related to notions and functions; 'new' vocabulary is introduced via themes or topics, as well as incidentally; attention may also be given to aspects of pronunciation and features of spoken and written discourse.

Previous chapters have suggested that the needs of a specific class of learners can never be perfectly met by a single coursebook, even when the coursebook has been carefully designed to cater for the needs of learners in that context. Supplementation, which means no more than 'adding something new', stems primarily from the recognition of a deficit: it is an attempt to bridge the gap between a coursebook and an official syllabus (or statement of aims), or a coursebook and the demands of a public examination, or a coursebook and students' needs. The publisher may have thoughtfully produced a number of add-ons (cassettes, workbook, reader and so on), and if these are available and affordable, the gap between learners and material may be much smaller than would otherwise have been the case. However, even where this is the case, many teachers feel impelled to provide additional material because they feel that *their* students need exposure to a greater range of textual material, for example, or more practice of particular kinds. They may also wish to provide differentiated materials, that is, materials that cater for different levels of proficiency or different needs within a class.

The decision to supplement the coursebook may also be prompted by affective considerations. Experienced teachers know that walking into class and saying: 'Good morning. Open your books at page 37' is not the best way to capture the attention of a group of learners, and many use 'warm-up' activities for this reason. They also know that there are other points in a lesson (and these are not always predictable) or a certain time in the week when learners just need something a little different. Maley (1998: 281), probably thinking of dreary days in Britain, refers to this as 'the wet Friday afternoon effect'. This is the time when learners are tired or apathetic or having difficulty, a time when learning needs to be made lighter, more fun – through a game, a song, a video.

Both types of supplementation – the cognitively-motivated and the affectively-motivated – need to be fully integrated into course plans and lesson plans if they are to be maximally effective. It is worth bearing in mind that warm-ups, carefully selected or devised, can serve their affective purpose *and* relate to the topic of the lesson; the same is true of 'lightening' activities used at other points in a lesson.

2 IDENTIFYING GAPS IN A COURSEBOOK

The following checklist, from Acklam (1994) (see Table 5.1, below), is designed to help teachers identify specific gaps in the coursebooks they are using. The checklist emphasises sufficiency (is there enough X?), variety and relevance. Such a checklist might also be used as part of a textbook selection process.

Table 5.1 Identifying gaps (text by R. Acklam first published in *Practical English Teaching*, 1994. © Mary Glasgow Magazines/Scholastic)

Checklist
❏ Is there enough grammar? Is it what your students need? Is it clearly presented?
❏ Is there enough pronunciation work? Is it what your students need?
❏ Is there enough vocabulary work? Is it what your students need?
❏ Is there enough work on phrasal verbs?
❏ Is there enough (authentic) reading material and variety, e.g. from magazines, novels, newspapers, letters, diaries, menus, advertisements?
❏ Is there enough (authentic) listening material and variety, e.g. monologues, group conversation, songs, people in everyday situations, e.g. shops, restaurants?

❏ Are there enough communication activities?
❏ Is there enough speaking and variety of speaking activities, e.g. role play, discussions, problem-solving activities?
❏ Is there enough writing and variety of writing activities, e.g. stories, letters, poems, form-filling?
❏ Is there enough 'personalisation' – a chance for students to relate the new language to themselves and their own lives?
❏ Is there enough revision?
❏ Is there enough controlled practice of new language?
❏ Is there a good variety of controlled practice activities?
❏ Is there enough freer practice of new language?
❏ Is there a good variety of freer practice activities?

Task 5.1

1. Suppose you are planning a course based on a given coursebook and you want to use a checklist to assess whether it will need to be supplemented and, if so, in what ways. What changes, if any, would you make to the checklist above?
2. Take a coursebook that you are familiar with. Use the (revised) checklist to assess it. Can you see any weaknesses in the book that were not revealed by the checklist? If so, what changes will you need to make to the checklist?

3   FORMS OF SUPPLEMENTATION

We can supplement a coursebook in one of two ways:

1. by utilising items, such as exercises, texts or activities, from another published source: a coursebook, a supplementary skills book, a book of practice exercises or a teacher's resource book;
2. by devising our own material; this may include the exploitation of authentic visual or textual items.

We begin by considering (1), since this has the obvious advantage of convenience.

3.1 Supplementation using published materials

Most books carry a statement saying firmly that no part of the work may be reproduced without the prior permission of the publisher. And yet the most common form of supplementation is the use of material from another book, most frequently in the form of photocopies, less often as an overhead transparency. Two measures have been taken to legalise this practice. The first involves payment: institutions can apply for a licence which permits restricted photocopying in return for a fee. The second is the publication of whole books or of books in which some sections are clearly marked 'photocopiable'. Photocopiable books tend to be much more expensive, of course, to counteract the reduced income through sales; the inclusion of photocopiable sections is at the same time an important concession and an appeal to the teacher's sense of fair play.

Supplementation through copying is an option when two conditions can be met: (1) facilities for reproduction are available and (2) appropriate source material is to hand. It is arguably only necessary when the advantages outweigh the disadvantages. Before the days of photocopiers and overhead projectors, teachers wrote on blackboards and asked students to copy what was on the board; and this still happens in many classrooms. Often a photocopier is a convenience rather than a necessity – and sometimes it can be a double-edged sword. It takes time; it can be frustrating (why is it that machines jam or run out of toner just before a class is about to start?); and the costs of producing multiple copies certainly add up. Moreover, loose pieces of paper are difficult to manage: students lose them or forget to bring them to class; and devising a suitable filing system can also be one task too many for busy teachers.

Financial and logistical considerations will not be an issue in certain kinds of supplementation using commercial materials. For example, a teacher might decide to use an oral activity from another coursebook or a teacher's resource book which can be explained and conducted without learners having recourse to written instructions or stimuli. The same applies to certain types of activity based on audio or video recordings: though the text requires playback facilities, the students' responses can be elicited by the teacher reading aloud (rather than having students read) the original questions or prompts, adapting these as necessary. Copyright and ethical issues would of course arise if written materials were reproduced, even if these had been adapted.

Some well-resourced institutions, while stipulating that a particular coursebook be used as the basic text, recognise the intrinsic limitations of a single textbook and purchase class sets of additional materials that can be used by teachers as and when the need arises. Detailed cross-referencing systems may even be drawn up to show which sections of these materials can be used to supplement a particular unit in a particular coursebook. Such guides are best compiled by a group of staff pooling their experience. Once a system has been established, however, it is not too difficult for a designated individual to keep it up-to-date by coordinating the suggestions of others on a termly or annual basis. This level of resourcing and institutional support obviously requires commitment on the part of management as well as the teaching staff.

3.2 Devising one's own material

Since it is easier to borrow something, even if some form of minimal adaptation is involved, what are the arguments for devising one's own material? The first and most obvious reason is that condition (2) above does not apply: suitable supplementary material is not available. The key word here is 'suitable'. Supplementary material has to meet the same criteria as coursebook material, but these are likely to be more strictly applied. Whereas time and effort spent adapting coursebook material to render it more suitable can be justified, this is less true of supplementary material. If the only potentially suitable published supplementary material that is available would necessitate large-scale adaptation, it is preferable to prepare one's own. Teachers know their own students and will be able to 'tune' the material to suit their level, their aptitude, their interests, their needs, and personalise it so that it seems even more meaningful.

Not everyone would agree that teachers should design their own material. Block (1991), who is in no doubt that they should, prefaces his arguments for what he calls DIY (do-it-yourself) materials design by reviewing the papers by Allwright (1981) and O'Neill (1982) discussed in Chapter 1. Despite their contrasting positions on coursebooks, both Allwright and O'Neill seem to agree that classroom teachers are not best equipped to write materials. Allwright puts this explicitly: 'the expertise required of materials writers is importantly different from that required of classroom teachers' (p. 6). Johnson (1972: 1) implies a similar view: 'Teachers choose and use instructional materials because they cannot (and ought not) [*sic*] prepare all the materials they need.' Behind this view seems to lie the assumption that materials are best prepared by professionals (i.e. knowledgeable and experienced writers) and by publishing houses which can ensure a high level of production (Sheldon 1988).

Teachers, it seems, have their own view. For instance, Nunan (1988a) reports that a survey of several hundred teachers in a large-scale ESL programme for adult migrants (Eltis and Low 1985) found that 73 per cent of the teachers 'regularly used materials produced by themselves' and 50 per cent claimed not to use commercially-produced materials at all (Nunan 1988a: 98). We might infer that the 50 per cent were so unhappy with commercially-available material that they felt driven to prepare their own, and that the other 27 per cent who regularly designed their own materials felt that it was desirable to supplement the commercial material they were using.

Similarly, Block's (1991) argument that teachers should prepare their own material derives in part from his dissatisfaction with published material. Teacher-prepared material, he claims, is likely to be more up-to-date and more relevant to students' needs and interests than equivalent coursebook material. For example, in order to provide a context for students to practise talking about what they did the previous weekend, he suggests that a teacher might record his or her colleagues talking about what *they* did. Such a recording, he notes, also has the attraction that, like other specially prepared materials, it has a 'personal touch' that students recognise and appreciate.

Though learners may still have a preference for 'a book' over handouts, the increasing availability of computer packages which enable teachers to design professional-looking materials and the possibility in more technologically developed settings of incorporating materials from the Internet can make teacher-produced materials an attractive (at least occasional) supplement to the coursebook.

In the next task, a development of an idea in Acklam (1994), you are invited to take the kinds of evaluative decisions that have been discussed in this and previous chapters in relation to a particular piece of lesson material. One difference between this task and that at the end of Chapter 4 is that in this case you are encouraged to include supplementary material, if you feel this would be helpful and appropriate.

Task 5.2

The lesson material below (see pp. 86–7) comes from an intermediate-level coursebook, and is intended for use with older teenagers/adults for whom balanced skill development (i.e. coverage of listening, speaking, reading and writing) is just as important as grammatical accuracy and vocabulary extension. If you do not normally teach this kind of class, try to imagine that you are standing in for a colleague who does.

1. You have one one-hour lesson each day with this class. Would you wish to spread the material over more than one lesson? If so, how many class hours would you base on the material?

2. Now follow these steps in planning one or more lessons based on the material. Remember a lesson lasts one hour.

   • Specify the aims of the lesson(s).
   • Write down the main stages in each lesson and describe their purpose, the nature of the activity, the interaction patterns (e.g. teacher to students, pairs, groups), which aids would be involved, and the time you estimate would be needed for each stage. This is essentially a skeleton lesson plan. You will probably find it easier to use a landscape format. A layout for such a plan is shown in Table 5.2 below.

Table 5.2 A layout for skeleton lesson plan(s)

Stage (brief description)	Objective	Procedure	Interaction	Aids	Time (minutes)
Lesson One 1. warm-up	activate vocabulary relevant to topic	topic introduced, then plenary brainstorming	T–Ss	blackboard	5
2.					

8 *Judging by Appearances*

VOCABULARY

Physical description

1 When we describe someone we tend to follow this order in our description: height, build, age, hair, face, complexion, extra features, dress. Study this example.

> My cousin, Paul, is a tallish man in his mid thirties. He is a bit plump and has got long straight hair which he wears in a pony tail. He has a round friendly looking face with a little scar on his cheek from a childhood accident. He has got bright blue eyes and wears glasses. He has got a beard. He isn't very smart and tends to wear shabby clothes.

2 Height and build
Match these adjectives with the definitions.

	frail		overweight.
	stocky		attractively thin.
Someone who is	slim	is	(old and) weak-looking.
	plump		unattractively thin.
	skinny		shortish but well-built.

3 Age

1 What ages do these words and expressions describe?

  A elderly **B** in your teens **C** a youth **D** a pensioner **E** middle-aged
  F a toddler **G** in your early/mid/late thirties

2 Tell your partner your age and the age of some family members without being exact about it.

4 Face

1 Find people in your class who have got round, oval and square faces.
2 What are scars, moles, wrinkles, lines and freckles?
3 What colour of skin do people have if they are pale, tanned or sallow?

5 Eyes

When we describe people's eyes we normally start with their size, followed by shape and colour, e.g. *She has got big round blue eyes*
                    SIZE SHAPE COLOUR

Put these sentences into the correct order.

1 Susan has got brown/large/round/eyes.
2 Klaus has got blue/bright/eyes/small.
3 Mary has eyes/green/large.
4 Mariko has/almond-shaped/large/dark brown/eyes.

What are eyebrows and eyelashes?

98

Figure 5.1 (above and opposite) Lesson material (Naunton, 1996, *Think First Certificate*, © Longman Group UK Limited/Addison Wesley Longman 1996, reprinted by permission of Pearson Education Limited)

6 Hair

When we describe people's hair, we normally give length first followed by colour and style, e.g. *He has got long dark hair in a pony tail.*

Match these adjectives with the pictures.

1 balding **2** straight **3** curly **4** bald **5** spiky **6** wavy

A   B   C   D   E   F

How is hair if it is in a bun or in pigtails?

7 Clothes

Match these adjectives with the definitions.

1	casual	**A**	old/worn a lot
2	scruffy	**B**	carefully dressed
3	shabby	**C**	well (expensively) dressed
4	smart	**D**	informal
5	neat	**E**	untidy/dirty

READING

Look at this short description of a character from a book. It is very effective, but how is it different from the description of Paul on page 98?

Eve was a small woman with a tiny waist and slender elegant legs. She had small hands with long tapering fingers. Her face was wide at the cheekbones and narrow at the chin, her forehead high, her upper lip short and her mouth full and lovely. Slightly tilted, her pretty nose was a little too small for her face. She had large hazel-green eyes and black eyebrows like Chinese brush-strokes, not unlike Sean's, and her thick, shiny, dark hair reached to the middle of her back. But she was very small, no more than five feet or five feet one at best. Liza didn't know her weight, they had no scales, but when she was sixteen Eve estimated seven and a half stone for herself and eight stone and a bit for Liza and that was probably right. Yet this tiny woman had somehow moved a man one and a half times her weight and nearly six feet tall.

And put him where? Somewhere in the wood. Liza decided, when she thought about it around that sixteenth birthday.

WRITING

You were a witness to a bank robbery in your town. You got a good look at the criminals when they took off their masks in the getaway car. Write about the robbery and include a full description of the criminals.

3. Next prepare a table with five columns which summarises, using the numbers of the exercises in the original material, the decisions you have taken and the reason for these. If your plan is for more than one lesson, draw a horizontal line under each lesson to keep the activities in each lesson separate from those in the next. Use the layout shown in Table 5.3, below, and follow the instructions given in each box.

Table 5.3 Summary of planning decisions

Lesson	Select	Reject	Adapt	Supplement
One	Write the number of each exercise you intend to use unchanged, and briefly indicate why it is worth retaining.	Write the number of any exercises you do not intend to use, and briefly indicate why.	Write the number of any exercises you intend to adapt, and indicate how they will be adapted, and why you think it would be desirable to adapt them in this way.	List the types of additional materials to be used (e.g. picture of X), and your justification for these.
Two, etc.				

Table 5.3 is a summary of the evaluative decisions you have taken and your rationale for these. It will enable you to compare your decisions with others, in later stages of the task.

4. If you are working in a group, compare your table (we will come back to the lesson plan later) with those of the other group members. If you are working alone, go on to the next stage.

5. Acklam (1994) includes a set of skeletal teacher's notes devised by a teacher who thought it necessary to supplement this material for the class she was teaching.
   Table 5.4 on the next page summarises the teacher's decisions (numbers refer to exercises in the original material). Compare these with your own.
   If you are working in a group, you will probably find it interesting and useful to discuss any differences between your plans and the teacher's and consider why the teacher may have taken the decisions she did. (The teacher's lesson notes are presented in Appendix 5.1.) You may then wish to reconsider your own plan. This process of comparison and reflection would be useful even if you are working alone.

Table 5.4 Summary of teacher's decisions

Lesson	Select	Reject	Adapt	Supplement
One	2	1	3	* warmer * additional visuals * listening * reading poems * writing poems
Two	4		5 6	* descriptions of family * role play
Three		Reading Writing	7	* warmer * survey * listening * discussion

Like materials evaluation, materials design needs to be based on principles. The remainder of this chapter provides an introduction to the process and principles of materials design, with particular reference to the design of worksheets and worksheet exercises. The development of material based on authentic texts, a particular type of supplementary material, is dealt with in the next chapter, which also extends the discussion of design principles.

4 THE PROCESS OF SUPPLEMENTARY MATERIALS DESIGN: SYLLABUS DRIVEN OR CONCEPT DRIVEN?

When the principal determining factor behind what you do is a syllabus – an official document or your own teaching plan (scheme of work) based on an analysis of learner needs – this will have an obvious influence on your approach to the creation of supplementary material. You may find yourself saying: 'I need something to practise X', where X is a point in your syllabus that is either not covered in the coursebook or is not dealt with adequately, in your opinion. If you know of something ready-made that will fit the bill, the problem is quickly solved. If not, you will need to design material specially for that purpose. We can call this kind of orientation *syllabus-driven* materials design.

Sometimes, however, since teachers never totally switch off, teaching material seems to suggest itself. You are reading a newspaper or flipping through a magazine and BAM! it hits you: 'I could use this with Form 3' or 'I could use this to practise Y.' Notice, though, the difference between these two thoughts. In the first instance, you can see that the material is likely to be relevant to the interests or needs of a specific class, but you will need to think about how to exploit it; in the second case, you can already see its linguistic potential, but you have no particular class in mind. What the two have in common is that the ideas that suddenly popped up were not the end of a conscious syllabus-driven search but rather the beginning of what we might call a *concept-driven* (or ideas-driven) process of materials design.

A rather broader definition of syllabus-driven materials design (one which extends to learner-generated syllabus items) would allow for the fact that learner questions or requests may also be a stimulus to materials development. The first of two worksheets on hypothetical meaning included in Jolly and Bolitho (1998: 98–104), for instance, was prompted by students' request for an explanation of the verb form in 'It's time the Prime Minister *listened* more carefully to her critics.' (This worksheet can be seen in Appendix 5.2.)

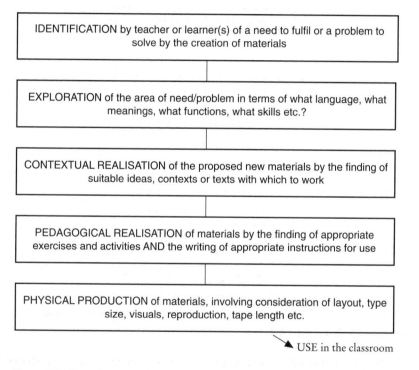

IDENTIFICATION by teacher or learner(s) of a need to fulfil or a problem to solve by the creation of materials

EXPLORATION of the area of need/problem in terms of what language, what meanings, what functions, what skills etc.?

CONTEXTUAL REALISATION of the proposed new materials by the finding of suitable ideas, contexts or texts with which to work

PEDAGOGICAL REALISATION of materials by the finding of appropriate exercises and activities AND the writing of appropriate instructions for use

PHYSICAL PRODUCTION of materials, involving consideration of layout, type size, visuals, reproduction, tape length etc.

USE in the classroom

Figure 5.2 Steps in materials design (Jolly and Bolitho 1998: 97)

Jolly and Bolitho's representation of the process leading up to the production of the worksheet is captured in Figure 5.2, above. While the sequence illustrated appears logical as a sequence, it is probably not an accurate reflection of reality. As Jolly and Bolitho point out, this is a simplified version of the process, in that (1) a materials writer may not go through all of these steps and may not follow the steps in exactly this order and (2) it fails to take account of the rewriting (revision) that is likely to follow feedback.

The diagram is also simplified in that it appears to conflate two rather different scenarios: one in which the need to produce materials gradually becomes apparent and one in which this is seen to be unnecessary (see Figure 5.3, below).

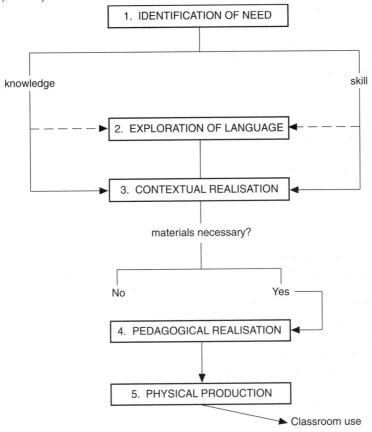

Figure 5.3 To produce materials or not?

At Stage 1, the teacher becomes aware of a need that cannot be satisfied on the spot. If that need is for *knowledge* and implies *presentation* of linguistic or cultural information, they will then reflect on what they know (Stage 2: Exploration of language) and perhaps consult one or more authoritative sources. The issue of whether or not to produce materials to deal with the need/problem will almost certainly not have been considered up to this point. If, on the other hand, the need is for *skill* and (further) *practice*, other than oral practice, will be required, then the teacher will have recognised this at Stage 1 and may well skip Stage 2. (There will, of course, be situations where both presentation and practice are felt to be necessary.) For the teacher who has presentation in mind the first decision comes at Stage 3: will an oral explanation and/or some examples (deductive presentation) be appropriate or would an awareness-raising approach be preferable, and if so, are supplementary materials called for? In either case, one or more appropriate contexts will have to be devised. When materials are deemed to be necessary, the two scenarios come together at Stage 4 (pedagogical realisation). Here the focus is on method, how learning can be facilitated or practice managed. In the penultimate stage, decisions are taken about layout and so on and the materials produced. The final stage, in the diagram, at least, is classroom use. However, we might wish to allow for input from colleagues at any point in this process.

We will come back to this design model in Chapter 9, in the context of a discussion of revision in the materials development process.

Let us now consider some of the general principles involved in worksheet design.

5 DESIGNING WORKSHEETS

5.1 The function of worksheets

Worksheets are a particular category of handout. Like re-usable self-access 'workcards' (a distinction made by Ur (1996: 192)), they are designed to facilitate learning through activity. A photocopy of a page of exercises from a book, a collection of cut-and-pasted exercises from different sources, a number of teacher-produced exercises – whatever their origin, their function tends to be the same: to raise awareness of how the language works through an activity of some kind and/or to provide additional practice.

Although teacher-produced worksheets frequently focus on specific points of grammar (and may therefore differ little from individual pages in the kind of workbook produced to accompany some coursebooks), they can be used for a broader range of purposes. These include awareness raising or practice in relation to:

- *handwriting* (for young children or learners whose native language uses a different script); this can include not only practice in forming individual letters but also joining letters, and writing on the line;
- *spelling* (e.g. the spelling rules governing the pluralisation of nouns ending in 'y' or the doubling of the terminal consonant in verbs);
- *punctuation* (e.g. inserting full stops and capital letters into an unpunctuated text; deciding which words in a text should be capitalised; combining sentences; changing indirect speech into direct speech);
- *pronunciation* (e.g. exercises which require learners to match words

containing the same vowel sound, mark stressed syllables, give the normal spelling of words written in phonetic transcription).

Vocabulary and grammar exercises are dealt with later in this chapter.

5.2 General issues in worksheet design

Whether you are preparing a worksheet that will consist of photocopied exercises or exercises you have devised yourself, there are a number of general issues that need to be addressed.

5.2.1 Awareness raising or practice?

While worksheet exercises typically provide opportunities for learners to apply what they know (i.e. practise), they can serve other purposes, the most obvious being to raise awareness of systematic features of the language (i.e. fixed rules), or the extent to which rules are variable. This distinction between practice and awareness raising corresponds to that sometimes made in reference to two approaches to grammar teaching. In a *deductive* approach, learners are given a rule and examples and required to apply that rule; in an *inductive* approach, they are given samples of language and expected to discover the rule for themselves. This is, in fact, the process by which we acquire many of the rules – morphological, syntactic, phonological, orthographic and discoursal – in our first language.

One question we therefore have to ask ourselves is whether we favour a deductive approach, which may seem convenient and efficient, or an inductive approach, which may be more time consuming but – many would argue – more effective, and therefore ultimately more efficient. Rules in books and teachers' explanations often employ abstract language which learners have difficulty in understanding. If they can work out and correctly formulate a rule for themselves, perhaps with a little help from their teacher, this is evidence that they understand it; moreover, the effort involved in working out the rule may well mean that the rule is better retained. Learners may have their own views, of course. For instance, Fortune's (1992) study of young adults' reactions to different types of self-access grammar exercises indicated a general preference for the more conventional.

In educational environments where a deductive approach is the norm and the teacher is expected to be the dispenser of knowledge, it may be necessary to explain to students how they might benefit from a different approach and introduce them to this in easy stages. This implies not only teacher support – comparable to helping someone while they are learning to swim – but also that what the students are required to do is within their capacity. What seems easy to the person who devises an exercise and therefore knows the answers may prove impossibly difficult for students. As with any materials development, piloting and revision are essential steps in the process.

The distinction between awareness raising (often termed 'consciousness raising' when grammar is involved) and application is an important one. With teacher education in mind, Ellis (1986: 92) warned against the too-ready assumption that making teachers aware ('of the options open to them and the principles by which they can evaluate the alternatives') will lead to improved practice. 'We do not know', he points out, 'to what extent this assumption is justified' (ibid.). Writing more recently, specifically about language learning, Fox (1998: 42) is a little less guarded:

> Whilst there is no automatic transfer from awareness of a feature to the ability to use that feature, there is certainly a likelihood that increased awareness will lead to increased proficiency – particularly of features which, once pointed out, are encountered frequently in real-life language situations.

The assumptions here are clear in the words 'frequently' and 'real-life', and although there is now some evidence of a carry-over from awareness-raising activities to production, we do well to be cautious, especially if we know that our learners have little opportunity for daily exposure to the target language in 'real-life situations'.

5.2.2 Accuracy or fluency?

A second issue concerns the relationship between the format of the exercises and the purposes they are intended to serve. If worksheets are intended for individual work and self-checking by students, then formats which require them only to respond to what is given (e.g. sequencing, matching, selecting) or are closed-ended (e.g. certain types of gap-filling or transformation exercises involving a change from singular to plural, declarative to negative, active to passive) are obviously more convenient than formats which require them to produce language. Convenience should not be an overriding consideration, however. What is important is that the exercise format should reflect the objective of the exercise. The types of exercise format just listed may be appropriate for developing accuracy, and therefore have value, but other types of activity will be necessary for the development of fluency. Worksheets which do not necessitate language production or which closely control what students produce will have at best an indirect effect on their ability to produce language fluently in less controlled situations.

5.2.3 Practice or testing?

A test of language form is at the far end of a continuum that starts with copying or highly controlled practice. In practice situations, we provide support, typically in the form of examples; in testing situations, we remove that support. In controlled practice situations, moreover, the focus is narrow, the choices very limited, and learners have an opportunity to consolidate their mastery of the language point through repetition. In discrete-item testing, on the other hand, the intention is to sample the learner's mastery of a range of language items, and each item will therefore tend to focus on a different point. Again, what counts is the objective: we need to be clear that the format suits the pedagogic purpose. Look at the examples in Appendix 5.3. Does the format always suit the apparent purpose?

5.2.4 Differentiation and motivation?

Since a worksheet will normally be used by learners working individually or in groups without the help of a teacher, a key question is how to cope with the problem of differences in proficiency levels within a class. One answer is to prepare different worksheets for different levels of learner. The alternative is to design a worksheet in which exercises are graded from easy to more difficult, a principle often followed in testing. This has two main advantages over the first suggestion: it is less work, and it avoids the possible negative effects of 'labelling' students (however subtly this is done, students recognise it for what it is). If everyone works with the same worksheet, weaker learners or more careful learners who work more slowly may only complete the first few sections, but if what they have done is correct they will nevertheless feel a sense of achievement, and thereby gain confidence. If later sections of the worksheet are at an appropriate level of challenge for the more proficient learners, they will also feel a sense of achievement. The relationship between age, level, achievement, motivation and confidence is, of course, complex. It has been frequently observed that 'success leads to success', and this might be a reason for trying to ensure that younger learners and those in the early stages of language learning experience success. However, we might wish to ponder whether for some, especially older and more advanced learners, success that is easily achieved will be as valued or as motivating as hard-won achievement.

If graded worksheets are set as groupwork, it is advisable that the members of each group be of roughly the same proficiency level. Although there is an argument for peer teaching in relation to certain types of activity, there is a strong possibility that in this particular case the more proficient students will dominate and complete the worksheet without reference to or discussion with their weaker peers. If plenary feedback is conducted, the groups containing weaker students should be given the opportunity to show that they can answer the easier questions.

5.2.5 Layout and other general considerations

Issues such as objectives, format of exercises and organisation apart, a number of more practical questions also need to be considered. For instance:

- Should the material be in the form of a disposable worksheet or a re-usable workcard? (Where there is a choice, it makes sense to produce a disposable version first and try it out; see 'Evaluation', below.)
- Should students write their answers on the worksheet? If so, how much space should be allowed for the answers?
- Are the exercise rubrics (instructions) clear? (It might be a good idea to get a colleague to look through these.)
- How can the worksheet be made to look visually appealing (e.g. through typographic variation or the inclusion of graphic elements)?
- Will you provide an answer key, check answers with the whole class or collect the answers in for marking?

5.2.6 Evaluation?

It is also worth asking how you will be able to evaluate the effectiveness of the worksheet. If you collect the worksheets to mark them yourself, you could look at the number of correct answers (in principle, the more the better, but if everyone completes the worksheet correctly within five minutes you might have to reconsider the level of difficulty) or at the sections or questions which seem to have posed most difficulty. You could watch students as they work, see how engaged they are in the task, how quickly they progress through the various exercises, and at what points they slow down or get stuck. You could also ask students how they felt about the worksheet and what suggestions they have for improvement. You could do all of these, and then prepare a revised version for use with the corresponding class next year, or carry over what you have learned from this experience to the preparation of further worksheets for the same class.

5.3 Computerised worksheets

The increasing availability of computers for student use in classrooms and self-access centres has made possible the provision of computerised worksheets. These have a number of advantages over handouts. Materials can often be modified by the learner to permit variation in the degree of difficulty (e.g. by determining the frequency of deletions in a cloze text). Immediate feedback is available. Self-checking is easy. Mistakes can be easily erased. Computers can give praise, but they do not blame. Moreover, the computer is endlessly patient: it will not push the learner to finish within a specific time; and it will repeat examples, explanations and exercises as often as the learner wishes.

6 DESIGNING YOUR OWN WORKSHEET EXERCISES

Let us suppose that no suitable supplementary exercise material is available and that you have therefore decided to prepare your own. This section offers advice on the preparation of grammar exercises and vocabulary exercises.

6.1 Designing grammar exercises

6.1.1 The objective of grammar teaching

Grammar teaching is motivated by two objectives: to transmit knowledge and to facilitate skill development. Figure 5.4 below is an attempt to capture this distinction.

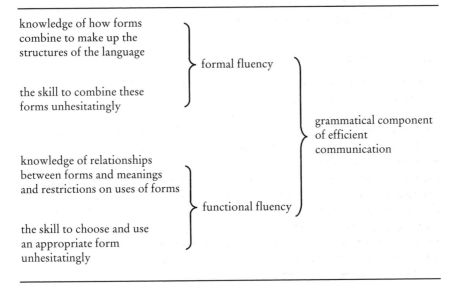

Figure 5.4 Objectives of grammar teaching

As Figure 5.4 indicates, the grammatical component of efficient communication requires the integration of different forms of knowledge and skill. Take as an example the acquisition of the so-called 'Third Conditional', e.g. 'If I'd known then what I know now, I wouldn't have agreed to do it.' The basic elements of this can be reduced to:

If + Past Perfect + Conditional Perfect (*would* + *have* + past participle).

A learner needs (1) to know what the various components of this structure are and how to combine them and (2) the ability to put the correct components together quickly. But he or she also needs (3) to know what the structure means and when it is appropriate to use it and (4) the ability to use it

spontaneously and appropriately. Note that, in the spoken medium, important aspects of fluency will be the use of weak forms (e.g. /əv/ rather than
/həv/ in 'wouldn't have') and contracted forms such as *I'd* and *wouldn't*.

By distinguishing between what are here referred to as 'formal fluency' and
'functional fluency', the diagram makes the further point that grammar
teaching has to relate to real-life language use, and therefore raises the issue of
contextualisation.

6.1.2 Contextualising grammar practice

We will return to the relationship between classroom language learning and
real-world language use in the next chapter, where we discuss authenticity.
Here, we look at the implications for the contextualisation of grammar practice and learner output.

If grammar practice – or the first stage in this – is seen as primarily concerned with the development of formal fluency (see the first half of figure 5.4
above) then context may not seem particularly important. Indeed, it may be
seen as a potential distraction. We can, however, acknowledge this while still
insisting that all the samples of language which learners are exposed to and
expected to produce should be realistic, that is, potentially usable and useful.
Thus, even though the focus may be on the *underlying* form or rule, the surface manifestations of that rule should have potential value in their own right.

The argument for contextualisation is, of course, incontestable in relation
to the lower half of the diagram. Grammar is a system for expressing certain
types of meaning. Used in combination with appropriate lexical choices, it
allows us to express meanings about ourselves and our world (real and
imaginative) or the world 'out there', that of events and information to which
we only have access through books, TV or the Internet. This distinction may
be somewhat artificial: Widdowson (1979b: 78) refers to the knowledge a
learner gains as part of his or her general education as 'part of the learner's
world'; however, the point is that in thinking of contexts for grammar practice, these two worlds will be the most appropriate reference points. Factors
such as the age of the learners, their existing knowledge, and the predictable
contexts in which they might use the target language would obviously influence
the choice of specific contexts and exercise items.

6.1.3 Knowledge versus skill

The point was made above that knowledge and skill combine in efficient
communication. However, teaching for knowledge is very different from
teaching for skill. Knowledge can be 'presented' or 'discovered'; it can also be
forgotten. Skill, on the other hand, can only be acquired through practice, and
once acquired is relatively easily maintained. The fact is that while we can
'teach' knowledge, we cannot teach skill. Skill has to be learned, and practice
is a central element in that learning.

Task 5.3 K

Look at the extracts from exercises in Appendix 5.3.

1. What do you see as the differences between extracts A and B?

2. Now look through the other extracts. For each extract, answer the following questions.

   What is the specific linguistic focus? Is the focus on knowledge or skill? on formal fluency or functional fluency? on learning or testing? If the focus is on knowledge, is the approach inductive or deductive? Is the language that the learner is expected to produce natural? You might find it helpful to draw up a table like the one below:

Table 5.5 Analysis of extracts from Appendix 5.3

Extract	Linguistic focus	Knowledge(K) or Skill (S)	Formal Fluency (Form) or Functional Fluency (Flu.)	Learning (L) or Testing (T)	Inductive (I) or Deductive (D)	Natural?
A	gerund					
B						

3. How do the exercises differ in format? Which formats do you prefer? Why?

4. Choose one exercise that you think would be worth extending. Add several items and ask your colleagues to comment.

5. Choose one exercise about which you have reservations. How could it be adapted? (Bear in mind that several of the exercises are extracts only.)

For feedback on your answers to the first two questions, see 'Tasks: Keys and Commentaries'.

6.2 Designing vocabulary exercises

In one sense, having a good vocabulary means knowing a lot of words. Many language learners have problems expressing themselves not because their grammar is weak but because they have a limited vocabulary. Since we can never teach learners all the words they will need, even if we could predict these, they have to be shown how to extend their word-stock systematically through their own efforts. Word-building exercises are an ideal focus for worksheets to be used out of class, but can also be exploited for cooperative work in class.

Much has been written about what it is to know a word. Lado (1956) makes a well-known and helpful distinction between knowledge of *form*, *meaning* and *distribution*. Knowledge of form would include familiarity with the pronunciation (including stress pattern) and spelling of a word, what part of speech it is, whether it takes affixes (and if so, which), and how it behaves syntactically. Knowing a word's meaning would include knowing not simply its denotation (dictionary meaning) but also whether it has any connotations, whether it forms part of a semantic set, and how it relates to other words (e.g. as a synonym, antonym, hyponym). Knowledge of distribution includes awareness of how a word collocates with other words, whether it belongs to a particular register, and whether it is stylistically marked (e.g as formal or slang). The awareness that a word can be looked at from these rather different perspectives can help us to set objectives for teaching and testing; it can also inform the way we look at teaching materials.

Appendix 5.4 contains a number of extracts which illustrate different exercise foci and formats. Look at the exercises and try Task 5.4.

Task 5.4 K

1. Look at each exercise in turn. What purpose is each intended to serve? (You could answer this question in a number of different ways.) Now consider the exercise format. What do learners have to do in each case (e.g. classify, match . . .)? Again, you may find it helpful to record your answers in a table like the one below for easy comparison.

Table 5.6 Analysis of extracts from Appendix 5.4

Extract	Specific linguistic focus	Type of lexical knowledge	Format
A	collocation		matching

2. Which exercises do you prefer? Why?

3. Choose two of the exercises about which you have reservations. How could these be adapted to make them more useful/interesting/challenging?

6.3 Commentary

The first part of the task above encouraged you to think about how vocabulary exercises can be categorised (according to their linguistic focus, the kind of lexical knowledge they are designed to develop or their format). Apart from the more obvious vocabulary-building exercises, the examples include what have been termed 'tidying up' exercises (Wallace 1981). Vocabulary learning is not just about learning more words; it is also concerned with knowing more about the words you already know (e.g. how they relate to other words with a similar meaning or which other words they are used with). 'Tidying up' exercises are ways of bringing miscellaneous items of knowledge into a systematic relationship with each other. This may involve not only organising existing knowledge but introducing new items to add to a 'word family' or complete a closed set. Though such exercises are an obvious way of exploiting a text, they are also useful for general revision purposes.

For a detailed commentary on the individual extracts, see 'Tasks: Keys and Commentaries'.

Task 5.5

1. Analyse the vocabulary exercises in any published materials that you have available. Is there any difference in the coverage of form, meaning and distribution in materials for different proficiency levels? Should there be?

2. On what techniques are the exercises based? Are there any variations on the techniques illustrated in Appendix 5.4? Any totally new formats?

Exercises abound in coursebooks and practice books. There is thus no shortage of examples on which to base your own exercises. As with any other materials writing, however, it is important to think about objectives as well as means and to ensure that the objective you have in mind can be achieved through a particular exercise format.

Task 5.6

The end-of-chapter task this time is fairly predictable, but there is a choice – and a little twist.

1 Prepare a worksheet (ideally, for a class you are teaching) containing at least three exercises. The worksheet:

   a. may focus on any linguistic system (grammar, vocabulary, phonology, orthography);

   b. should focus on a genuine problem for learners;

   c. may include exercises from published materials;

   d. must include at least one exercise that you have prepared yourself.

2. Ask your colleagues if they can spot the exercise(s) you have designed. Ask them also for any suggestions on how the worksheet might be improved.

7 FURTHER ADVICE AND IDEAS

Certain forms of supplementation have been only briefly referred to in this chapter. Ideas for warm-ups and other short activities can be found in Ur and

Wright (1992). For further ideas on catering for mixed levels, see, for example, Hubbard, Jones, Thornton and Wheeler (1983: Ch. 10) and Prodromou (1992b). Teacher-prepared tests are, of course, another form of supplementation. For advice on the preparation of classroom tests, see, for example, Heaton (1990).

The literature on grammar teaching is quite extensive. For further discussion of deductive and inductive approaches and exercises, see, for example, Rutherford (1987); Harmer (1991); Batstone (1994). Sources of exercises include Wright (1994); Bolitho and Tomlinson (1995); Thornbury (1997). On vocabulary, see, for example, Wallace (1981); Gairns and Redman (1986); Schmitt (2000).

8 SUMMARY

The focus of this chapter has been the supplementation of coursebooks through the provision of additional exercises. These can be 'borrowed' from other published materials or specially written for the target learning group. When there is a choice between these two options, the latter, while more demanding, has the advantage that it should result in materials that are more relevant to the needs of the specific group in question. Teachers who take the decision to prepare worksheets to provide additional practice of this kind need to take account of a number of general considerations. These include the relationship between objectives and format, learner differentiation, layout and the need to evaluate the worksheet. Teacher-made worksheets tend to deal with grammatical features and the chapter has discussed factors that might influence the design of grammar exercises and illustrated a variety of exercise types. However, the worksheet approach also lends itself well to individualised work on other aspects of the language, and this has been exemplified through a secondary focus on vocabulary exercises.

Chapter 6

Using the real

The nature of authenticity: authentic texts; criteria for the selection of authentic texts; text-types; text selection and teaching purpose; principles; exercise- types; authentic tasks; spoken communication activities; authenticity and difficulty; task difficulty – materials dissemination – concordances: the value of concordances; using concordance data – exploiting the Internet: as a source of material for teacher-directed learning; as a medium for self-directed learning; Web-based teaching; designing course materials for the Web

In the previous chapter, the argument was put forward that teachers should prepare their own supplementary materials in the following circumstances:

- the coursebook does not fully meet the specific needs of the learner group, and
- no suitable published supplementary materials are available (or these cannot be copied or bought).

That chapter dealt with the preparation of supplementary exercise material. This chapter not only has a different focus, it is also intended to be relevant both to teachers who base their teaching on a coursebook and to those for whom that is either not the preferred option or not an option at all.

One of the assumptions underlying the chapter is that teachers who, through necessity or choice, use a coursebook will sometimes wish to supplement the book in other ways, for instance by providing a greater variety of texts, or by introducing authentic texts or tasks if these are not included in the coursebook. The first part of the chapter therefore deals with the concept of authenticity, and offers guidance in the selection of authentic texts and the preparation of tasks based on these. For teachers who design most of their own material these will obviously be central concerns.

Another assumption is that teachers in both groups who are keen to provide learners with authentic texts will also be willing to explore other ways of providing access to samples of language that reflect real-life language use and encouraging authentic language use. The second section of the chapter deals with the exploitation of concordance data that is one output of computer-based language corpora. This is followed by a section on the use that can be made of the Internet.

What links these three foci is the belief that language learning (in the first and additional languages) is facilitated by four interrelated conditions. The first of these conditions is exposure to suitable samples of the language in sufficient quantity (suitability being a matter of quality as well as appropriateness to the learner). The second is opportunities for practice (receptive as well as productive), that is, engagement with language samples and other language-users. The third is motivation, which may exist independently of conditions one and two but may also be stimulated by these. And the fourth is feedback – not necessarily in the form of error correction, but certainly a response indicating whether or not one has been understood. By providing opportunities for learners to interact with *real* materials, create materials and communicate with others about those materials, and by structuring that experience so that feedback is available, we may be able to do more than just establish a fertile environment for classroom learning. We can also hope that out of these conditions springs the motivation for learners to want to carry on communicating and learning out of class.

1 THE NATURE OF AUTHENTICITY

A useful summary of the authenticity debate is provided by Clarke (1989a). Although, as Clarke points out, there has been something of a shift in focus from text to task, belief in the importance of authentic texts runs deep and this therefore provides the starting point for this section.

1.1 Authentic texts

Nunan (1988a; see pp. 99–102) offers the conventional definition of authentic texts: '"Authentic" materials are usually defined as those which have been produced for purposes other than to teach language' (p. 99), for example print materials such as newspapers or timetables, or spoken materials such as public announcements. If we see authentic-text materials as not simply samples of the kind of language use that learners may need to cope with outside the language classroom but also as potential models of use, Nunan's definition might be further refined to include the more contentious dimensions of speaker/writer and listener/reader highlighted in the following definition: 'communication *by and for native* speakers, writers or readers in that language' (Breen, Candlin and Waters 1979: 1; emphasis added). This raises another issue, of course, that of what constitutes an appropriate model, a question to which there might be different answers in different contexts.

Strictly speaking, an authentic listening text would be neither scripted nor edited; in practice, poor quality, length and other pedagogic considerations lead to spoken texts being re-recorded and/or edited for use in classrooms. Written texts may similarly be retyped and edited. While it might be argued that these changes can substantially alter the way the original text was conceived or delivered and affect comprehensibility (Grellet 1981), the pedagogical argument has generally prevailed. The key issue in relation to text authenticity, however, is how far it is reasonable to go in the direction of rendering a text accessible to learners.

Task 6.1

Think about the changes you have made (or would be prepared to make) to authentic written texts in order to make it easier for your students to cope with them.

1. Which of the following are unjustified, in your view?

2. Can you think of other forms of adaptation that you would consider unacceptable?

> a. cutting out a newspaper/magazine article and photocopying it (loss of information on visual context in which it appeared);
> b. retyping an article (change in visual appearance of text);
> c. reproducing only part (but a continuous part) of the original text;
> d. editing out sections of the text to simplify the argument or content;
> e. editing out linguistic elements (e.g. sentences, phrases or words) that are not syntactically necessary and would pose difficulty.

The main concern in relation to these kinds of adaptation is that the more changes are made the less 'authentic' the text becomes. Authenticity is felt to be important because it gives learners a taste of the real world, an opportunity to 'rehearse' in a sheltered environment, hence the less authentic the materials we use the less well prepared learners will be for that real world. This is also the argument advanced against specially written or simulated authentic texts. Although discourse analysis has helped us to identify the features of authentic speech and writing, and we can deliberately build certain features into specially devised materials so that they resemble the real thing, they can never *be* the real thing, as a comparison between, say, scripted speech and a transcript of real speech immediately reveals. Does this matter? Some, such as Nunan (1988a), would say it does: that 'comprehending and manipulating scripted dialogues does not readily transfer to comprehending and using language in real communicative situations' (p. 100), that there will be not only phonological differences (e.g. articulation and intonation) but also differences at the level of syntax, discourse patterns and patterns of interaction. However, to recognise these differences is not to argue for the total exclusion from the classroom of scripted material, since this can be used – alongside authentic text – for quite different pedagogic purposes (Nunan 1988a).

1.2 Criteria for the selection of authentic texts

A number of criteria need to be considered in selecting authentic texts for classroom use, the most obvious of which are:

- relevance (to syllabus, to learners' needs)
- intrinsic interest of topic/theme
- cultural appropriateness
- linguistic demands
- cognitive demands
- logistical considerations: e.g. length, legibility/audibility
- quality (as a model of use or as a representative token of a text-type)
- exploitability.

Relevance is a *sine qua non*. However interesting a text may be, if its use cannot be justified on the grounds of relevance (whether of topic, genre or linguistic features), it should not be used at all. The corollary also applies: if a text is patently not going to interest learners, however relevant it is, it should be replaced by one that will. Relevance and interest are relative, of course, and potentially a matter of presentation and exploitation as well as content. With a little ingenuity, it may be possible to use an unpromising text in ways that make it seem relevant or more interesting. For this effort to be worthwhile, the text would also need to be suitable in other respects.

In some contexts, cultural appropriateness is seen as the absence of any features (illustrations or verbal references) that offend against the religious, social or political mores of that culture; more broadly, it might be seen as the framework within which the materials are set, and the extent to which settings, interactions and characters are familiar. With regard to a specific text, therefore, cultural inappropriateness may relate to the topic, the attitude of the writer to the topic, or specific allusions. It may be possible to edit out or replace certain allusions; if the text is deemed to be inappropriate in a more general sense, then there is little that can be done. (For a fuller discussion, and an alternative view, see the section on 'Materials and Culture' in Chapter 10.)

The extent to which there is a rough match between the linguistic and cognitive demands of the text and the capacities (language proficiency, cognitive maturity, knowledge) of the learners is an obvious consideration. Cognitive considerations will include the familiarity of the subject matter and key concepts, degree of abstractness and text organisation (including the ordering of information and the salience of discourse markers). On a linguistic level, glossing of key lexical items can help, and some difficulties can be removed through judicious editing. Editing (e.g. of whole paragraphs) can also reduce a long text to something usable within a limited time-frame. Too much editing, on the other hand, especially within paragraphs or sentences, can not only result in the loss of some of the features that make a text authentic but also eliminate some of the links that make it a cohesive whole – and thereby render it more difficult to process (see Tomlinson's (1998a) comments on simplification, quoted in Chapter 4). Potential problems relating to the legibility of a written text (e.g. its (small) size or the fact that it is handwritten) or to the audibility of a recorded text may necessitate the production of a more accessible version of the original or, if these logistical difficulties combine with other disadvantages to make the text basically unsuitable, lead to the decision to select an alternative text.

Two final criteria should be mentioned. Since texts are seen by students (if not always by teachers) not simply as something on which to polish their listening/reading skills but also as something from which they can learn language, it is important that they are suitable as examples (e.g. of a particular text-type – a letter requesting information, or an abstract of, say, a journal paper) and/or contain examples of specific language features. In other words, a text should be an appropriate sample of language use and a model, in some of its features at least, for student production. We should remember, however, that authentic texts were not written to serve as practice grounds or hunting grounds for language learners. They were written to convey information, transmit ideas, express opinions and feelings, entertain. Good texts tell us something we do not know; they contain interesting content; they provoke a reaction. They are multiply exploitable because they lend themselves readily to tasks which are interesting as well as useful.

1.3 Text-types

One reason for teachers to go outside a coursebook for texts is that they wish to expose their students to more examples of a particular text-type, and to illustrate the variations within this, or to provide exposure to a greater range of text-types.

Task 6.2

1. Can you add to the following list of text-types? You might also wish to distinguish between subcategories of some of the items, such as letters.

   - novels, plays, cartoons, nursery rhymes
   - letters, postcards, notes
   - newspapers and magazines – and particular sections in these, such as advertisements or letters to the editor
   - reports, statistics, diagrams
   - travel brochures, guidebooks, timetables

- instructions, road signs
- menus, bills
- telephone directories, dictionaries

2. Which of the text-types on your (expanded) list have you not used? Are there any of these which it might be useful for your students to work on?

1.4 Text selection and teaching purpose

The primary purpose for choosing to use an authentic text is that it is authentic. Beyond that we may use a text for a number of different purposes. The next task encourages you to consider in a preliminary way possible objectives underlying text-use and some of the procedures that might be used to fulfil these objectives.

Task 6.3 K

Here are five teachers (A–E) talking about their reasons for using texts in class. Read the extracts, then try the tasks that follow.

A. *I want students to have a model (for instance, examples of a new structure or a particular kind of letter) so that they'll feel more confident about attempting new things in the language. The principle of listen/read first and then speak/write seems a basic one to me.*

B. *Students will only learn to understand native speakers of the language if they're exposed to plenty of samples of authentic language, different voices, etc.*

C. *Sometimes my students have difficulty talking or writing about topics because they lack imagination or inspiration. I find that if I give them a listening or reading text first that often helps to get the ideas flowing.*

D. *I tend to use texts to develop a specific receptive skill, be it listening or reading. And I normally have particular aspects of the skill in mind – for instance, the ability to distinguish the main points, to get the gist, as it were, or the ability to use contextual clues or existing knowledge to make informed guesses about the meaning of unfamiliar lexical items. Sometimes, I use explicit means (i.e. consciousness raising); at other times, I use what you would probably call implicit means – that is, I get students to carry out particular operations in the hope that these will become instinctive. For example, if I wanted to help students to process written text more quickly, I might either analyse a text with them so that they can see how texts are typically structured in the target language – bearing in mind that there are differences across cultures, or if I were working implicitly, I might simply set them a task which **required** them to read quickly. Normally, of course, I'd move from the explicit to the implicit,* *which would then be a way of practising or applying their conscious knowledge. So, using the same example, consciousness-raising analysis of text structure would be followed by practice in skimming.*

E. *I see texts as linguistic quarries. My main concern in working with texts – real texts, that is, not texts specially written for language learners – is to draw attention to points of language which are either of interest in themselves (specific structures, lexical items, cultural allusions) or provide a starting point for consideration of related language features. A lot of what I do – and my students seem to find this fascinating too – is in the area of synonymy, antonymy, idiomatic expressions, etc. The general idea is to enrich their vocabularies, of course, extend their linguistic repertoires. We dig at the text together; they then decide what they want to take from it. For the kind of students I teach, upper intermediate and advanced, this seems to work pretty well.*

1. Which of the teachers seem most concerned that texts should be authentic?

2. Each of the extracts makes reference to an end (the objective) of using texts and a means. Go through them again and mark the relevant sections O (i.e. objectives) and M (i.e. means) respectively.

3. The objectives listed below are reformulated (and reordered) versions of those expressed by teachers A–E. Match the teachers' objectives with the reformulated versions in the table below. One has been done for you.

Objectives	
Language skill-oriented develop general comprehension develop specific receptive skills	. . . . .D. . . .
Language system-oriented facilitate productive use of specific language items develop general language proficiency	. . . .
Other facilitate production	. . . . . .

4. Which of the views expressed is closest to your own?

Beyond beginner level, all language teachers in adequately resourced contexts make use of texts. However, they differ both in what they do (method or means) and in what they hope to achieve (objectives or ends). Clearly, different procedures are likely to produce different results. What we need to ensure is that there is a match between our objectives and our means. Here are a few general principles that might be helpful.

1.5 Principles

1. Students will find it easier to cope with 'real-life' listening/reading if they are exposed to authentic texts in class.
2. In much of the listening that we do in real life we are involved as interactants. We listen and we speak. We know why we are involved in the interaction and our role and that of others in the interaction. Even if we are not directly involved, as when we are 'eavesdropping', standing in a queue or sitting near someone on public transport, we know what the situation is and we have access to various kinds of contextual information, such as facial expression, physical closeness and touch, that can usually help us to make sense of the relationship and of what we hear. In other kinds of listening (e.g. telephone conversations, public announcements, radio broadcasts, lectures), where the speaker knows we need additional help to compensate for what we cannot see and/or for the lack of potential for interaction, this will be provided through explanation, repetition, and so on. In the classroom, when audio recordings have been used, this has not always been the case. Audio recordings are, of course, an important way of providing for classroom listening practice. However, it needs to be recognised that in relation to recorded conversations learner-listeners will be at a severe disadvantage compared to someone present during that conversation because they lack contextual information. Unless one of the specific purposes of the activity is to encourage learners to make guesses about the situation, the topic, the attitude of the speakers to the topic, the relationship between the speakers, and so on, as much of this information as would be known to someone present during the conversation should be made available to the learner. From all this we can derive a very brief principle: put the learner in the picture.
3. If we are to simulate real-life text-processing (reading or listening), the *first stage* of an approach to text should involve *a focus on meaning*. In our first language, we listen/read with a purpose. That purpose always involves extraction of meaning (information or opinion), although it may also include supplementary expectations, such as pleasure through humour.
4. *The meanings that we ask students to extract should be related to the meanings the intended reader is expected to derive from the text* – i.e. the writer's intention. Students' text-processing proficiency can be judged by their capacity to extract this meaning (and arguably no other). The nature and extent of the meanings involved will, of course, be partially determined by text-type.
5. Students are more likely to cope successfully with text-meanings if they are given help with content and/or language.
6. Since students are also language learners, it follows that the *second stage*

should involve *a focus on language*. This may be intended to serve various purposes:

(a) provision of models: e.g. study of the use of a particular tense;
(b) language enrichment: text items provide a starting point for work on, e.g. synonymous or antonymous items or lexical sets;
(c) input to another activity: a text is used almost as a pre-text or preliminary to an activity in which the focus is on another language skill (e.g. a written text may be used as input to discussion). In this case, the initial text may serve both to stimulate thought on the topic and to feed in relevant ideas and language.

In 'the bad old days', a teacher might have said: 'Read/listen to the text and answer the questions'; these days, the orthodox approach takes the form 'pre-reading/listening – while reading/listening – post reading/listening'. The principles above reflect this orthodoxy, 2, 3 and perhaps 5 relating to the pre-reading/listening stage, 4 to the while-reading/listening stage, and 6 to the post-reading/listening stage.

1.6 Exercise-types

Let us imagine that a good (suitable) listening or reading text is available – in other words, a text which satisfies the text-selection criteria discussed in a previous section and which will serve a teacher's teaching objectives. It may be a reading or listening text in a coursebook, accompanied by an inappropriate set of 'comprehension questions', or it may be something the teacher has found him- or herself. In either case, it will be necessary to prepare questions or tasks. The principles above may be helpful at a general level, but it is still necessary to consider how specific objectives can be translated into task-types.

Grellet (1981) is probably the most comprehensive source of ideas for the teacher wishing to develop text-based materials. As Table 6.1 (overleaf) indicates, her approach is to identify specific reading subskills (many of which have an equivalent in listening); she then provides copious illustrations of the types of exercise that can be used to develop each of these skills. See Grellet (1981: 14–25) for a discussion of each of these exercise-types.

Task 6.4

1. Does Grellet's taxonomy seem to you to be a satisfactory way of describing the skills involved in reading? Look first at the major headings.

2. Can you think of any techniques which are not listed here? (You might like to refer to other discussions of reading, e.g., Nuttall (1982/1996).)

3. Look through the reading materials in your coursebook or the reading materials you have prepared yourself. Is there anything that you now feel you ought to include?

Table 6.1 Reading comprehension exercise-types (based on Grellett 1981: 12–13)

Reading techniques		
sensitivity: • inference: through context; through word-formation • understanding relations within the sentence • linking sentences and ideas: reference; link words	improving reading speed	from skimming to scanning: • predicting • previewing • anticipation • skimming • scanning
How the aim is conceived		
aim and function of a text: • function of the text • functions within the text	organisation of the text – different thematic patterns: • main ideas and supporting detail • chronological sequence • descriptions • analogy and contrast • classification • argumentation and logical organisation	thematisation
Understanding meaning		
non-linguistic response to the text: • ordering a sequence of pictures • comparing texts and pictures • matching • using illustrations • completing a document • mapping it out • using the information in a text • jigsaw reading	linguistic response to the text: • reorganising the information: reordering events; reorganising the information using grids • comparing several texts • completing a document • question-types • study skills: summarising; note-taking	
Assessing the text		
• fact versus opinion • writer's intention		

One of the many ideas contained in Maley's (1998) discussion of current and desirable future developments in materials design is that of a typology of generalised procedures that can be used with raw texts. They are, in essence, ideas that teachers can use in devising student activities. As with any good typology, the number of ideas that can be generated by each option is limited only by the user's imagination.

1. *Expansion*: students add something to the text (e.g. adjectives, sentences, comments, a beginning or ending).
2. *Reduction*: students shorten the text in some way (e.g. by turning it into telegraphese, by combining sentences, by rewriting in a different format; see also 3 and 8, below).
3. *Media transfer*: students translate the text into a different medium or format (e.g. drawing, table, poem, or recast a letter as a newspaper article).
4. *Matching*: students 'match' the text with something else (e.g. a title, another text, a picture).
5. *Selection/ranking*: students select a text (e.g. for inclusion in a teenage magazine) or part of a text for a particular purpose (e.g. words to act as a title); or rank texts according to a given criterion (e.g. formality).
6. *Comparison/contrast*: students identify points of similarity or difference (e.g. words/phrases, facts, ideas).
7. *Reconstruction*: students reconstruct the original text (which has been e.g. reordered, gapped or presented in a different medium).
8. *Reformulation*: students express the same meaning in a different form (e.g. retelling a story, rewriting in a different style).
9. *Interpretation*: students engage with the text on a personal level (e.g. in response to prompts about their own experience or the images/ associations thrown up by the text) or think about what questions they might wish to ask the author.
10. *Creating text*: students use the text as a starting point for the creation of their own texts (e.g. parallel text on a different theme, re-using words from the original text, using the same title for a new text).
11. *Analysis*: students carry out a linguistic analysis of the text (e.g. frequency with which different tenses are used, listing all the words referring to a particular topic, such as the sea).
12. *Project work*: students make use of the text in a more extended practical activity (e.g. a text in which an issue is presented leads to the design of a questionnaire, which is administered to other students).

(based on Maley 1998: 288–91)

The procedures are illustrated in pages 291–4 in Maley's article.

In each case, Maley suggests, the normal pattern would be for individuals to do the activity first themselves, then to compare what they have done in pairs or threes, and finally for the outcomes to be shared with the whole class.

Task 6.5

1. Are there any techniques in Maley's list that you hadn't thought of?

2. Can you add further examples for any of the options?

3. Look at the tasks that accompany extract F in Appendix 3.3 and classify them according to Maley's typology. Which of the task-types suggested by Maley might precede, follow or replace the original tasks?

4. Do the same for the tasks in Appendix 6.1 or in a randomly chosen lesson in the coursebook you are using.

One of the points emphasised in Grellet's (1981) introduction to her book is that reading should be linked to other skills. Examples include reading and writing (summarising in a letter what one has read); reading and listening (comparing an article and a news bulletin); reading and speaking (debates, the arguments for which have been researched). This brings us to the issue of task authenticity.

1.7 Authentic tasks

The narrow concern with text authenticity that characterised the early years of the communicative movement has since given way to a concern for the nature of tasks and for learners' attitudes to texts and tasks (see, e.g., Candlin and Murphy 1987; Nunan 1989; Crookes and Gass 1993a, b; Willis 1996).

Nunan (1988b: 4) provides a generally accepted definition of authentic tasks which takes real-world behaviour and learner need into account: 'tasks which replicate or rehearse the communicative behaviours which will be required *of them* in the real world' (emphasis added). Authentic tasks can be contrasted with *pedagogic* tasks (e.g. controlled grammar practice activities such as gap-filling or transformation exercises), which focus on the development of accuracy rather than language using.

One point of particular interest in Nunan's definition of authentic tasks, though he does not pursue it, is the specific reference to learners' own realities. This poses a common problem for syllabus planners and materials designers: how to predict the behaviours that will (and will not) be needed? Form-filling, for instance, might seem a potentially relevant activity, but the classroom teacher is probably in the best position to know whether a specific group of learners are likely to need to complete a car-hire form, a visa-application form, a dating-agency form – or none of these. The obvious solution would be to exclude the kinds of tasks which will most obviously not involve the learners in relevant kinds of communication or, more positively, to concentrate on the likely needs of the majority – but even here there are problems.

One of these has to do with the relationship between text and task. Hall

(1995), for instance, makes the point that the authenticity of a text is not in itself sufficient to make the work based on it either interesting or valuable; what counts is the reader's response. If a learner is already familiar with the content of the text he or she is expected to read in the language class, then the 'need' to read will derive merely from the requirement to jump through the hoops (exercises and activities) provided by the teacher. If real-life reading is our yardstick, then we must bear in mind that this is self-motivated: that a reader reads because he or she wishes to. For Hall, therefore, 'An authentic response depends on the existence of *an authentic need*' (p. 12; emphasis added).

While this is a persuasive argument, it ignores the fact that a good deal of reading for study purposes (and probably much of the reading that is done in work contexts) is not motivated by a wish to read but a need to read, which students and those who need to read in the course of their work accept. Moreover, learners may have different expectations of classroom activities and their real-world parallels. Thus, a second problem, if it can really be seen as this, is that learners may take a different perspective from theorists. There has been research into adult learners' preferences which suggests a preference for conventional form-focused activities (i.e. pedagogic tasks) over more communicatively-oriented activities (see Nunan 1988a for a summary of some of this research). Taking this into account, Nunan (1988a, 1991) suggests that learners may themselves *authenticate* particular activities which, using measures such as those discussed above, would not pass the authenticity test.

Our response to this should not be: 'Good, so it doesn't matter what kinds of task (or text) we use, as long as learners seem happy with them.' If we can predict that learners will need to engage in real-world interactions, whether face-to-face or through the written word, then we owe it to them to devise appropriate rehearsal activities (tasks). But this concentration on the real (authentic tasks) should not blind us to the fact that there may be two routes to success in carrying out such activities. One involves the acquisition, through discrete practice exercises (pedagogic tasks), of the necessary knowledge and skills, with the final task necessitating the integration of these enabling competences. The alternative is to provide a progressively more complex series of tasks, with feedback at each stage. The latter approach has been strongly advocated in recent years (see, e.g., Willis 1996).

Task 6.6

1. Think of the tasks that you typically set on texts. Which of these are authentic and which pedagogic? Do the latter prepare for the former? Should they?
2. What are your students' views about text and task authenticity? If you don't know, how would you find out? (Be as specific as possible.)

1.8 Spoken communication activities

The 'information gap' is now well established as a means of stimulating class-room communication. For instance, jigsaw listening and jigsaw reading both require learners to share their piece of the puzzle with other learners in order to solve a problem. Other types of commonly used paired activities which exploit this principle include the following:

- 'Describe and draw': one person describes a picture, the other attempts to reproduce it; the same principle applies to following instructions on how to get from A to B on a map.
- 'Describe and arrange': one person describes a fixed set of items, the other organises movable items accordingly (e.g. cut-outs of furniture in a room or photographs of people) – for this activity, two copies of the same sets of pictures will obviously be needed.
- 'Spot the difference': the kind of observation puzzle sometimes found in newspapers, where two versions of the same picture (hand-drawn or photocopied) differ in a specified number of details. This is more interesting when items are added as well as deleted from both pictures.
- making plans: both students have diaries with certain fixed appointments; the task is to find a time when they can do something together.

The degree of difficulty involved in any of these tasks will depend partly on the nature of the task but more particularly on the lexis required to describe/understand. In one version of 'Describe and arrange', for example, the task might be to arrange photographs of people or food items or landscapes in a particular order, but the photographs themselves might be so similar that very detailed descriptions are required. It is not difficult to cater for quite different proficiency levels within a class in this way.

'Opinion-gap' activities also have an obvious real-world origin. We differ in our tastes in clothes, colours, food; we differ in what we think of books, films, music; and we differ in our judgements of people and events. We will also have different preferred ways of dealing with common problems and different views on how we should act in given situations. Unlike information-gap activities, activities that exploit an opinion gap are open-ended in the sense that there is no right answer (Clark (1987) calls them 'divergent' as opposed to 'convergent' tasks); and as a result, some students may find them less satisfying. (The instruction to 'try to persuade others to agree with you' may be a way of extending an open discussion meaningfully and bringing it to a positive conclusion.) Activities that would fall into this category would include:

- discussion: e.g. based on a question, a visual or auditory stimulus, a social problem, an 'agony aunt' page
- debates

- priorities exercises: e.g. ranking a list of occupations according to their social usefulness
- story completion.

Prabhu (1987), whose Bangalore project used both information-gap and opinion-gap activities, also refers to 'reasoning-gap' activities. These involve processing information in order to solve a given task. An example would be working out from a railway timetable the quickest way to reach a given destination. For school-age learners, such tasks can obviously serve broader educational aims as well as providing for communication practice.

1.9 Authenticity and difficulty

In language learning, as Nunan (1988a, 1991) points out, difficulty has traditionally been seen in terms of language items, and careful selection or 'control' of these items has been the principal means by which input to learners has been graded.

The adoption of the principle of authenticity as a central tenet of communicative language teaching has posed a particular problem as far as grading is concerned. If only authentic texts are used and the principle of authenticity is adhered to strictly, then no linguistic editing (or control, in this sense) is possible.

Two ways of resolving this dilemma have emerged.

1.9.1 'Grade the text'

In the first approach, where the emphasis is on linguistic appropriateness, texts are selected which are of approximately the right linguistic level for the learners, without worrying overmuch about specific linguistic items. While this may seem relatively unproblematic for an experienced teacher with a feel for the kind of language that a particular group of learners should be able to handle, text difficulty cannot be assessed purely on the basis of linguistic analysis. The difficulty of a spoken text may be attributable to the rate at which a speaker speaks, for instance, to his or her accent (and perhaps the familiarity of the learners with this accent) and articulation, to the fact that there are several speakers whose speech overlaps, or to white noise; and particular difficulties are involved in listening to recordings, when the clues available in face-to-face speech are absent. Both spoken and written texts may prove difficult, as noted earlier, if one is unfamiliar with their content, key concepts or the cultural setting.

1.9.2 'Grade the task'

The second approach is to select texts on the basis of their inherent interest and devise tasks which are judged to be within the competence of the learners, to grade the task and not the text (Grellet 1981). Following this principle, even newspapers can be used with beginners.

In practice, the two tactics are frequently combined in a single strategy: that is, a text is selected which is thought likely to interest learners and be of an appropriate level of difficulty, without being 'easy'. The pedagogic justification for not choosing an 'easy' text or one from which all difficulties have been edited out is that in responding to relatively simple tasks, the learner's focus will tend to be on taking only what is needed from the text for a defined and limited purpose (an 'authentic' approach in itself).

1.10 Task difficulty

Nunan (1989: Ch. 5), whose discussion of task difficulty draws attention to the complex interaction between the various contributory factors which combine to determine task difficulty, refers to input considerations (i.e. the text, and the support this provides for the listener/reader), the nature of the task, and learner factors such as linguistic/cultural knowledge, confidence and previous experience with similar tasks.

Linguistic output considerations (what the learner may be required to say/write) are no doubt implied in this discussion, but by making them explicit, as in Figure 6.1 below, and distinguishing them from non-linguistic features of the task, we ensure that they are fully taken into account at the task-design stage.

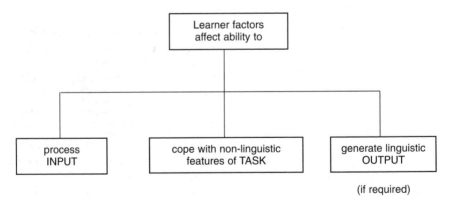

Figure 6.1 An input–output view of task difficulty

One advantage of separating linguistic output from the other features of task difficulty is that it encourages a focus on the conditions (e.g. time constraints) under which the task is to be carried out, but also on the cognitive processes involved. Prabhu's experience with the Bangalore project suggested that key factors affecting task difficulty included the degree of abstractness and the need for precision and reasoning (Prabhu 1987). Candlin and Nunan (1987, cited in Nunan 1989: 110) have proposed a system of grading adapted from Bruner, in which there is a four-stage progression from 'attending and noticing' to 'transferring and generalising'.

This kind of analysis is not only relevant to the selection or design of suitable tasks for a specific class of learners; as Nunan (1989) points out, it also makes possible the manipulation of one or more elements to create tasks which pose different levels of challenge.

2 MATERIALS DISSEMINATION

Arguing that the time spent by teachers on materials design can be justified, Block (1991) presents a six-stage process leading to the sharing of material. The example given is the exploitation of a reading text, but this might equally well be a satellite TV news programme, a radio interview or any general-interest material in any medium.

1. The teacher finds an interesting article in a news magazine.
2. The teacher spends over an hour putting together a reading exercise, a language activity derived from the text, and a discussion activity.
3. The teacher uses the text and activities in class, and then makes a few adjustments in the activities.
4. The teacher posts several copies of the text with the activities on a board in the teachers' room.
5. Several teachers use the text and activities in their classes.
6. At some point, the text and activities are either put in a long-term bank (in which case, they are considered to be relatively 'timeless') or thrown away (in which case they are considered 'dated').

(Block 1991: 215–16)

He makes the point that for this to be 'cost-effective' in terms of preparation time at least six colleagues need to contribute to the bank of material. This obviously necessitates an institutional culture in which colleagues are prepared to cooperate – and give as well as take. This problem apart, there is the practical difficulty of keeping track of the use of a specific piece of material. Where staffrooms operate with this kind of common resource, it can be very frustrating to find that a class in which you are intending to use 'your' material has already used that material (especially if you only discover this in the course of the lesson). On the positive side, it should be recognised that this kind of sharing has the potential additional benefit that the original material is gradually extended and refined as a result of trialling with different classes and by different teachers.

Task 6.7

1. Choose an authentic text which you feel would be appropriate for a specified group of learners.

2. Devise two or more tasks on the text.

3. Describe the intended context of use to a colleague, explain your choice of text and tasks, and ask for comments.

You may find it helpful first to look at some of the references at the end of this chapter.

For some teachers, materials development of this kind is more than just an occasional activity. Chapter 7 deals with systematising the design process.

A word of warning: because authentic texts are inherently rich in their possibilities, it is tempting to base a whole battery of activities on a single text. Don't. As Maley (1998: 288) wisely points out, 'there is no point wringing the text dry just for the sake of completeness'. You may have lost your learners long before they reach the final activity.

3   CONCORDANCES

3.1 The value of concordances

Descriptions of language in use have benefited greatly from the development in recent years of huge computerised databases (e.g. the British National Corpus at the University of Oxford, the COBUILD corpus at the University of Birmingham and the Nottingham/Cambridge University spoken English corpus at the University of Nottingham). Using such a database to examine a specific language item (e.g. the verb 'do'), it is possible to determine both the range of ways in which the item is used and the relative frequency of these, information which can be a useful input to course planning and materials design. Made available to learners, print-outs (or 'concordances') of extracts from such data can also offer an interestingly different basis for awareness-raising activities. They can be used to help learners formulate their own rules for the use of an item. They can also reveal – and help learners notice – patterns of use that might not otherwise be apparent (Willis 1998). For instance, a study of concordance lines focusing on 'break out' would show that the subject of the verb 'break out' is typically something unpleasant, 'wars', 'fights', 'strikes', 'riots' or 'fire' (Fox 1998). Moreover, in relation to grammatical features, concordances can compensate for the limitations of coursebooks. The concordance of 'than' below (see Figure 6.2), from Tribble and Jones (1990: 41), while short on examples of *more* ADJ *than*, contains 'plenty of examples of the comparison of adverbs, often neglected in course books, and of *rather than*, as well as the common idiomatic uses ... *than ever*, ... *than you think*, and the structure *better to* (verb) *than to* (verb)' (ibid.).

* pstick. She looked so much better	than	the fat, spreading South London moth
* safe rule is never to get closer	than	the overall stopping distance shown
* pping at Marks & Spencer is easier	than	ever, with a Chargecard. When you'r
* peed; you may be going much faster	than	you think. Do not speed up to get a
* ditions. Your speed will be higher	than	you think – 50 mph may feel like 30
* on of peace obviously looms larger	than	ever before in human history. And h
* ng involved an in– crease of less	than	5,000 million tons of coal equivalen
* ibute (reckoned in calories) less	than	four per cent to the world total. In
* drawing a trailer, or a bus longer	than	12 metres, must not use the right-h
* after conversion from holding more	than	15% of the shares in the successor
* ookshop of their choice from more	than	3,000 throughout the UK and Ireland.
* e Board? A W will do much more	than	that. We will hold meetings with Mem
* ers stay down at any time for more	than	three minutes without a train arriv
* ervation at intervals of not more	than	two miles and they apply to all lane
* atch in fascination as more often	than	not he missed his mouth and the carr
* coming up behind much more quickly	than	you think. Make sure that the lane
* enticeship – I deduce that, rather	than	know it – sometime, it must have be
* ith him for most of the day rather	than	several visitors all at once, which
* heelers are much less easy to see	than	larger vehicles and that their rider
* offer the customer better service	than	our competitors.We believe that on
* take the bend a little bit sharper	than	him; so I took off, was going towar
* n your right is moving more slowly	than	you are. Never move to a lane on yo
* that, um something which is worse	than	in other countries, or . . . <Dian
* , especially when you are younger	than	usual. So I like to think I'm helpi

Figure 6.2 A concordance of 'than' (Tribble and Jones 1990: 41)

Concordances can also be a corrective to the prescriptiveness of course-books. Fox (1998: 32) suggests:

> a selection of appropriate lines can be given to students, who can then see for themselves what is happening. They will find sentences exemplifying what is traditionally taught – and that's good: it gives them some rules they can apply and know they will not go far wrong. But they will also find sentences that deviate from what they have been taught – and discussion should help tease out what is happening: how so much depends on the speakers and their perceptions.

In the same vein, Carter, Hughes and McCarthy (1998) point out that the design of the Nottingham corpus of spoken English, which incorporates a description of the context of use, permits finer or different distinctions to be drawn than were previously possible, for example that the choice of 'going to' or 'will' depends as much on 'interpersonal and social-context sensitive factors' as it does on 'strength of prediction' (p. 68).

3.2 Using concordance data

A teacher could simply take a print-out into class and talk learners through it (Tribble and Jones 1990). Though this might be informative, it might also be overwhelming, and it is possible to imagine other uses that are a little more imaginative and potentially more effective. A first step, as Tribble and Jones suggest, would be to add a heading and a set of questions to the print-out. The dataset could also be edited by deleting repetitive examples. This latter problem might be reduced by using a sampler, that is, a smaller, representative set from the main database. Tribble (2000) recommends for teaching purposes the British National Corpus sampler (1999), a two-million word sample from the much larger database; this is also available as a CD-ROM.

A number of exploitation techniques are also suggested and exemplified by Tribble and Jones (1990, Ch. 4). For instance, if the intention is to draw learners' attention to the range of uses of a particular lexical item, an edited selection of these can be generated with the keyword deleted and learners asked to supply the missing keyword. Matching exercises can be created by reordering the elements that follow the keyword (see Figure 6.3 below). Groupwork activities can be based on groups being given the same task but a different set of data. Technical advice is also included on how to produce and manipulate the concordance data – with scissors, paste and correction fluid as simple alternatives for those who prefer them.

In this concordance something seems to have gone wrong with the printer! The contexts after the word *such* have come out in the wrong order. Can you put them back in order so that the first part of each context matches the second part? Write a number in the brackets at the end of each context to show which ending goes with each beginning. The first one has been done for you.

```
1   Burnley; 'but think how she felt, such  things  as salad, vegetables and bre (12)
2   d not mind. To him the old man was such  thing as a ones meal. The recipes  th (..)
3   nd  this applies  to other countries such  richness of choice that a Book Toke (..)
4   r  on clothes. – Empty containers, such   as his nickname or what foods he lik(..)
5   the road to warn drivers at places such   a little girl, she was only eleven,  (..)
6   ything she should know about him, such  as aerosols or tins.  A combination (..)
7   gifts  animals  give  us  painlessly. such times the boy did not laugh.  He was (..)
8   thin a year or two from illnesses   such  dinners, optimism is restored, and o (..)
9   e remains. Friend– ships  bloom  at such  as skin cancer or pneumonia which the (..)
10  ct under the sun.  This  is world of such as Aus– tralia, New Zealand and Can (..)
11  dish–Suppers   There really is no such an   object of fascination that he se (..)
12  red accompaniment to the meat, are such   as bends and brows of hills where t (..)
13  d rosewood and mahogany floor. At such  as milk and eggs.   The proposition (..)
```

Figure 6.3 A matching exercise using concordance data (Tribble and Jones 1990: 41)

Willis (1998) suggests that teachers (or their students) can create their own concordance exercises based on texts with which students are already familiar. Willis' paper includes five examples of actual classes in which she used what she calls 'hand concordancing', that is, the creation of a mini-concordance based on available texts (which may be learner-generated texts) by the learners themselves. The focus of each concordance was determined by Willis herself with reference to a computer-generated frequency list – in this case, a list based on the Bank of English, the University of Birmingham corpus. Participants produced the concordances, on overhead projectors or on the board, and Willis devised the analysis tasks.

One of the examples provided by Willis relates to an analysis of uses of 'in'. The students (described as 'weak remedial beginners') had read three short articles from the *Guinness Book of Records* about the largest, the smallest and the most expensive houses in the world, and were then asked to write out the phrases containing 'in' and classify these as 'place', 'time' and 'other'. In the *Guinness Book* texts, all the phrases were found to relate to place or time. The students were then asked to look through materials they had worked with earlier in the course and find further examples. This led to a number of discoveries: for example that 'in' can be used to refer to groups of people ('in your family'), languages ('in English') and fixed phrases ('in fact'). It also has an adverbial use: for example, 'Will you join in?' 'Hand your books in.' Willis comments: 'This search for more examples gives a broader picture of the uses of the common word. In other words, it is making full use of the pedagogic corpus so far covered by the learners' (p. 57).

The possible benefits of the kinds of language-analysis activities she describes are summarised below:

Learners can:

- become aware of the potential different meanings and uses of common words;
- identify useful phrases and typical collocations they might use themselves;
- gain insights into the structure and nature of both written and spoken discourse;
- become aware that certain language features are more typical of some kinds of text than others.

(Willis 1998: 55)

Concordance print-outs need to be handled with care, however. Students may find the fragmentary nature of the lines and the disparateness of the samples disorientating. An appropriate first step would therefore be to explain what a concordance is and how working with concordance print-outs may help them. (See Thompson (1995) for suggestions for introductory exercises.)

They may also feel daunted if they are presented with too much material. Even though these disadvantages can be overcome by getting students to do the concordancing themselves, they may still be reluctant to spend a great deal of time on a single point of language. Fascinating though such material may be for us as teachers, we need to remember that most learners are pragmatically inclined.

Task 6.8

The following two examples from Carter et al.'s (1998) paper illustrate phenomena which they refer to as 'heads' and 'tails' respectively.

> **The women**, they all shouted.
> **That chap over there**, he said it was OK.
> **That house on the corner**, is that where they live?
> **This friend of ours, her daughter, Carol**, she bought one.
> **Robert, this friend of mine I work with**, his son was involved in a car crash just like that.

(Carter et al. 1998: 82–3)

> He's a real problem is **Jeff**.
> She's got a nice personality **Jenny has**.
> It's too hot for me, **Singapore**.
> I'm going to have burger and chips **I am**.
> It was good **that book**.

(Carter et al. 1998: 70–1)

1. Would you see a value in presenting learners with material of this kind (a) for awareness-raising purposes (b) as preparation for production?

2. If you decided to use it for (a), what insights would you expect students to gain, and what specific questions or tasks would you set to guide them towards these insights?

3.3 Further reading and sources of help

For further discussion and examples, see, for example Aston (1997), Boswood (1997), Fox (1998), Willis (1998), Carter, Hughes and McCarthy (1998); Johns and King (1991) is a thematic collection, and Tribble and Jones (1990) a book-length treatment. Published extracts for teaching purposes include the Collins Cobuild Concordance Samplers (e.g. that on 'Reporting' by Thompson (1995)) and the British National Corpus Sampler (1999), available as a CD-ROM. Thurstun and Candlin (1997) focuses on a small number of lexical items judged to be of particular relevance for those studying English for academic purposes. Tribble (2000) cites two Web-based 'sources of inspiration': Cathy Ball's 'Tutorial: Concordances and Corpora' at http://www.georgetown.edu/

cball/corpora/tutorial.html and Tim Johns' Data-Driven Learning Pages at http://sun1.bham.ac.uk/johnstf/ddl_lib.htm.

For do-it-yourself concordancing, Tribble (2000) recommends the following software programs, the first being the more comprehensive: M. Scott (1996, 1998) *WordSmith* – for more information, see http://www.liv.ac.uk ~ms2928/homepage.html and M. Barlow (1996, 1998) *MonoConc 1.5* (for student use) and *MonoConc Pro* (for research) – for more information, see http://www.athel.com

4 EXPLOITING THE INTERNET

As Forsyth (1998: 170) points out, 'the Internet is about links':

> The origin of the Internet was to set up links between like-minded people, seeking and sharing information. It was American. It was military. It was science. Then it became education, information and available . . . There is an expectation that using the Internet provides random access to information and that this constitutes learning. (ibid.)

The increasing availability of home computers means that many people now use a computer as an alternative to a library. Encyclopaedias, dictionaries and other reference materials can be bought as software packages or CD-ROMs; but the Internet also offers convenient and seemingly limitless access to information on the World Wide Web (WWW) – a continuously expanding body of information placed there by institutions or individuals in print, graphic, audio or video form. Recognising the educational potential, educational institutions are not only supporting learning by making Internet access available to students but also exploiting the Net as a delivery mechanism for programmes or part-programmes. The possibilities offered by the Net for electronic communication also make it relatively easy for students and staff to communicate individually and for students to communicate with each other when a task set by a teacher requires this. A growing number of institutions, particularly at tertiary level, have also established their own internal networks (Intranets) for communication and teaching-related purposes.

The first part of this section picks up both parts of the final sentence in the above quotation. It considers how the information resources of the Internet can be exploited by teachers or by learners working independently of a teacher in such a way as to promote language learning. It also expresses a reservation about the assumed relationship between random use and learning. This is followed by a brief discussion of how the Net can be utilised as a delivery system for specially-designed materials. The latter allows, of course, for the fact that a teacher might refer students to additional resources available on the Net, i.e. guided Net-exploration.

4.1 The Internet as a source of material for teacher-directed learning

In a traditional programme based on a textbook or materials supplied by the teacher, it is the teacher who structures, synthesises, selects and sequences. While these teacher roles will still be important in a programme which exploits the Internet as a source of material, there is also considerable potential for learners to be involved in decisions concerning the choice of material or to look for their own material to supplement that provided by the teacher (see also Chapter 8).

Examples of this kind of directed use of the Net would include:

4.1.1 Learners are directed to or find for themselves information on which they can draw for essays, projects and presentations

Asking learners to find information for themselves has an obvious educational benefit: they take on the role of independent researchers and develop skills in this; but it also has potential disadvantages. Inexperienced researchers can waste a great deal of time looking through materials which are not particularly relevant, they can get lost or distracted – and when the time available is limited, as it usually is, this can seriously affect the value of what they produce.

There is also an issue of quality. Whereas conventionally published information has been in some sense vetted, there is no such control over material on the Internet. Jor (1999) raises one set of issues: 'How can students learn to evaluate information on the Web? How do teachers deal with abuse of Internet resources such as pornography, dangerous and false information, lies and libels, etc?' (Jor 1999: 24).

Anticipating these problems, the teacher can either direct students to a quality-controlled directory, such as the Yahoo directory or dmoz.org (where quality controls are operated according to quite strict criteria) or pre-select a limited range of suitable websites, but give students freedom to determine which of these they wish to make use of. Morrall (1999), thinking more specifically about Internet materials specifically designed for learning, warns that teachers should first try these out and check that answers are correct and feedback appropriate before recommending them for student use.

A further and very common problem (and this is not confined to second-language learners, who may be understandably unsure about their linguistic competence) is that students produce a cut-and-paste version of what they have found. It is important to point out in advance that plagiarism is unacceptable and show students how to avoid this both by appropriately referencing any quotations and by paraphrasing and summarising, again with reference to the source.

4.1.2 Two or more institutions collaborate cross-nationally on a project

The aims of such collaboration are typically to develop the linguistic skills of the participating students (even when one institution is located in an English-speaking country), to further cross-cultural understanding, and to obtain a broader perspective on the topic of investigation. When this cooperation is at undergraduate or postgraduate level, it may also provide access to sources (e.g. in another language) that would not otherwise have been available. Although collaborative projects can be difficult to manage (see, e.g., Shive 1999 for a report on two projects involving tertiary-level students in the USA and Hong Kong, where the difference in time zones made it difficult for students to be on-line at the same time), the potential benefits for language learners in terms of cultural insights and linguistic confidence are clear. The Windows on the World website at http://www.wotw.org.uk, which was designed to help schools in Europe to find partners for cross-cultural projects, gives information about and examples of e-mail projects (Thorne, A. and Thorne, C. 2000). Reports on projects can also be found at http://www.stolaf.edu and http://hut.fi/~rvilmi/project.html (Eastment 1999). Appendix 6.2 lists the websites (recommended in Shive 1999) of a number of North American organisations that facilitate school-based information-technology learning exchanges.

4.2 The Internet as a medium for self-directed learning

While indiscriminate browsing ('surfing the Net') may not be ideal, many language learners are making use of the Net without being guided in this by a teacher. They are finding their own resources for learning. The motivation that drives this kind of self-directed learning is perhaps analogous to that which leads a learner to look for a pen-pal, read English newspapers, novels or special-interest magazines, listen attentively to the words of recorded songs, or even – in one rather special case in my experience – induce a young man studying English in the UK to spend his weekends taking train journeys because they offered the opportunity of conversation with native speakers. Behind these examples may lie rather different motivations, of course. A similar variety of motivations will be reflected in Net-use.

Morrall (1999) reports on a survey, carried out in the Centre for Independent Language Learning of the Hong Kong Polytechnic University in autumn 1998, of the experiences of tertiary-level students (50) and teachers (20) in learning and teaching English via the Internet. Although small in scale, the study produced a number of interesting results, some of which are listed below.

In relation to English language learning:

- 72 per cent said that learning English using the Internet had made them more independent learners;

- roughly half of the students surveyed had communicated with native speakers using e-mail or ICQ (a messaging system that allows people to chat in real time);
- 36 per cent had used the Internet to learn English (some students were not aware of how to exploit the Net for this purpose, and Morrall speculates that others may not have thought of their communication with native speakers in this light).

On a more general level:

- 96 per cent considered that their research skills had improved (Morrall expresses reservations about this finding, commenting that the students may have been equating their ability to locate information with improved research skills);
- 74 per cent of the students and 65 per cent of the teachers had sometimes felt that their computer knowledge was inadequate when using the Internet;
- 72 per cent felt that the Internet encouraged them to study in more depth than was necessary;
- 56 per cent of the students found that the use of the Internet, e-mail or ICQ increased their motivation to study;
- roughly half of the students had used the Internet, e-mail or ICQ to study at home.

Many of these points will be picked up in the discussion below.

4.2.1 Utilising language-learning materials on the Net

It is important for teachers and learners to be aware that a growing bank of materials specifically designed for language learning and teaching can be found on the Net. For learners, these include materials in familiar categories, such as grammar explanation, practice, and common errors, vocabulary and idioms, pronunciation, listening, reading- and writing-skills development, but also games, crossword puzzles and quizzes. Probably the best-known site is Dave Sperling's ESL Cafe at http://www.eslcafe.com, others being http://www.wordcentral.com and http://www.comenius.com/fable/complete.html. Among the references in Eastment (1999) are two sites listing language-learning resources, the *TESL Journal* site at http://www.aitech.ac.jp/~iteslj and the Frizzy University Network http://the city.sfsu.edu/~funweb. Jor (1999) – see also http://humanum.arts.cuhk. edu.hk/~cmc/eltmatters has also made a categorised selection of some 200 websites relevant to the learning and teaching of English. Although some of these have particular relevance to the Chinese context, the majority will be of more general interest. Particular categories of learning material listed by Eastment include the following:

- *reading*: http://deil.lang.uiuc.edu/web.pages/readinglist.html (University of Illinois list of authentic reading materials); http://www.ed.uiuc.edu/impact_homepage (short texts at intermediate and advanced level)
- *listening*: http://www.esl-lab.com (Randall Jones's listening lab, with more than 100 listening clips in RealPlayer format)
- *writing*: http://owl.english.purdue.edu (Purdue University: work-sheets and guided-writing exercises)
- *grammar*: http://www.go-ed.com/english/grammar, http://www.ucl.ac.uk/internet-grammar (University College, London).

4.2.2 Communication practice

A second and important way in which the Net can be and is increasingly being used by students is as a medium of communication. Through an electronic mail service (e-mail) or instant messenger services, such as ICQ or AOL, which permit real-time chat, language learners can make contact with other users of the language, native and non-native, the texts that are produced being genuine instances of communication. 'Keypals' may be found through the ESL cafe (see above) and such websites as http://www.englishclub.net/e-friends and http://www.summersongs.net. Comenius at http://www.comenius.com provides this service for a small fee.

Students may also have located one or more special-interest groups. If they have joined the type of group known as a newsgroup through an institutional server or an Internet provider, they will be able to access the discussion between members of that group at any time by simply going to the site, where all the messages are stored. If on the other hand they have joined a listserv (by simply sending an e-mail saying they wish to join), they will be receiving all the messages sent by other subscribers to that list. These groups use the same technology as e-mail. If learners have access to the Net but have not yet explored its potential for sending and receiving messages, they may find this an exciting new way of learning. Eastment (1999) provides a number of helpful references for lists. These include a student list organised by Latrobe University, Australia, which offers a range of topics and, in some cases, different levels; see http://www.latrobe.edu.au/www/education/sl/sl.html. More generally, discussion lists can be accessed at the Deja News site at http://www.dejanews.com; for a directory of lists, see http ://www.liszt.com.

In the introduction to this chapter, the point was made that learners need exposure to quantities of material and quality material. Lists and newsgroups can provide the quantity, but, as Eastment points out, there may be problems as far as quality is concerned with newsgroups: 'Unless the group is carefully chosen, the quality of both language and content can be poor, and sometimes offensive' and 'At their best, they are an excellent source of up-to-date information, ideas and comment . . . At their worst, they are trivial, tacky or irrelevant' (p. 14).

4.3 Web-based teaching

In the past, the kinds of computer-based materials briefly referred to in Chapter 5 would only have been available within the physical confines of an institution, in the classroom or in a dedicated self-access centre. One of the great benefits of the Internet as a delivery system is that it offers considerable flexibility to both learners and teachers in terms of when they work and, especially if they are equipped with a home computer and modem, where they work. As Jor (1999: 25) points out, 'it creates new learning spaces and expands learning hours'.

Software programs are now available (one of the most popular being Web CT – CT stands for 'course tools') which allow an institution or an individual teacher to utilise the same technology for a restricted set of users. Course descriptions, syllabuses, assignments, reading lists can all be placed on a 'delivery platform', obviating the need for photocopying. Source materials, such as published articles or specially designed instructional materials, can also be presented in this form. A 'bulletin board' or 'noticeboard' is available for announcements or discussion on topics set by the teacher or suggested by students. Students can have their own Web pages and use this to 'publish' their own work, on which other students and the teacher can give feedback. Informal student–student interaction is also possible, through a 'chat' facility.

Forsyth (1998), whose focus is on the Internet as a delivery system, suggests that before developing materials for the Internet we should ask ourselves two questions:

1. What is there about the programme that would make it desirable to use the Internet as a delivery system?
2. What is there about the Internet that makes it suitable for this programme?

Although these questions may seem to be two sides of the same coin, they are distinct. The first can be seen as a question about costs and benefits, and the answer might relate to easier access to the programme for potential students, and as a result, perhaps, a larger student enrolment for the institution. The second question is concerned with programme content and process; it asks in what ways an existing programme could be improved by making use of the Internet or, in the case of a new programme, why the Internet might be seen as a preferable delivery system to, for example, face-to-face teaching. Implicit in the second question is the view that the Internet should not be seen as simply an alternative way of delivering the 'same' programme. Programme design for the Web requires a rather different approach from face-to-face teaching (see below) and, especially when what is envisaged is a complement to traditional face-to-face teaching, necessitates careful evaluation of the strengths and limitations of both the media involved and the 'isolation' of the learner.

4.4 Problems and issues in teaching by the Web

A number of issues relating to Web use for learning have already been alluded to: for example the amount of information; the time involved in out-of-class learning in sifting through this; the quality of that information. Other problems and issues (raised by Jor 1999 and Morrall 1999) are discussed below.

4.4.1 Teacher and student competence in IT use

Learning–teaching by the Web requires learners and teachers to acquire new skills. Learners need to be capable of using key functions relating to searching, referencing and, to a lesser extent, downloading; teachers need a higher level of the same skills and, if they wish to create materials, design skills (see 'Designing course materials for the Web', below). Even when they can carry out these operations confidently, many teachers are likely to need continuing technical support, for example in relation to programming, graphic design, and site maintenance and improvement.

4.4.2 Time

When class time is spent using the Web to search for information or to download it on to students' machines, it might be argued that this time is lost for teaching. Time is also an issue for students who are expected to engage in Web-based discussion with other students out of class and for teachers, who may be trying to manage and contribute to such discussions in different classes. In the latter case, the answer no doubt lies in the right balance between in-class and out-of-class activity; to find that balance is far from easy.

4.4.3 Evaluating the effectiveness of Web-based teaching

For some, technology has its own appeal, and their enthusiasm may lead them to assume that learners are bound to be equally excited about this new approach to teaching and learning. This is not necessarily the case. Nor is it the case that what is new is always better. Even if learners do appear to be more highly motivated, carefully controlled comparisons will be needed to show that Web-based teaching (which will depend largely for its effectiveness on the quality of the materials) consistently produces a higher level of performance.

4.4.4 Attitudes

Attitude change may be needed on the part of teachers and learners. Students who already use Net functions such as e-mail or ICQ may be not only unwilling to switch to a new and unfamiliar and possibly inferior system in order to communicate with a teacher or fellow students; they may also be suspicious that if they use the package supported by the institution, their use of the Net will be monitored (Morrall 1999). If, however, students are allowed to opt out, 'the teacher will be unaware of the students' learning activities, unable to take part in their discussions, and unable to accurately assess the[ir] problems and learning' (Morrall 1999: 12).

As with the use of computers in the classroom, Web-based teaching can encourage learners who have hitherto been dependent to become more autonomous (see Morrall's 1999 survey, cited above). However, as is the case with other initiatives directed towards the same end, this entails a willingness on the part of the teacher to let go. Teachers must be prepared to become managers and mentors, and for the purposes of Web-based teaching acquire the skills to carry out these roles at a distance, as it were. Helpful insights into what is involved can be found in Sandholtz, Ringstaff and Dwyer (1997, cited in Jor 1999), which includes case studies of computer use in the classroom.

Moreover, enthusiasm for information and communication technology (ICT) is not universal among teachers. There are institutions, even education systems, where it is expected that teachers will use ICT and support is available. There are also institutions and for the time being, at least, education systems where ICT use is the exception. In both situations there are teachers who feel at odds with the environment in which they work. Either their pioneering efforts are unrecognised, unrewarded and unsupported or they feel under threat. Within the latter group there is concern about the time needed to master the technology and suspicion, perhaps tinged with a hint of fear, that computers are being allowed to take over. And yet a computer is a tool for learning, just like a textbook. The central message of this book has been that teachers must choose their tools carefully, use them purposefully, and put them aside when their use would be inappropriate. As far as the use of computer technology is concerned, might not our expectations be exactly the same? One view that has been expressed is that 'machines can never replace dedicated teachers and innovative administrators who love to work with students' (Jor 1999: 25); however, Jor (ibid.) goes on to quote Clifford's prophecy at a TESOL conference: 'Computers will never replace teachers . . . But teachers who use computers will replace those who don't.' For some of us, even at the beginning of a new millennium, it is still difficult to conceive of a world in which all learners will have access to computers, but even if that does become a reality it is far from certain that non-use of computers by some teachers will in itself result in their replacement by a new breed of technocrats. Learners attach great value to the personal qualities of a teacher, and in partic- ular to his or her sensitivity and responsiveness to their needs and difficulties. If teachers who elect not to use computers are replaced, it will be because they have shown themselves impervious to the changing needs and expecta- tions of their learners, and, as a symptom of this, the possibilities that ICT offers for enhancing learning. It is perhaps worth noting that 14 of the 20 teachers surveyed by Morrall (1999) thought the Internet could help them to teach more effectively, the remainder being undecided. In many cases, indecision may well be due to lack of technical know-how and lack of awareness of how computers can help teachers as well as learners. For instance, software programs are being developed which can reduce the time teachers spend on repetitive tasks such as marking (students submit an electronic text; the teacher can generate rapid feedback on common errors by calling up ready-formulated comments and explanations). Teacher education initiatives focusing on awareness raising in relation to this kind of development and training in specific ICT competences, if accompanied by moral and technical support, might go a long way towards converting the as yet unconverted.

4.5 Designing course materials for the Web

4.5.1 Purposes

Why would a teacher who is seeing students regularly want them to use the Internet? There are a number of possible answers to this question, depending on whether we are thinking of the Net as a library resource, a way of accessing specially-prepared materials, or a means of communication. In relation to materials, these include:

- It offers access to materials that would not otherwise be available.
- It allows the learner to work at his or her own pace on materials provided by or suggested by the teacher and, if the system allows this, check his or her own progress; it thereby offers conditions that are facilitative of autonomy (although the materials themselves may be just as prescriptive as non-Net materials!).
- It allows for discreet differentiation and individualisation (e.g. a teacher might set different tasks for different students without others knowing this, or ask more capable learners to deal with a greater quantity of material).
- It saves the time and money that would have been spent on photocopying.
- It allows for learning through (and as a result of) communication.
- It allows for learners to have easy access to what other learners have discovered or produced.
- It is motivating.

A further benefit is that learners are encouraged to assume control over their own learning, making use of what is provided by the teacher and other resources. Now in a one-to-one relationship with the teacher, the learner is also liberated to ask questions and admit to difficulties that might have been concealed in the public arena of the classroom.

4.5.2 Categories of material

If the materials that are made available on the Web are intended to supplement a coursebook, they would include the types of material referred to in Chapter 5 and earlier in this chapter: practice materials (but also, perhaps, explanations) and authentic written texts, with tasks. In addition, there might be snippets of cultural information and 'fun' activities, such as games and crosswords, to induce learners to play with the language. Further suggestions include:

- *Dictionary access*: if the materials include printed texts, these can be linked to a dictionary, so that the learner can quickly check the meanings of any words with which they are unfamiliar. A dictionary could also be used as a self-checking device (e.g. following a task relating to word-meaning or pronunciation).
- *Mazes*: ideally suited to the computer, mazes present the learner with a problem and a set of possible options. Following the selection of one of these options, feedback and/or more information is given and another set of choices offered. Having made a decision, the student is not allowed to go back – though the maze may well contain loops that involve a return to the same point (and therefore a chance to learn from one's mistakes). Like the original print versions (see e.g. Rinvolucri and Berer (1981) and Farthing (1981) for examples), screen-based mazes offer an interesting form of purposeful reading practice or, if some of the material is contained in a sound file, for listening practice; the decision points also serve as stimulating discussion prompts. Vallance (1998) describes a business simulation which utilises a maze format.
- *Listening*: time spent listening out of class is time saved for more inter-active activities in class. Moreover, learners have the freedom to listen as often as they wish; a tapescript can also be made available. Listening material – in the form of RealAudio files – can be accessed using Real-Player software.
- *Video-watching*: video is a possibility, but it is really only practicable in contexts where there is a fast server and where the relatively small number of users accessing the system ensures a rapid connection time. As technology improves, so will the prospects for using video.

4.5.3 Design considerations

As Forysth (1998) points out, the materials that form the basis for a face-to-face programme are likely to be skeletal because it is the teacher that fleshes them out. In developing materials for teaching using the Net, the natural inclination might therefore be to start from the existing skeletal materials and elaborate these for transfer to the Net – in effect, to produce a print-based version of the existing programme. This assumes, almost certainly wrongly, that students will be content to scroll carefully through the pages as if they were reading a book, but without the flexibility that a book offers for flipping back to reread something or skipping a whole section.

Three points follow from this:

1. *The material should be designed screen by screen (like a Powerpoint presentation) and be as user-friendly as possible.* For instance, as a general rule, font size should be 12 points minimum and line length between 45 and 55 characters. There are two schools of thought on page length. One view is that each screen should carry a relatively small amount of information to minimise screen scrolling and that short, easily digested paragraphs should be used. Although this may seem like good advice, it is more time-consuming to download several short pages than one or two longer pages. Moreover, it is possible to insert links at the top of a page of text to each of the paragraphs or sections below. Readers who know what they are looking for can then skip directly to that paragraph or section. For helpful advice on how to write for the Web, see Jacob Nielsen's website at http://www.useit.com.

2. *Links are important.* The speed of the Net means that it is ideally suited to flipping and skipping. It can also allow the reader to access several 'books' simultaneously. What makes this possible are the links that are carefully built in at the point of design. These can be links to other sections of the material or to related materials (equivalent to cross-references); to definitions of key terms; to examples; and to tasks. The first phase of materials design should therefore be primarily concerned with outline planning: determining content, breaking this down into subsections, and creating links between these and to support materials. For site design, see http://info.med.yale.edu/caim/manual/contents.html.

3. *As with a book, an index can be invaluable.* This might take the form of, for example a site map, which indicates the contents of the site, or some other kind of navigation aid, such as an A–Z index, a categorised index, or a timeline. Incorporating a site search engine – which means that the computer does the searching – is also desirable. To access a free site search engine, contact www.picosearch.com.

Interaction also needs to be planned in. This might take the form of a self-testing mechanism (e.g. multiple-choice pre-test and post-test) that satisfies the learner's need for instant feedback or a task which is either linked to a commentary or requires a tutor response.

As with any materials development project, piloting and revision are essential stages. Useful information can also be gleaned from watching learners using the materials. Where the material is in the public domain, the inclusion of the designer's e-mail address on every page may encourage users to send feedback.

Confirmation of the relevance and value of these general guidelines is provided in a recent paper by Vallance (1998), reporting on the use of a specially-designed set of business English materials with 65 students in various parts of the world. Not surprisingly, students had different levels of technical expertise, and Vallance expresses doubt concerning the ability of some to scroll through pages and download sound files. However, the technical features of the material also attracted comment: some students would have liked to return to previous pages (an option deliberately denied them in Vallance's maze activity); the pages were also felt to contain too much information. Other aspects of the material were well received, such as the fact that an explanation was available when they had given an inappropriate response, and an opportunity to try again in a similar situation; the students also liked the unexpected touches of humour.

The way in which the materials were used by the students is also of interest:

- Seventy-five per cent of the students preferred to work on their own.
- When they were working in pairs, the more confident dominated, and their partners remained passive and bored.
- Traditional approaches to learning persisted ('informal observation . . . indicated that students tended to read out loud the function phrases offered . . . even though models were provided for students to download' (p. 40)).

'It is ironic', Vallance notes, 'that using the Internet in its current format seems to reinforce the reading skill at a time when it was imagined that an oral culture based on television and telephones would reduce the role of the written word' (ibid.).

Thorne, A. and Thorne, C.'s (2000) account of the setting up of a British Council website for the dissemination of material on British Studies includes a discussion of the planning considerations as well as examples of materials. The website can be accessed at http://elt.britcoun.org.pl.

Task 6.9

1. There is a great deal of jargon associated with ICT, and it may sometimes seem as if those in the know are using it to score points off those who are not. This can leave the latter feeling extremely uncomfortable. In this section an attempt has been made to introduce the most common technical terms and either explain these or use them in self-explanatory contexts. If some of these concepts are still unclear, why not ask for clarification? (Eastment (1999) offers helpful definitions of all the common acronyms.)

2. Three forms of Internet exploitation have been discussed: i.e. (a) teacher-directed use of the Internet by students (b) self-directed student use (c) Web-based teaching. Do you have any experience of any of these? If so, what has that experience taught you and what ideas and examples can you add to those given in this section?

3. Choose one of these three areas of Internet use that you would like to experiment with or find out more about. For instance, under (a) you might like to carry out a survey of teacher use and/or student reactions; under (b) explore the extent and nature of student use and elicit some recommendations for other students or browse through some of the language-learning Websites referred to; and under (c), prepare for a learner assignment by pre-selecting some suitable websites or do a detailed plan for putting course materials on your Web server.

4. If you are working on this task as part of a course, the obvious follow-up to (3) would be a presentation of what you have found out or done – and feedback on this from your classmates. If you are working in a self-directed way, you might still want to share what you have been doing with your colleagues.

5 FURTHER READING

It is unfortunately beyond the scope of this book to include reference to all forms of 'real' material and even less possible to deal with all forms of supplementation. Obvious gaps are non-text documents, games, and songs. Whole books have, of course, been devoted to some of these topics. See, for example, on games, Wright, Betteridge and Buckby (1984) and on songs, Murphey (1992). Ur (1981), Klippel (1984), Pattison (1987), Watcyn-Jones (1981) and Hadfield (1990) are well-known sources of ideas for spoken communication activities, some of which are games. Maley and Duff (1982) and Wessels (1987) are invaluable resources for teachers wishing to make use of drama activities.

Teachers wishing to develop text-based materials are advised to dip into general methodology textbooks (e.g. Harmer 1991; Nunan 1991, 1999; Hedge 2000) and books dealing with the teaching of specific skills (e.g., on listening, Anderson and Lynch 1988; Ur 1984; Underwood 1989; Brown 1990a; Rost 1990; and on reading Grellet 1981; Wallace 1992; Hood, Solomon and Burns 1995; Nuttall 1996). Suggestions for activity-types can also be found in, e.g., Widdowson (1979b, 1979c), Robinson (1991: Ch. 6) contains references to other useful sources. On video, see, for example Geddes and Sturtridge (1982), Lonergan (1984) and Allan (1985).

Keeping abreast of developments on the Internet is even more of a problem. A current TV advertisement claims that there were only 50 websites in 1990; ten years on, the figure has been put at more than 10 million, of which perhaps 1000 may be devoted to language-learning activities, resources or materials (Eastment 1999). For some teachers and some learners, the shift from a coursebook to learning resources has already taken place, although not in quite the form envisaged by Brumfit and Allwright some twenty years ago. Eastment (1999) reports that more than 300 CD-ROMs designed for EFL are now available, with many more to follow. Since teachers have tended to be book people, guidance on how to use the new technologies as tools will be welcomed by many. In addition to the books referred to above, colleagues and practising teachers have recommended the following for guidance and ideas: Warschauer (1995), Sperling (1997), Warschauer and Kern (2000), and Windeatt, Hardisty and Eastment (2000), which has an associated website at http://www.oup.com./elt/rbt.internet. Although not specifically concerned with language teaching, Jonassen (2000) may also be of interest.

6 SUMMARY

The focus in this chapter has been on the real: authentic texts, authentic (realistic?) tasks, examples of real language use extracted from computer databases, and, in relation to the Internet, real communication and the accessing of yet more authentic texts. The strongest argument for exposing learners to real language (in the form of texts and corpora) and facilitating their engagement in real communication (e.g. through inter-institutional Internet projects) is compellingly simple. Motivation. This language is alive. It comes off the page (or screen), surprising, entertaining, puzzling. It comes through the window on the breeze, bringing intriguing sounds and scenes from the world outside. It opens doors into the homes and lives of strangers who may yet become friends. This is the language of real people. To understand and to make them understand, we must know this language.

Chapter 7

Systematising materials design

Systematising brainstorming – systematising the structure of activities and lessons: role play; 'standard exercises' for use with reading and listening texts – materials for self-access centres (SACs): categories of material; learner involvement; design criteria – from lesson materials to course materials: a last resort; advice, principles, models; problems

One of the arguments against teachers producing materials is that it is a very time-consuming process. One answer to this very real problem is that suggested by Block (1991), and referred to in the last chapter, that teachers share the burden and the benefits. Another possibility, and this may be adopted by a group of teachers or an individual, is to develop 'templates' or models which, by providing a structured basis for the development of activities, whole lessons, units of work or even courses, can obviate the need to start from scratch on every occasion.

This chapter brings together a number of suggestions for systematising the design process.

1 SYSTEMATISING BRAINSTORMING

In McGrath (1992) I outlined an approach to lesson planning based on a simple framework for systematising brainstorming. The most productive starting point is a text, written or spoken, although a visual (such as a picture story) or a stimulus combining visual and text (such as a magazine advertisement) might also be used. Thinking of the needs of a particular class and ideally working with one or more colleagues, the teacher brainstorms ideas for the exploitation of this text, and enters these in the kind of grid shown in Figure 7.1 (overleaf).

Following this kind of systematic brainstorming, the ideas likely to be of most relevance to the whole class need to be selected, grouped and organised in a rough sequence. For instance, after a theme-setting orientation activity there might be a focus on the meaning of the text, and finally some language work.

Listening	Phonology
Speaking	Grammar
Reading	Vocabulary
Writing	Discourse
Other (e.g. culture, study skills, etc.)	

In the case of a written text, one obvious possibility is to draw students' attention to specific *grammatical* or *lexical* features, perhaps using these as a basis for further practice. The highlighting of *discourse* features, such as temporal or logical sequencers, or the use of anaphoric (back-refer-ring) 'which' or 'this' in the context of work on the development of *reading* strategies, might also form part of the preparation for *writing*. If the teacher first reads (part of) the text aloud, before giving it to students, it could be used for *listening* (and perhaps note-taking) practice. These are, of course, very general ideas, which would need to be much more concretely specified (e.g. the grammatical feature identified, the writing task specified). Working with a real text rather than an imaginary one, it should be relatively easy to come up with at least one idea in most of the boxes.

Figure 7.1 An ideas grid for lesson planning (text by I. McGrath first published in *Practical English Teaching*, 1992. © Mary Glasgow Magazines/Scholastic)

Appendix 7.1 shows how ideas prompted by a specific text and organised within the grid were then ordered into a lesson-planning sequence. The appeal of this approach to lesson planning lies in three features:

- it results in a lesson which is unified around a single text (and thus deals with the potential problem of 'bittiness');
- it obliges the teacher to be specific about learning objectives;
- it ensures a variety of knowledge/skill foci within a single lesson and, with careful record-keeping, a balanced coverage of language systems and skills across lessons.

One further feature of the worked-out example in Appendix 7.1 is also worth noting: the fact that in the penultimate stage learners are offered a choice. Differentiation within classrooms tends to mean catering for different *levels of proficiency*, with the teacher often determining the level at which learners should work. In this example, differentiation is on the basis of *linguistic focus* rather than level and it is learners who choose what they wish to do on the basis of interest or self-perceived need.

Task 7.1

1. Select appropriate stimulus material and try out the ideas grid technique. Limit yourself to 15 minutes at the brainstorming stage (any longer would probably be a luxury for a teacher planning several lessons for the next day).

2. Prepare any written supplementary material.

3. Get feedback on your ideas, preferably at stage 1 (above) as well as stage 2.

2 SYSTEMATISING THE STRUCTURE OF ACTIVITIES AND LESSONS

2.1 Role play

One simple example of a principled and systematic approach to activity design can be found in the role-play cards suggested by Cunningsworth (1984, 1995) (see Chapter 4). In the approach advocated by Cunningsworth, the conversational turns are specified and assigned. The realism of the resulting interaction thus depends not only on each speaker's ability to take a turn smoothly and produce something appropriate but also on the task designer's predictions of what will be said. In the following example supplied by a teacher of Russian (Figure 7.2, overleaf), roles are allocated and guidance is given as to the purpose and general direction of the conversation, but because there is less control at the level of who should say what when, the conversations that result are likely to be the result of genuine negotiation, sound more spontaneous and therefore constitute a more useful form of practice. Although these materials were originally designed for the purpose of testing how far students could integrate what they had previously practised in more controlled, discrete activities, they could obviously be used as part of a teaching cycle to provide feedback to students on specific features that might need further practice and as a basis for exploring alternative linguistic means of achieving the same communicative function.

Person B's card is exactly the same as Person A's except that he or she is told 'You should assume the role of Person B.' Preparation of the cards, especially if a word processor is used, is therefore quick and easy once a decision has been made about the topic(s) and general structure of the conversation.

One potential drawback of the example in Fig. 7.2 is that the conversation seems to be controlled by A, who is charged with asking questions about B's likes/dislikes and home town. Though this may well be appropriate for this particular situation, it is desirable in general either to build in explicit opportunities for both speakers to initiate conversation (and not only by asking questions) or to tell students that this is expected at the briefing stage. In the testing context in which this example was used, students participated in two role plays, and this allowed for some variation in role.

Conversation 1

SHOPPING IN MOSCOW

Person A is Russian and Person B is English.

Person B, a student on his/her first visit to Moscow, is staying with a Russian family. Person A, the host/hostess, asks about his/her likes and dislikes as far as food and drink are concerned in order to decide what to buy for the next few days. They make a list and then go together to buy these things. On the way, Person A asks about the town in which Person B lives in England.

YOUR SHOULD ASSUME THE ROLE OF PERSON A.

Figure 7.2 Role cards for teaching and testing (Vasilyeva-McGrath 1997)

A much more elaborate framework for lessons built around role play is provided by Richards (1985). This consists of six stages:

1. Learners participate in a preliminary activity in which the topic and situation are introduced.
2. They then work through a model dialogue on a related topic which provides examples of the type of language which will be required.
3. Assisted by role cards, learners perform the role play.
4. Learners listen to recordings of native speakers performing the role play with the same role cards.
5. Follow-up activities exploit the native speaker performance.
6. The entire sequence is then repeated with a second transaction on the same topic.

(Richards 1985: 87–8, cited in Nunan 1988b: 10)

While stage 1 reflects a general principle of communicative methodology (activate learners' existing schema, i.e. experience of similar situations) and stage 2 might be seen as activating or adding to their knowledge of appropriate 'scripts', i.e. what is typically said (in this case in English) in this situation, stages 3–6 are of particular interest. Learners first attempt the task themselves; they then have an opportunity to compare their performance with that of native speakers (on the same task), and are led to perceive both the differences between the two and specific features of the native speaker performance; and finally they have an opportunity to apply the new insights in a second attempt at a similar task. This movement, represented in Figure 7.3a, below, can be compared with the more traditional teacher-centred IRF (Initiation–Response–Feedback) model illustrated in Figure 7.3b, in which the teacher initiates, the learner responds, and feedback is provided:

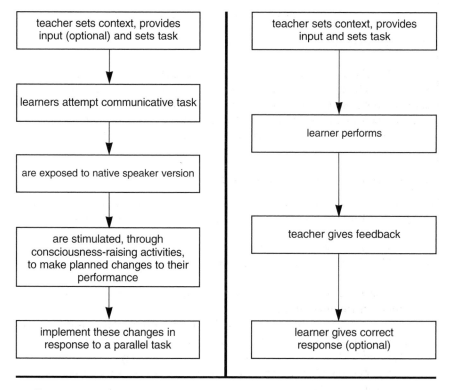

Figure 7.3a Task cycle in a learner-centred approach

Figure 7.3b The IRF sequence

In Richards' template, learners have an opportunity to hear a native speaker version; indeed, this constitutes their 'feedback'. They then decide which elements of that feedback they wish to incorporate in their second attempts. And the second performance is not simply a classroom ritual but a motivated attempt to improve on the first. In other words, the learner determines what use to make of the input. In Figure 7.3b, on the other hand, the teacher clearly controls the output.

2.2 'Standard exercises' for use with reading and listening texts

One of the factors which led to the search for materials-design templates was the pressure on teachers of ESP courses to design much of their own material. As Scott, Carioni, Zanatta, Bayer and Quintanilha (1984) observe, teachers simply do not have the time to create new exercises every time they come across a worthwhile new text. Their answer was to create a 'standard exercise' (Figure 7.4, below) that would guide their students (tertiary-level learners from a wide range of disciplines) 'towards more efficient and critical reading strategies' (p. 115). Students were expected to read at least sixteen texts per semester using the same exercise each time.

1. Read only the title of your text. Predict and write down at least five vocabulary items – key words – which you expect to see in the text. Use a dictionary if necessary. The key words can be noted down in English or in Portuguese.
2. Skim the text quickly (maximum one minute), looking for key words in the text. Use all typographical indications, your previous knowledge, cognates, and repeated words. Now write down, in no more than fifteen words, the main theme of the text.

Re-read the text as often as necessary to answer the following questions:

3. What seems to be the author's main intention: to persuade you or just to inform you?
4. Write down any words which look important in the text (key words) which you did not know before reading it. Beside each one, write down your idea of what it probably means.
5. Write down the main idea of each paragraph, using only one sentence for each main idea. If the text consists of more than seven paragraphs, write down the main idea of each main section. Avoid translating and try not to mention insignificant details.
6. Divide the text into sections. Is there an introduction? If so, where does it end? Is there a conclusion? If so, where does it start? Explain your answer.
7. Write one sentence reporting something which you learned from the text.
8. Critical reaction: whose interests does this text reflect? Which country, which social class, or which institution? Who would find the publication of this text desirable? Is the information in the text applicable to your own situation?
9. Indicate your interest in this text using a scale of 1 to 5 (5 = very interesting; 1 = very boring).
10. How many times did you need to use a dictionary to answer the questions so far?
11. Write down the number of each paragraph which you feel you couldn't understand properly, or aren't sure you understood.

12. Try to work out why you found the paragraphs you listed in the last question so difficult. What was the main reason?

 a. lack of previous knowledge of the topic
 b. a grammatical problem (which one?)
 c. inefficient reading strategies
 d. difficulty in separating main points from details
 e. difficulty in identifying the introduction or conclusion
   etc.

13. Now estimate your comprehension of the text (e.g. 30 per cent, 80 per cent).

Figure 7.4 Standard reading exercise (Scott et al. 1984: 116, translated from the Portuguese by the authors)

Task 7.2 K

1. What is the rationale, do you think, for the structure of this exercise and each of the questions?

2. In your experience (as teacher or student), how do you think university students would react to being asked to use an exercise of this kind repeatedly?

A summary of the rationale for the exercise and the response of the Brazilian students with whom the exercise was used can be found in the 'Tasks: Keys and Commentaries' section at the back of this book. Dickinson (1987: Appendix C (III)) contains an adaptation of the exercise for use with listening texts.

Another factor leading to the design of standard exercises was the growth of self-access centres (SACs) (see below) and the need for an economical means of producing materials for self-directed learning. This was the situation of Scott et al. and also of Walker (1987), whose own standard reading exercise is based on that shown above (see Appendix 7.2). Sheerin (1989) provides further examples of a number of different standard task sheets for use in SACs: e.g. for book reviews (p. 66) – see Appendix 7.3; radio/TV programme reviews (p. 88); and tasks based on recorded discussions (pp. 86–7). Gardner and Miller (1999) make the point that 'generic' self-access worksheets, which provide instructions and suggestions for working with a range of authentic material, offer the promise of economy, but may be less appealing than 'specific' worksheets to learners who are pressed for time or feel the need for more guidance.

The idea of the standard worksheet for use in self-access centres has been adopted for classroom use. Kissinger (1990), who acknowledges a debt to Lonergan (1984), has produced a framework for use with video recordings (see Appendix 7.4). Axbey (1989) has done the same for audio recordings and written texts.

The underlying structure of Axbey's framework is the now orthodox three-stage *pre-reading/listening, while reading/listening, post-reading/listening*. The second stage is, however, subdivided and each of the resulting four stages is further specified:

BEFORE READING/LISTENING
1. Draw upon *existing knowledge*.
2. Exploit *areas of interest*.
3. Encourage *prediction* of content, language and function.

FIRST READING/LISTENING
4. Confirm and *check predictions*.
5. Understand *global meaning* and shape.

SECOND READING/LISTENING
6. Understand *main points*.
7. Deal with *vocabulary*.
8. Be aware of *writer's/speaker's purpose*.

AFTER READING/LISTENING
9. Give a personal *response/evaluation*.
10. Encourage *self-awareness* of difficulties.

Figure 7.5 Standard reading/listening exercises (Axbey 1989)

Appendix 7.5 contains a worksheet which may help to clarify some of the substages here. Note that not only does the worksheet follow the four-part substructure and the ten-point superstructure presented above, many of the questions have also been framed in such a way that they could be used with other texts of an informational nature.

Task 7.3

1. Compare Axbey's framework – let's call it (1) – with (2) that of Scott et al. (Figure 7.4, above) and (3) Walker (Appendix 7.2). Which would you find easier to use if you were developing materials of this kind? Are there any features of the other frameworks that you would like to incorporate in the one you have chosen? Bear in mind that the end-product should be as generalisable as possible. You may also like to refer back to the discussion of principles underlying an approach to authentic text in Chapter 6.

2. Look at Appendix 7.4, which contains a standard worksheet for use with (recordings of) TV news programmes. Would you want to make any modifications to this?

3. Design a standard worksheet for use with another genre of text, spoken (recorded) or written (e.g. advertisements, soap operas, public announcements or notices). Try it out and see how it works.

The aim of the standard exercise devised by Scott et al. (1984) was to help students develop reading strategies and skills in a situation where there was no teacher to mediate between student and text; as they acknowledge, it cannot work at the level of specific points of language. The approach suggested by Axbey, while less economical in terms of teacher time because it requires the teacher to produce a 'new' set of questions for each text, nevertheless provides a familiar underlying structure for both teacher and learner; at the surface level of the individual text, moreover, it allows sufficient freedom for teachers to exercise creativity – and learners are therefore unlikely to get bored. Although Scott et al.'s students did not complain about the repetitiveness of the procedure they were expected to follow, we have to allow for the possibility that students will get bored if the materials that make up a course are too systematised. Hutchinson and Waters (1987: 107) caution:

> Avoid the assembly line approach, which makes each unit look the same, with the same type of text, the same kind of illustrations, the same type and number of exercises. If it doesn't send you to sleep writing them, it will certainly send your learners to sleep using them. A materials model must be clear and systematic, but flexible enough to allow for creativity and variety.

3   MATERIALS FOR SELF-ACCESS CENTRES (SACS)

An SAC, which may serve a whole institution or simply be housed in a corner of a classroom, is like a library in that it is essentially a materials resource. Unlike a library, however, most of the materials in an SAC will probably need to be specially prepared.

3.1   Categories of material

3.1.1   Published materials

Published materials can, of course, be utilised in a number of ways. At the very minimum, there will be books for extensive reading, and perhaps graded reading schemes. There is likely to be a special 'library' section containing reference materials such as dictionaries, grammars, advice on language learning; there may be test practice materials; in better resourced centres, there may also be listening stations where students can use the tapes that accompany coursebooks or supplementary skills books focusing on listening, video booths, and computers with a choice of software. Some publishers produce materials specifically intended for use by learners working independently; others, as

Gardner and Miller (1999) warn, label their materials as if this were the case when they are simply classroom teaching materials with an answer key.

3.1.2 Authentic materials

Authentic materials also have a place. The following list of categories of materials that may be useful is based on Gardner and Miller (1999: 102–3): newspapers; magazines (related to predictable or known areas of interest); user manuals (for technical equipment); leaflets and brochures (e.g. from government departments, travel agencies, banks, etc.); foreign mission information (embassies, non-government agencies); material from international companies and airlines; letters, faxes and e-mails (with permission); videos (films, documentaries); and songs (some centres now have karaoke rooms). Lectures and speeches being given locally can perhaps be recorded; willing native or near-native speakers may also be persuaded to record talks, give interviews or tell stories. A satellite dish may bring live TV programmes direct into the centre and/or permission can be sought to include off-air recordings of TV and radio programmes (this may involve the payment of a licence fee).

It is not difficult to understand why the potential quantity and diversity of material available can create logistical problems (e.g. storage space, cataloguing, the need to get rid of outdated material periodically); but there are also additional time and cost implications in relation to packaging some of these raw materials so that language learners can derive real benefit from them. This is, of course, the argument for the kinds of standard exercise discussed above.

3.1.3 Adapting and supplementing published materials

The centre is also likely to contain published material that has been adapted or supplemented in some way. Books or workbooks can be cut up and mounted in a durable form (though the publishers' permission may be needed for this) to offer a set of single-focus activities and permit a much larger number of students to use the material. Such cut-up materials can be combined with teacher-prepared answer keys or, in the case of grammar exercises, for instance, an introductory explanation written by a teacher, perhaps in the learners' mother tongue (Sheerin 1989). Materials of this kind may be self-standing or deliberately designed to supplement the coursebooks in use within the institution and coded to cross-refer to these. Material originally intended for classroom use may require more extensive adaptation so that it can be used by learners working independently. (For a carefully detailed illustration of such an adaptation followed by a supporting rationale, see Dickinson (1987: 70–8).)

3.1.4 Specially-prepared materials

While published and authentic materials can thus form the cornerstones of an SAC, there will always be a need for material that is more precisely tailored to the needs of students working on their own. For anyone contemplating writing materials for a self-access centre, Sheerin (1989) provides a useful practical starting point. As is the case with other volumes within the *Oxford Resource Books for Teachers* series, this is basically an inventory of examples preceded by an author's introduction. The examples can be used, as Sheerin points out, as they stand, but they are 'intended primarily as "prototypes" for different types of self-access activities in different areas' (p. 9). The activities are organised into three main categories. The emphasis of the first is on learner training (i.e. helping learners to assess their own needs and develop a study plan). This is followed by activities at different levels focusing on receptive skills and productive skills. Sections within this category are graded and activities are included on handwriting, spelling, punctuation and pronunciation. The final category is entitled 'building blocks' and contains activities on grammar, vocabulary and 'key functional areas' (ibid.).

As can be seen from the examples in Appendix 7.6, each of the photocopiable activities contains (1) information that helps the learner to decide whether the activity is likely to be suitable (2) pre-task information or instructions (3) post-task materials, such as a key, tapescript or commentary (4) comments or suggestions directed at the teacher. The examples also indicate that self-access materials can go beyond familiar closed formats (yes/no, true/false and multiple-choice questions). Activity-types represented include:

- practice/testing activities, e.g. exercises, dictation, cloze tasks
- learning/awareness-raising activities, e.g. discovery tasks, information guides, study guides
- reflective/creative activities, e.g. reactive listening, book reviewing, story writing
- social/peer matching activities, e.g. communication tasks.

(list based on Sheerin 1989: 10)

3.2 Learner involvement

Learners can contribute authentic materials to an SAC; they can also be encouraged to contribute materials that they have prepared themselves (Gardner and Miller 1999). This kind of involvement may bring its own rewards, linguistic and attitudinal; it may also result in their being willing to take on more responsibility for their own learning. Unfortunately, time constraints can mean there is 'initial enthusiasm . . . but weak response' (Gardner and Miller 1999: 107). See, however, the activity from Gardner and Miller (1999) reproduced in 'Learners as Teachers' in Chapter 8.

One further way in which learners can contribute to the development of self-access materials is through their feedback. Gardner and Miller (1999: 113) make the following suggestions:

Feedback can be collected in a number of ways (which are not mutually exclusive). New materials can be trialled with willing self-access learners. In-house materials can contain a request for feedback. Published materials can have a request attached to them (e.g. a sticker on the cover). Generic feedback forms can be made available for use with any materials alongside a drop-off box. A more general suggestions box will collect feedback on materials along with other things.

They add: 'Another form of materials evaluation is the rate at which take-away materials (e.g. worksheets and information sheets) disappear'; and, wryly: 'This form of evaluation also occurs for materials which are not intended to be taken away' (ibid.).

3.3 Design criteria

Criteria for the design of self-access materials have been proposed by Sheerin (1989) and Dickinson (1987). Such materials should, they suggest, have the following characteristics:

1. *Clearly stated objectives*: to facilitate learner selection and indexing.
2. *Clarity of instructions*: in a monolingual situation, the L1 might be used; examples will often be necessary.
3. *Attractive presentation*: illustrations, colour and the use of a reasonable-sized typeface can all help to encourage learners to work with the materials.
4. *Clear layout and pathways*: indicating how different components fit together and how these relate to other materials (see also 7, below).
5. *Manageability and feasibility*: the scope of each unit of material should be limited so that it does not require a huge investment of time and effort; similarly, activities involving cooperation between learners should be simple to organise.
6. *Support*: to help learners to make sense of the materials (e.g. illustrations, explanations, glossaries, transcriptions of spoken texts).
7. *Advice*: on how to work with the materials and a choice of procedure (offering students different options allows them to choose one that suits their own preferred learning style).
8. *Worthwhile*: 'it should be possible to learn something by doing the activity, and that "something" should be worth learning' (Sheerin 1989: 24).
9. *Feedback*: the form this takes will vary according to the type of activity: keys and tapescripts allow learners to check their own answers; for less closed activities, a commentary might be more appropriate. When written tasks lead to 'free production', sample answers can be provided or a way of displaying these can be found; and a forum created for the performance of oral tasks.

10. *Balance and variety*: there should be roughly the same quantity of material for each main focus and at each level and this should be varied in objective and activity-type.

For further suggestions on, for example, the organisation of a self-access centre, the classification of materials, how the writing might be organised and the involvement of students, see Sheerin (1989: Ch. 1). Dickinson (1987: Ch. 4 and Appendices C and D(1)) also contains much useful practical advice. Tibbetts (1994) describes the approach taken to setting up a self-access centre in a secondary school in Hong Kong, and Forrester (1994) a self-access language-learning course designed to help Hong Kong secondary-school students prepare for tertiary-level study. Gardner and Miller (1999) is a wide-ranging volume incorporating both theoretical and practical perspectives; it includes four very short case studies.

Whereas Sheerin's approach to materials development is based on the task sheet, used independently of or in combination with other resources, such as reading or listening materials, some of the individual papers in Section 3 of Gardner and Miller (1994) represent pedagogic developments made possible by technological advances. Gardner (1994), for instance, proposes a solution to the problem of passive video viewing in the form of a computer-based management system (the aXcess Video System) which enables a learner to locate a specific point on a videotape, access accompanying instructional materials, and obtain feedback on his or her responses. Flowerdew (1994) reports on the development of a computer-assisted package designed to help students with style and tone in the kinds of letters they might need to write in connection with job-seeking. The paper includes a detailed description of how particular authoring programmes (Testmaster, Gapmaster, Choicemaster and Matchmaster (Jones and Trackman 1988, 1992)) were used for this purpose. Mak (1994) describes the process leading to the design of a multimedia computer simulation, highlighting some of the problems associated with this.

Teachers with a particular interest in computer-based materials development will find further ideas and advice in Boswood (1997) and such specialist journals as *CALL Journal*, *Simulation and Gaming Journal*, *System* and the newsletters of the IATEFL Special Interest Group for Computer Assisted Language Learning and its TESOL equivalent.

4 FROM LESSON MATERIALS TO COURSE MATERIALS

4.1 A last resort

Although economic and practical constraints may also require teachers to produce their own materials, the decision to develop original materials is typically taken when a new course is being designed for which no suitable textbook(s) can be found. The materials may be for use by the writer(s) and/or other teachers within their own institution or be intended for (non-commercial) publication and more general use by a group of similar institutions. Where English is the target language, this is likely to be a course of English for Specific Purposes since a huge range of published materials exists for the teaching of General English (GE). Bautista (1995: 157), for instance, recalls:

> We urgently needed to prepare ESP textbooks for two reasons: our old textbooks were grammar and literature-based and the ESP textbooks on the market, aside from being too expensive, were not 'Filipino' enough and seemed to be pitched too low for our students.

(See also other papers in section III of Hidalgo, Hall and Jacobs (1995).) Ultimately, organised and developed, the materials that result may become the equivalent of one or more coursebooks; during the initial development phase, they may be used in conjunction with materials from miscellaneous published sources, gradually replacing these as development proceeds. Even when this cautious, gradualist approach is adopted, the time, effort and skills required for materials development should not be underestimated. As Hutchinson and Waters (1987: 125) advise, 'materials writing is best regarded as a last resort, when all other possibilities of providing materials have been exhausted'. The effort involved is agonisingly well captured by Rozul (1995: 213), again writing about the development of ESP materials in the Philippines:

> Once we had done the preparatory work, the actual writing was a slow and painful process that involved thousands of man hours of actual writing, revising and researching. The main bulk of the work was the actual writing. This involved the thinking and re-thinking, the wording and re-wording, the writing and re-writing of drafts and drafts and drafts of seemingly endless exercises, activities and tasks.

Many of the considerations that influence the design of original material for an activity or a whole lesson also apply to sequences of lessons (units of work) and whole programmes; however, planning beyond the lesson is a much more complex undertaking because of the variety of factors involved. A number of suggestions have been made for ways of making this process more thoughtful and more systematic, and therefore more efficient.

4.2 Advice, principles, models

Although we are not here concerned with commercial publication, publishers may have useful advice to offer. Anyone writing for other teachers (or for publication) would do well to heed the advice of Methold (1972), whose suggestions are based on years of experience as a publisher in Asia. 'Many materials fail', he points out, 'not because they are bad in themselves, but because they are bad in the situation in which they are used' (p. 94) – in other words, they fail to take local needs or conditions into account (see points 2 and 4, below). Good materials, by contrast, will have the following characteristics, according to Methold (1972). They will:

1. set out to teach a predetermined body of knowledge, e.g., what is contained in a syllabus (some might wish to take issue with this);
2. be divided into teachable segments (i.e. take account of both time constraints and the quantity of material that can be included in a particular lesson);
3. take into account such principles as variety, weighting (of more important points), the content validity of exercises, and the need for recycling;
4. take into account local conditions (the classroom environment, conventional teaching and learning practices, and teachers' linguistic and methodological competence).

Teachers writing a course that they will teach to their own students will of course take local realities into account; the more distant one is from the reality of the classroom in which the materials will be used, the more important it is to inform oneself about that context and the eventual users (see also Chapter 2).

It is to be expected that experienced writers will also have a few words of wisdom, at least, to offer the less experienced. Hutchinson and Waters (1987: 26), for instance, advise:

- use existing materials as sources of ideas
- work with other people, if possible
- don't expect to write materials that are perfect the first time
- don't underestimate the time needed
- pay attention to the appearance of the materials.

Principles are perhaps even more valuable than advice, and Tomlinson (1998c) has proposed an extensive set of principles, each of which is discussed in some detail. The following headings from his introduction (1998c: 7–21) sum up these principles.

1. Materials should achieve impact.
2. Materials should help learners to feel at ease.
3. Materials should help learners to develop confidence.
4. What is being taught should be perceived by learners as relevant and useful.
5. Materials should require and facilitate learner self-investment.
6. Learners must be ready to acquire the points being taught.

7. Materials should expose the learners to language in authentic use.
8. The learners' attention should be drawn to linguistic features of the input.
9. Materials should provide the learners with opportunities to use the language to achieve communicative purposes.
10. Materials should take into account that the positive effects of instruction are usually delayed.
11. Materials should take into account that learners differ in learning styles.
12. Materials should take into account that learners differ in affective attitudes.
13. Materials should permit a silent period at the beginning of instruction.
14. Materials should maximise learning potential by encouraging intellectual, aesthetic and emotional involvement which stimulates both right and left brain activities.
15. Materials should not rely too much on controlled practice.
16. Materials should provide opportunities for outcome feedback.

One of the noteworthy features of this list is its length, which is a reflection of its breadth. Although a relatively small number of the principles relate specifically to language learning (e.g. 7, 8, 9, 13, 15), others express more general beliefs about desirable curricular aims and learning and how these might be facilitated; the need to take learner differences into account is also recognised.

For novice writers, principles are probably most valuable when they are illustrated with examples which indicate how the principles can be translated into practice. Tomlinson's approach is to indicate how the principles could be applied; Nunan (1988b: 1) shows how the principles below were realised in a particular set of materials.

1. Materials should be clearly linked to the curriculum they serve.
2. Materials should be authentic in terms of text and task.
3. Materials should stimulate interaction.
4. Materials should allow learners to focus on formal aspects of the language.
5. Materials should encourage learners to develop learning skills, and skills in learning.
6. Materials should encourage learners to apply their developing language skills to the world beyond the classroom.

Principle 1 is particularly apposite for those who are putting a course together in a hurry and using whatever materials are readily available. As Nunan observes, not altogether neutrally, 'it is not uncommon for teachers to . . . select or devise learning activities because they are conveniently to hand, because they have worked well with a previous group of learners, or because they have been recommended by a colleague' (p. 2). The other principles, with the possible exception of principle 5, are probably self-explanatory. Principle 5 relates to the need for materials to incorporate tasks and activities directed towards developing learners' ability to organise and evaluate their own learning as well as strategies for learning. For further discussion, see Nunan's extended commentary on and exemplifications of these principles; see also Peñaflorida's (1995: 173–80) illustrations from her own materials for medical students at a university in the Philippines.

It is important to bear in mind that however reasonable such principles might seem, they do not represent an objective truth. Even if they are underpinned by research, that research may not be widely generalisable or it may reflect conditions that have since changed. A set of principles for materials design is therefore best thought of as a personal rationale: a key-point justification for the decisions that are to be taken based on beliefs about learning and how this can best be facilitated. Thus, Nunan's list of principles, which is firmly based on beliefs which have come to be associated with the communicative approach, gives emphasis to authenticity of text and task (see Chapter 6); interaction; the need to strike a balance between a focus on form (accuracy) and opportunities to express meaning (fluency); learner training; and – perhaps as one aspect of this – self-directed learning.

The explicitness found in Nunan's writings about the principles underlying a particular set of design decisions is of particular importance when materials are to be used by other teachers. Rossner (1988: 143), discussing teachers' expectations of materials, sees the impact of communicative principles as being most clearly visible in the following.

Materials will:

1. provide 'comprehensible input' for generalised rehearsal of skills and 'activation' of learners' interlanguage repertoire;
2. raise learners' awareness about language, communication, learning, etc.;
3. provide experiences of communication in the new language similar or parallel to those likely to be encountered beyond the learning situation.

The emphasis in (1) on desirable conditions for language learning derives from the hypotheses put forward by Krashen (1982) and others. Point (2) reflects a cognitive perspective, in part a reaction to the behaviourist learning theory that underpinned audiolingualism. And in (3) we can perhaps see a hint of the kind of learner-centredness that many associate with communicative teaching. Rossner himself amplifies (3) in this way, putting the emphasis on the nature of learner communication and what drives this:

The missing ingredient . . . in most language teaching environments, is the opportunity for learners to experience the second language in circumstances where there are genuine needs and intentions to communicate in ways that parallel their experiences of using their first language. In other words, the nub of communicative ideology is that learners need, in the classroom, to have opportunities of being involved as both speakers and listeners (or readers and writers) in the communication of facts, opinions, and ideas with specific interpersonal intentions in mind, and taking account of a given set of situational factors using the second language.

(Rossner 1988: 140–1)

Nunan (1988a: 199) reports that experienced teachers adopting a learner-centred approach prefer materials with the following characteristics.
The materials

1. can be exploited in a variety of ways;
2. reflect the outside world (authenticity of text and task);
3. foster independent learning by making students more aware of the learning process (e.g. self-evaluation is built into the tasks);
4. are suitable for different levels of individual proficiency and preferred learning styles;
5. can act as a model for the development of teachers' own variations on these materials;
6. reflect the socio-cultural context within which they will be used.

Characteristics 2 and 6 bear an obvious relation to Rossner's point 3.

Hutchinson and Waters' (1987) approach to the formulation of principles, like that of Rossner, is to start from the intended effect of the materials, or as they put it, 'what materials are supposed to do' (p. 107). Their principles are paraphrased below.

Materials should:

- act as a stimulus to learning (e.g. texts are interesting; there are opportunities for learners to use their existing knowledge and skills; both teacher and learners can cope with the content);
- help to organise the teaching–learning process (e.g. there should be a clear and coherent structure which helps the teacher to plan lessons and learners to feel a sense of progress and achievement, but the structure should not be so rigid that monotony results);
- embody a view of the nature of teaching and learning (i.e. reflect the beliefs of the writer);
- reflect the nature of the learning task – in this case, *language* learning (i.e. represent the complexity of language learning but also its manageability);
- provide models of correct and appropriate language use.

Their 'extended' model for designing materials is reproduced below, as Figure 7.6. 'The aim of this particular model', they note, 'is to provide a coherent framework for the integration of the various aspects of learning, while at the same time allowing enough room for creativity and variety to flourish' (p. 109).

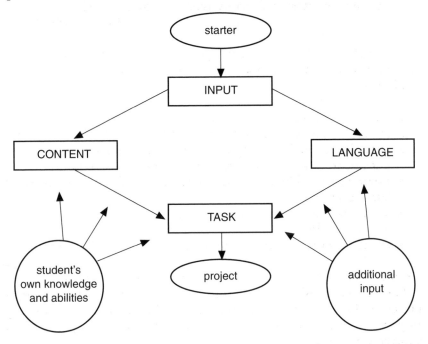

Figure 7.6 Hutchinson and Waters' (1987: 118) materials development model

The following summary of the four components that form the nucleus of the model is based on their commentary on pp. 108–9:

1. *input*: This may take the form of a text, dialogue, video recording, diagram, etc. It provides
   • a stimulus to activities
   • new language items
   • models of language use
   • a topic for communication
   • opportunities for learners to use their information-processing skills
   • opportunities for learners to use their existing knowledge, both of the language and of the subject matter.
2. *content*: Texts convey information and feelings; non-linguistic input can also be exploited to generate meaningful communication.

3. *language*: Learners need the language with which to carry out communicative tasks and activities. Good materials allow learners the opportunities to take the language of a text to pieces, study how it works, and then practise putting it together again.
4. *task*: Since the ultimate purpose of language learning is language use, materials should be designed to lead towards a communicative task in which learners use the content and the language knowledge they have acquired in the previous stages.

Since the focus is on enabling learners to carry out the task, the language and content selected from the input are determined by the demands of the task. For an extended example showing how the model was used to generate a text-based unit of materials, see Hutchinson and Waters (1987: 120–5). For accounts of other materials development projects based wholly or in part on the model, see the papers in Hidalgo et al. (1995) by Fortez (1995), Rozul (1995), and Peñaflorida (1995).

The strength of the Hutchinson and Waters model lies in its simplicity and its coherence. One possible limitation includes the lack of any kind of analysis of existing knowledge (content or linguistic), though there is scope (in the extended model) for learners to draw on their own content knowledge and ability to carry out the task, and for a teacher to provide additional input at a later stage if this seems necessary. Moreover, there seems to be an assumption that productive competence is the ultimate aim of language learning. There are a great many learners outside English-speaking countries for whom a reading knowledge is the primary study objective and there is therefore no reason why the task should not be receptive (listening or reading).

The Hidalgo et al. volume mentioned above was written for teachers with little or no experience of materials writing (hence its main title, *Getting Started*); and is of particular interest because several of the contributors had had no comparable writing experience prior to the writing projects they describe in their chapters. In order to avoid reinventing the wheel – and perhaps a cruder version of this than has already been designed – it is wholly appropriate that inexperienced writers should look to the more experienced for guidance. Peñaflorida, for example, whose article describes her own model, acknowledges a debt to Hutchinson and Waters, a series of workshops given by Maher (1988) and Nunan (1988b).

Task 7.4

1. If you have done any extended materials writing of the kind discussed in this section, list the beliefs about language and learning that have had most influence on the materials you have produced. Did you arrive at these ideas as a result of your own experience or have you been influenced by others? (If so, by whom and in what ways?)

If you have little or no experience of this kind, take another look at the sets of principles included in this section; then draw up your own list of principles. Try not to make this too long.

2. If you are working in a group, compare your list with those of others in the group, and explain your choices.

4.3 Problems

As we saw in the previous chapter, adopting the principle of (text) authenticity is not unproblematic. But a specific set of problems faces the teacher trying to create a set of learning materials based on authentic texts, as implied in the approach proposed by Hutchinson and Waters. The abandonment of a structural syllabus (the linguistic backbone of the audiolingual method) leaves open the question of how materials should be graded and sequenced; moreover, as Nunan (1991) has pointed out, there is a further problem of how materials can be integrated.

4.3.1 Integration and flexibility

With regard to integration, three 'solutions' have been developed: (1) *theme* or *topic*-based materials (2) a *text*-based approach in which the focus is on a particular genre of text (e.g. narrative) and (3) the *storyline* (Nunan 1991).

Each of these proposals has advantages and limitations. Particular problems relate to tensions between 'horizontal' and 'vertical' integration, and between integration and flexibility. For instance, the lessons or units that make up theme-based materials have an internal (vertical) coherence that derives from their relationship to the common theme; at a more macro (horizontal) level, however, the sequence of themes is likely to be quite arbitrary (Nunan 1991). The text-based approach, as characterised above, has the same strength and potential weakness. And the storyline, as normally used, despite being a strong cohesive device both horizontally and potentially vertically, suffers from a number of other problems (e.g. learners may not like the story, may have difficulty remembering details, may find that it palls over time, or may read on for themselves – and be resistant to spending class time on the same material later).

When teachers complain that materials are too inflexible what this normally means is that they cannot easily omit sections or deal with lessons or activities in a different order. For the materials designer, this demand for flexibility on the one hand and the requirement to provide a planned series of learning events is a real challenge. On the face of it, of the three approaches referred to above that based on themes would seem to offer the greatest flexibility in terms of teachers being able to replace the original materials with their own, supplement the original materials and perhaps reorder the original elements. However, the problem of the relationship between themes remains. If the materials are to be more than just a collection of resource materials, they need to be ordered in some way beyond the level of the theme. There may be, for instance, a progression in the themes themselves, from the very familiar (e.g. talking about oneself; the local environment) via the rather less familiar (e.g. the national level) to the unfamiliar (contact with people from other countries). There may be a (parallel?) shift from, depending on learner level, Past to Present to Future. There may be a progression in terms of functional repertoire (i.e. certain functions are recycled and new exponents introduced). Task complexity may also increase. What is important is that learners have the feeling that each theme offers them the opportunity to learn something new and integrate this with what they have already learned. In other words, the integration of themes should not be merely at a conceptual level but at the level of the language to which learners are exposed and what they are required to do with this and their existing resources.

If we extend the discussion to courses based on non-book materials, then there are other possibilities. Young (1980) describes a set of modular materials developed for an intensive course for advanced learners in which the plot of a story serves not simply as a horizontal link but also forms the basis for vertical links to a menu of optional materials dealing with grammar, register and topics. The approach adopted seems to deal with many of the problems inherent in a coursebook story: learners do not have access to the materials in advance; they are exposed to an episode of the story each day; each episode ends with a 'cliffhanger' which is resolved in the next; and episodes are in a variety of formats (spoken, written, videoed) to provide for register variation. Moreover, the modular approach described, in which teachers choose on a daily basis from sets of grammar, register, topic and communicative practice materials, allows individual teachers a considerable degree of flexibility to devise a course which meets the needs of their group of students. (For alternatives to the episodic storyline and fuller discussion, see also Low (1989).)

4.3.2 Final thought on principles

Earlier chapters have, like this, emphasised the importance of underpinning principles. As Tomlinson (1998d: 148) notes, 'good materials are those which are consistently informed by the same set of believed-in principles'. At the same time, Tomlinson (ibid.) warns, we should not go to extremes in our adherence to principle:

> [C]losed principles can lead to inflexible procedures which cater for a minority of learners only. So a belief that listening is the primary skill in early language acquisition can lead to an edict that beginners should not see the target language written down; or a belief that practice makes perfect can lead to a plethora of mechanical drills which fail to engage the energy or attention of the majority of users of the materials.

Thinking of a team of writers working on materials development, he acknowledges that the solution to this dilemma 'is not easy; but I think it lies in the overt establishment of agreed and justifiable principles followed by procedural compromises ... driven by one or more of the established principles' (ibid.). In other words, one principle may, in a particular situation, be outweighed by another; thus, the final decision remains a principled one.

5 FURTHER READING

As Low (1989: 153) points out, 'designing appropriate materials is not a science, it is a strange mixture of imagination, insight and analytical reasoning'. While imagination and analytical reasoning are qualities that can perhaps be stimulated and developed through careful study of published materials, insights come from a variety of sources. One of these is our own observation and experience (what appears to work well and why); another is feedback from others on the materials we have produced (including watching others teach with the materials); and a third is through reading. There are, as we have seen, sources of general advice in the form of principles and models. However, in relation to the design of materials for the teaching of specific language skills or systems, the materials designer will also need to go to books on teaching methodology. The best of these provide analyses of the skill/system (i.e. a profile of what a skilled user of the language knows and can do) as well as suggested ways of developing this knowledge and skill in learners in the form of procedures and activity-types. Though it is not one of the purposes of this book to provide advice on writing for publication, the experience of published writers (and this includes those whose writing has been in the context of development projects) can be of use to those writing merely for their own classrooms. The following are likely to be of interest: British Council (1980) – a collection of reports on projects in materials design; papers in Hidalgo et al. (1995); and the collections of papers by published writers edited by Byrd (1995b) and Tomlinson (1998a).

It is important not to forget, in an age in which learners are increasingly exposed to sophisticated visual materials, that visual design is important. One concern in visual design is thus to make materials attractive to learners through impact and aesthetic appeal; but pedagogic considerations are also important. For instance, the route through learning activities and the relationship between them needs to be clearly indicated. This is in part a matter of page layout, but also headings, numbering, the use of icons and so on. Software packages, such as Pagemaker, are helpful and, again, careful study of published materials is rewarding. See also Wright (1976, e.g. pp. 128–36) and Ellis and Ellis (1987).

6 SUMMARY

This chapter has attempted to build on the last by dealing with that rather large – and as far as guidance is concerned – rather empty space between coursebook-based teaching and writing for publication. Commercial materials for specific-purpose language teaching exist, but the economics of publishing demand that these are written to appeal to as large a number of people as possible. This tension means that many specific-purpose teachers – as well as those dissatisfied with the general materials that are available – still find themselves spending a good deal of time on materials preparation. The chapter has suggested that while materials writing will always be a demanding activity, there are ways of systematising the process which offer the promise of economies for the materials designer, security for the learner and stimulation for both. Systematisation does not have to involve mechanical repetition. It can mean the thoughtful, planned deployment and permutation of particular elements (activity-types, language items) within an overall structure. Farmers rotate their crops; the managers of the top international football clubs rotate their players; and teachers can try to maintain interest by providing opportunities for learners to use and recombine what they know in new contexts and to practise what is new through familiar activity-types.

To put this a little less prosaically, what we should be aiming for is a creative interplay between an underlying structure which embodies the beliefs of the teacher and the goals of the teaching and the means through which the beliefs and goals are realised. The structure will be relatively constant, but the means (content and procedures) need to be varied to maintain student interest.

Chapter 8

Getting learners involved

Utilising learner language: retrospective error focus; prospective error focus; learner transcriptions of their own stories; learner-generated texts for use with other learners; drama; transcript comparison; picture description for exam preparation – learner-produced exercises and worksheets – learners as teachers: learners as teachers of other learners; learners as teachers of teachers – learner-based teaching – caveats

In discussions of learner-centred teaching, the suggestion has been made that learners should not only be involved in choosing lesson materials (e.g. Wright 1987, Tudor 1993) but that they might also *adapt* or *produce* materials that can be used as the basis for teaching (e.g. Clarke 1989b, Swales 1992) and even present these materials themselves (e.g. Assinder 1991, Hall 1995). The decision to involve learners in materials generation may have initially been prompted by necessity (e.g. dissatisfaction with available materials or lack of resources for copying); more positively, it may have also been a response to humanistic ideas or a recognition that learners are also a source of knowledge (Deller 1990, Campbell and Kryszewska 1992). Once it has become an established practice, however, learner involvement in materials preparation can be seen to have clear benefits for all concerned.

This chapter brings together some ideas for stimulating students to generate their own materials. Examples are taken from short articles in the teachers' magazines *Practical English Teacher* (now unfortunately defunct) and *Modern English Teacher*; from *ELT Journal*; from the books *Lessons from the Learner* (Deller 1990) and *Learner-based Teaching* (Campbell and Kryszewska 1992); and from my own teaching. In addition to their more general function of illustrating some of the benefits of involving learners in materials generation, these examples are intended to encourage reflection at a practical level (*How can these ideas be used/adapted/extended? What other forms of material can learners produce?*).

The activities are organised in four main sections: '1. Utilising learner language'; '2. Learner-produced exercises and worksheets'; '3. Learners as teachers'; and '4. Learner-based teaching'. The sequence reflects an increasing readiness on the part of the teacher to share responsibility with learners for materials production. Indeed, the final section, on learner-based teaching, discusses a vision – of a classroom in which teaching-learning is based largely or entirely on learner products – that goes well beyond normal notions of learner-centred teaching.

1 UTILISING LEARNER LANGUAGE

There are a number of different ways in which learner language can be utilised as learning–teaching material:

1.1 Retrospective error focus

Teachers have for some time exploited learner language in the form of lists of frequent or typical errors, which are normally presented to learners after the activity in which they have occurred (e.g. a piece of writing, a spoken task), and used as a stimulus to self-correction or general awareness raising. The assumption is that this will have an effect on the accuracy of future production. In using this procedure myself, in both monolingual and multilingual classes, I have found it helpful to observe the following principles:

1. Present the errors in written form (written on the board or reproduced so that students have individual copies) – unless the focus is specifically on phonological features.
2. Embed the errors in sufficient context (e.g. for errors of collocation such as 'do a mistake', a phrase may suffice; for errors relating to tense or the use of articles, say, it may be necessary to reproduce a couple of sentences).
3. Mix in a few correct examples (also from learners), so that there is scope for learning from discussion of these as well as from the incorrect examples; this also changes the tone of what might otherwise be perceived as a negative and rather depressing activity.
4. Do not indicate which learner has made a specific error (in adult classes, learners may be quite willing to volunteer self-correction).
5. Try to group instances of similar errors so that there is a degree of reinforcement.
6. Don't make the list too long.

It is a good idea to keep the lists and to label them with a note of the date, the class and the activity from which they were taken. Not only can they be useful as a basis for supplementary exercises, oral quizzes or written tests with the class that generated these errors, they can also prove useful in predicting the errors of future classes on the same or a similar activity (see next section).

1.2 Prospective error focus

Learners in communicative classrooms sometimes complain that they are asked to do tasks for which they feel inadequately prepared. With experience, and especially if one sets the same types of productive task for successive classes, it becomes possible to predict difficulties and the kinds of errors that are likely to be made. For such classes, the error-list procedure described above can sometimes be turned on its head, for example by presenting learners in advance of the activity with a gap-filling pre-task which will force them to make the kinds of choice that are likely to be involved in the task to follow. If the required forms are known to the learners, this awareness raising should result in more accurate completion of the subsequent task; where the forms are not known, this provides a suitable opportunity for pre-teaching.

Task 8.1

1. Do you collect students' errors? If so, how do you use them?

2. What do you think of principles 1–6? What advice would *you* offer to other teachers?

As the next few activities illustrate, the task of noting down students' utterances need not fall only to the teacher. All the activities that follow involve students in transcribing spoken text (their own words or those of others), for which they would therefore require access to a cassette recorder (ideally with earphones). They have been used successfully with students who are reasonably well motivated (typically adult learners studying in a private language school or university) and whose language level is intermediate or above.

1.3 Learner transcriptions of their own stories

Learner stories, oral or written, about real events can provide fascinating material for a language class. I have asked adult learners of intermediate level to take turns (one per lesson) in telling a story (e.g. an interesting/funny/surprising experience while on a visit to the UK/USA) to the rest of the class. Such stories not only prompt questions and discussion; because they offer real insights into people's lives, they can also bring students, and students and teacher, closer together.

The story itself is recorded while it is being told (a small 'tieclip' microphone would be best) and then used in two ways: (1) the learner who has told the story listens to the recording (ideally in a language laboratory or listening centre), transcribes it using double spacing, writes in corrections of his or her errors, underlines any sections about which he or she feels unsure, and then gives the recording and transcript to the teacher; (2) the teacher listens to the recording, checks the corrections, and responds to the underlined sections. Comments on phonological features (e.g. specific sounds, stress, intonation) are best handled in an individual interview, if time permits.

Learners sometimes complain about oral practice: 'We just talked', and although as teachers we may feel that practice is in itself valuable, we also have a responsibility to provide feedback. This procedure allows first for feedback from other learners on general comprehensibility or the content of the story but it also has at least four further benefits in terms of subsequent processes:

1. since there is an opportunity for self-correction, learners can preserve 'face';
2. teacher feedback is private;
3. teacher feedback is economical and focused since it deals only with those features which the learner (a) cannot self-correct (b) sees as problematic;
4. teacher feedback is more comprehensive than it would be if the teacher were simply to comment orally immediately after the story.

1.4 Learner-generated texts for use with other learners

Forman and Ellis (1991), who describe their work with students in the English language department of a university in Malaysia, also suggest recording students' stories, but put the resulting stories to rather different purposes. The recommended procedure for what would probably be a one-off activity is as follows:

1. Students are told they are going to write a story based on their own experience.
2. They are given a set of standard prompts to guide planning: *When did it happen? Where were you? Who were you with? What were you doing before it happened? What happened? Who was involved? What did you do after it happened? What happened in the end?*
3. Small groups are formed and each student tells his or her story; other students fill out the details by asking the storyteller about their reactions and feelings.
4. The group decide which is the best story and work together to develop this.
5. Each group's story is told to the rest of the class; the class ask clarification questions and suggest recommendations for improvement.
6. Each group writes up a final version of its story, which can subsequently be recorded.
7. The group devises comprehension questions on the story.

The recordings and the questions are then used as listening materials for students at lower levels within the institution. (The written texts could also be used, presumably.)

Among the benefits of this procedure noted by the authors are the following:

1. the stages leading up to the writing phase (1–5) help students to generate ideas and stimulate the writing process;
2. the drafting and redrafting of the stories replicates real-life writing;
3. students' questions on their own stories focus on points that they feel to be important.

To these, we might add the fact that learners with different strengths and weaknesses (e.g. in speaking, writing, grammar) can all benefit from an integrated activity of this kind; that the activity is personalised; that student discussion is purposeful; and that the resulting stories should be of real interest to the other students with whom they are used.

In a variation on this idea, learners write for future learners. Bicknell (1999) describes a project in which, prompted by the question 'Before you came to the United States, what questions did you have about West Virginia University and Morgantown?', learners wrote Web pages about the institution in which they were studying and the local community. As with the previous example, there is a clear purpose and audience for the writing, and the process is collaborative, but there is a difference at the point of production. 'Posting' learner products on an Intranet is, in one sense, equivalent to displaying them on a classroom wall, but in Intranet form they are more easily accessible and therefore more likely to be read carefully; posting them on the Web puts them in the public domain, and opens up the possibility of a response from interested readers elsewhere. There are, in fact, websites specifically intended for this purpose (Slaouti 2000): the Pizzaz pages at http://darkwing.uoregon.edu/-leslieob/pizzaz/html; e-mail project pages at http://www.ota.dni.us/web-farm/emailproject/email.htm and http://dir.yahoo.com/Recreation/Games/Internet_Games/Web_Games/Interactive_Fiction.

1.5 Drama

'Drama activities' such as role play and to a lesser extent simulation are now quite widely used to provide opportunities for students to use language spontaneously and creatively. However, few teachers will have thought of going as far as Wessels (1991), who set up an EFL course (ten hours per week for three months) based entirely on drama techniques. Students (maximum fourteen in the class) were upper-intermediate to advanced level, of mixed nationalities, and were following the course, in a UK college of further education, instead of or in addition to a general EFL programme.

Wessels describes the various activities and stages leading up to the production of a play for other students in the college – not Shakespeare or even a modern classic, but a play which was entirely the result of student imagination and improvisation. One product of this collaboration was a script; other products being recordings of scenes on audiotape and video, and photographs. These materials were subsequently available for use with students on general EFL programmes, one script even being worked up for publication as a reader (*Soap Opera*, Wessels 1999). The popularity of the course led to the provision of a similar course for students at lower intermediate–intermediate level.

1.6 Transcript comparison

Storytelling can also be prompted by visual aids. For example, I have used very short silent extracts from video recordings (e.g. of the popular *Mr Bean*) to elicit student descriptions of what happens (and, if I stop before the end, what is going to happen). In advance of the lesson I have shown the video clip to a native speaker of English (this need not be a teacher of English) and asked him or her to record a description of the events.

Following class viewing, the activity can be organised in three ways: two or three individual students are asked to give descriptions, which are recorded; or students are divided into groups and each group records its description; or students work in a language laboratory and record descriptions. A transcript is then prepared of the recording(s). If the whole-class form of organisation is adopted, this can be a cooperative activity with the recording being played back and individual students other than the speaker writing up sections on the board.

Two stages of transcript comparison follow:

1. Students carry out a comparison of at least two transcripts (if two transcripts have been written on the board, this can again be a whole-class activity). The transcripts are compared on the basis of content as well as form. In relation to language, the emphasis is not on accuracy (though any obvious errors can be corrected), but on how different individuals have chosen to express the same idea.
2. In the second stage, the recording is played of the native speaker of English describing the same scene. This is also transcribed and any key differences between this and the other versions discussed.

This procedure is similar in some respects to that described in Richards (1985) and discussed in Chapter 7.

Normally, when students are asked to look closely at native speaker texts, these are intended to guide their own production; in this activity, students start from what they wish to say and use the native speaker sample to assess their own choices. In this situation, choices are likely to be better or worse rather than right or wrong. One of the most powerful insights for learners tends to be that native speakers do not necessarily speak in complete sentences.

1.7 Picture description for exam preparation

Graham (1994) describes a procedure in which, following pairwork and class practice, upper-intermediate and advanced students preparing for the First Certificate and Proficiency exams of the University of Cambridge Local Examinations Syndicate (UCLES) prepare a one-minute description of a picture or photograph, which is recorded in a language laboratory or on the student's own cassette recorder and then transcribed. Certain groundrules are established in advance: students are not allowed to write anything down before making the recording, but they can work on the recording repeatedly until they are satisfied; the transcription must be a faithful record of what is said, but they can write in corrections in a different colour. The teacher gives individual feedback, and also prepares whole-class practice on any areas of general difficulty. Graham points out that though she conducts a lesson of this kind every week and although it takes up one hour of the seven and a half hours available, it is a popular activity: 'The students find it hard work, but it has proved so popular that other classes have asked for a similar lesson' (Graham 1994: 29). One reason may be that it relates very clearly to one of the elements in the oral paper of the examination.

Task 8.2

This section has described a number of ideas for exploiting learner language as learning material.

1. Look back through the activities. What other points of similarity are there? How do they differ?

2. Have you done anything similar? If not, could you? Would you?

2 LEARNER-PRODUCED EXERCISES AND WORKSHEETS

As noted in Chapter 5, teachers prepare worksheets to provide extra practice, usually on points of grammar, less commonly on vocabulary, and even less commonly on other aspects of the language. Such teacher-produced worksheets may be no more than photocopies of exercises taken from books other than the main coursebook; alternatively, the exercises may have been designed by the teacher. While the former may be convenient (if one knows of a convenient source and photocopying facilities are available), these two conditions do not hold for everyone. Yet the alternative, teacher-made exercises, can be very time-consuming.

Teachers do not have to produce their own worksheets. Swales (1992) provides examples of student-generated material at three levels. These include the following:

- Students produce flashcards (hand-drawn or using magazine pictures), for which captions are provided by the teacher or other students under the teacher's guidance. These can be organised into sets such as furniture items, vegetables, etc. (*beginner*).
- Each student prepares a paragraph describing a recent news event in which all the main verbs are in the form of an infinitive; their partner has to supply the correct form of the verb (*intermediate*).
- Students design a questionnaire for use with other students (*advanced*).

The following procedure and principles are suggested:

1. exercises should be kept relatively short (e.g. five gap-filling sentences);
2. the exercise designer marks the answers of other students and discusses with them any wrong answers;
3. the teacher circulates during the exercise-writing, answering and feedback stages and helps to settle any disputes;
4. students rewrite their exercises in the light of feedback from other students.

The value of such an activity is summarised as follows: (1) it provides feedback to the teacher on whether students have internalised target structures (or whatever else they have been working on); (2) there is a high level of student involvement. Swales also claims that 'students . . . have never questioned the validity of the exercise' (p. 59).

Where there is a source of suitable exercise material, this can provide a starting point and model for learners to produce more of the same. McGrath (1994) suggests a follow-up to class oral practice of the pattern 'What would you do if . . . ?' in which groups devise further problem scenarios to be put to other groups. Clarke (1989b) shows how learners can be guided to devise a computer-based vocabulary sorting task for other learners.

Task 8.3

1. Have you tried getting your students to prepare material for use by other learners? If so, what did you get them to do; how did you organise the activity; and what did you learn from this (e.g. were there any problems that would lead you to do things differently another time?)?

2. One of Swales' colleagues suggested that students might also prepare exercises to help other students prepare for tests or exams. What do you think of this idea?

3. Can you think of variations on any of the ideas suggested by Swales or any other types of material that students might produce?

3 LEARNERS AS TEACHERS

3.1 Learners as teachers of other learners

Implicit in the argument for learner-made materials is an acceptance of the learner as a potential teacher of other learners. Whitaker (1983) argues that comprehension questions on texts should be devised by learners (for other learners) rather than by teachers or materials writers. Clarke (1989b) proposes an extension of this idea, preparation by learners of a transcoding activity, which would require their classmates to render the information from the text in an appropriate form (e.g. graph, table, diagram). Lynch (1991) takes the argument a step further, suggesting that (listening) tasks which require learners to assess and discuss among themselves the sufficiency of the input they have received for the purposes of task completion, and ask the teacher for further input if necessary, not only involve a role shift but legitimate the very act of asking the teacher questions. It is perhaps worth noting that the starting point for Lynch's paper was a research study of secondary-school pupils in Scotland (i.e. L1 users of English) who, it was hypothesised, were underachieving because they failed to give any overt signals (such as asking questions) when they did not understand. Gardner and Miller (1999), thinking of learner involvement in the production of materials for a self-access centre, give the following example of a classroom-based activity:

> Arrange learners into small groups according to their interests in developing some self-access materials e.g. listening, speaking, psycholinguistics, etc. Provide the groups with some samples of existing self-access materials, and guidelines on the format to use … Learners then arrange times when they can get together to produce materials. They need to prepare the materials, pilot them, then meet with the teacher to discuss what they have produced.
>
> (Gardner and Miller 1999: 135)

Teachers also test, but what they test reflects their ideas of what is important. When no coursebook progress tests are available, learners might be asked to construct tests for each other (with the teacher providing guidance in the form of 'model' test types) (Clarke 1989b). This will not only stimulate them to review what they have been learning, it may also reveal important differences between learner and teacher perceptions of what is significant.

Clarke (1989b: 135) presents five principles (paraphrased below) which underlie his view of learner involvement in materials adaptation and development. Four of these highlight learner roles:

- *Learner commitment*: creative involvement in the adaptation of materials engages the learner's interest and leads to a greater degree of commitment.
- *Learner as materials writer and collaborator*: working cooperatively with other learners to produce materials means that learners are active

collaborators in the learning environment rather than merely 'language receivers'; working on the tasks prepared by others in the class also leads to a higher degree of commitment than might otherwise be the case.

- *Learner as problem-solver*: devising a task for other learners is a meaningful activity for the problem-setter; language is both the focus of the task and the means by which it is achieved.
- *Learner as knower*: when constructing tasks based on given materials, learners are in the position of 'knower' rather than 'assimilator'; when required to research a task in order to produce material, they become 'expert'.
- *Learner as evaluator and assessor*: the act of adapting and producing material makes learners better able to make judgements about the relevance and interest of what they have been doing and their own level of achievement; the resulting insights can be used to shape future materials.

The ultimate in role-shifts occurs when learners take over the teaching. Assinder (1991) describes her approach to video-based lessons in the 'Current Affairs' component of a full-time course in Australia for non-English-speaking students preparing for higher education. This component occupied six hours (two mornings) each week, and the group in question comprised twelve students of mixed nationalities ranging in level from lower-intermediate to upper-intermediate. Some weeks into the course, Assinder realised that what she was doing in preparing a worksheet to exploit a video could just as well be done by the students themselves and mentioned this idea to the students. They reacted positively. Having discussed what a good video-based lesson might contain, possible question-types, and negotiated a time (two hours) for the preparation of a one-hour lesson and the drafting of a worksheet (to be typed up later by a member of the group) on which the lesson would be based, the class divided into two groups, each with a different video-clip (a news item of five–ten minutes) and a video recorder. Assinder's account of what happened next is worth quoting in detail:

> Firstly, the groups watched the video items for gist. The students then talked about what they had seen and heard and how they would approach the task, and organized who would do what. One group delegated a video operator, a note-taker, a 'dictionary consultant', a 'question-committee', someone to take down dictation, and a typist.
> The students tried to isolate new vocabulary and to check spelling and meaning: they consulted each other; they used dictionaries. They talked about the topics and had lengthy discussions about their perceptions of the situation, negotiating meaning until they were satisfied that they all had a good general understanding. They watched and listened, they talked, they listened again. They summarized, re-phrased, circumlocuted, took notes, took dictation, and took responsibility for themselves and for the group.

The groups argued about which items of vocabulary would be most useful for the other group to learn; which segment would be most representative of the whole programme to transcribe for the cloze exercise, and which words should be gapped. Individuals argued about the appropriacy of different questions for comprehension and/or discussion; they fought over what they had 'heard', meaning, pronunciation, and points of grammar. In most cases a consensus was reached. As a last resort, in cases of unresolvable conflict, I was called upon to act as a consultant or mediator.

(Assinder 1991: 219–20)

The subsequent three-hour session consisted of two one-hour lessons led by the student groups followed by feedback and general evaluation of the experience. 'The response', says Assinder, 'was overwhelmingly positive, and the students asked for more of the same' (p. 220). Towards the end of the course, instead of teaching each other, the two groups taught other (intermediate, general EFL) classes. 'This too was considered by both parties to be useful and successful' (p. 223).

Assinder notes that getting the students to prepare and present lessons gave her a much deeper insight into their individual strengths and weaknesses (not only linguistic). The data collected during this monitoring formed the basis for weekly class feedback and remedial work (for some of which she drew on audio and video recordings of the presentations) and for individual counselling sessions.

She lists eight effects of involving the learners in this way:

1. increased motivation
2. increased participation
3. increased 'real' communication
4. increased in-depth understanding
5. increased responsibility for own learning and commitment to the course
6. increased confidence and respect for each other
7. increased number of skills and strategies practised and developed
8. increased accuracy.

These effects are explained in terms of the interest and relevance of the subject matter; the nature of the task and the fact that it was group-based; the responsibility given to the students; the availability of feedback on points of language (in class and in individual tutorials); and the opportunity for students to teach each other.

3.2 Learners as teachers of teachers

As will be apparent from a number of the examples given in this chapter, learner-centred teaching provides endless opportunities for teachers to learn more about their learners (and learning). This reaches its logical conclusion in Prodromou's (1992a) suggestion that in a context where a native English-speaking teacher is teaching a monocultural class, students can also be set the task of preparing in teams questions to ask the teacher about the local culture. (A teacher new to the country may be allowed to use the services of a student informant.) Prodromou comments: 'This kind of activity makes for a more reciprocal relationship between the culture of the teacher and that of the students. It involves a built-in recognition of the value of the learners' culture and the value of their contribution to the learning process' (p. 48) – as well as helping the teacher learn more about the culture, and perhaps avoid cultural faux pas. (For further discussion of materials and culture, see Chapter 10.)

Task 8.4

1. Many of the activities described so far in this chapter have been justified by reference to the benefits to the learner (and, sometimes, the teacher). Are you persuaded that greater learner involvement of these kinds is, in principle, a desirable direction to take?

2. Do you see any problems in practice, in your own teaching situation?

4 LEARNER-BASED TEACHING

Thus far, we have been assuming that learner-generated materials would have their place alongside more conventional materials. Campbell and Kryszewska's (1992) experience of teaching English in Poland, to learners as diverse as university teachers of different specialisms on the one hand and children on the other, led them in the direction of what they call 'learner-based teaching'. They explain:

> All humanistic approaches to teaching accept that some language input can be based on the experience, knowledge and expertise of individual students. What is novel about learner-based teaching is the idea that *all* activities can be based on that wealth of experience, be they grammar exercises, exam preparation, games or translation ... The learners themselves are responsible for the information input, thereby ensuring its relevance and topicality for each particular group.
>
> (Campbell and Kryszewska 1992: 5; original emphasis)

Appendix 8.1 contains three examples. Example A, which is intended for use with students at elementary level, would clearly be suitable for learners of any age. Example B, intended for students at lower-intermediate level, makes two assumptions: that all learners share the same first language and that the teacher is as competent in that language as the learners are themselves. Example C casts learners in the role of teachers.

Many of the elements of the rationale for learner-based teaching can also be found in the sources discussed earlier in this chapter – for instance, the benefits of groupwork (group solidarity; peer teaching and correction); learner involvement (in the preparation of materials and the comments of other students on these materials); content relevance; and ongoing needs analysis, feeding into remedial work. Campbell and Kryszewska mention also the element of unpredictability: 'Not only do the learners not know what is coming before the lesson starts, but they are often unable to predict how the lesson will develop' (p. 9). It is, of course, conceivable that not all learners would feel comfortable in such a situation.

Other disadvantages are obvious and are acknowledged. Learners may be resistant to such an approach; there may be limiting factors, such as an externally-imposed syllabus or examination; and there are very specific demands on the teacher (for instance, the need to keep careful records of what is done, and to be very clear about intended outcomes and the steps by which these can be achieved). For teachers working within an externally-defined course framework, the answer may be to use learner-based activities as a complement to other, textbook-based work; for teachers who are more autonomous, it is probably still desirable to introduce such ideas gradually, a principle that applies to many of the activities included in this chapter.

The preposition in the title of Deller's (1990) book, *Lessons from the Learner*, makes a clear point. The 'appetiser' (preface) then sets the tone: like many teachers, she says, she used to file away potentially interesting material but never had the time or energy to go through it and select for her classes; now she continues to store away such material but periodically gives it to her students to classify or select from. The introduction outlines the rationale and the approach:

> [T]eachers . . . set up activities where the learners generate the material and then use it for other linguistic activities . . . In practice this often means a reversal of the usual process, i.e. starting with the freer activities which are then used for more controlled practice. For example, the learners can create such things as jumbled stories, cloze exercises and transformation exercises for each other, from material they have previously produced themselves. This material has the advantage of being understood by them, feeling close to them, and perhaps most importantly of all, being theirs rather than something imposed on them. As a result they feel more comfortable and involved, and have no problems in identifying with it.
>
> (Deller 1990: 2)

The movement from text production to exploitation is illustrated in exercise D in Appendix 8.1. The unpredictable outcomes of activities such as this do not simply mean that lessons are more interesting for learners: 'if there are times when we can't predict the material, we give ourselves the opportunity to . . . be stimulated by our learners and experience new ideas and situations' (Deller 1990: 1–2).

Activities are grouped in the book into eleven familiar, if rather miscellaneous, categories: ice-breakers, creative drills, writing, error-correcting and so on. As in the example above, there are brief indications of the level and number of students for which the activity is suitable, and the time and materials required.

In that it emphasises the importance of learners doing and not simply being – in other words, offering opportunities for them to control what happens to them in the classroom and make choices – Deller's book has the same starting point as that of Campbell and Kryszewska. One important difference, however, lies in the authors' attitudes to coursebooks. Campbell and Kryszewska note that their students use the coursebook 'mainly at home for self-study' (p. 7); Deller's view is that classrooms should include *more* activities of this kind rather than being entirely based on them. (Section 2 of her book illustrates how the concept of student-generated activities can be applied to a coursebook unit.)

An alternative typology of the activities in Deller and Campbell and Kryszewska (paraphrased below) is offered by Tudor (1996: 15–16):

1. activities in which learner knowledge is utilised as a source of input
2. activities in which the learners' L1 is used
3. direct learner involvement in activity development and organisation
4. affectively-based activities.

This categorisation not only brings out the learning-centred processes involved, as Tudor notes; it also constitutes a set of design principles for teachers wishing to create their own activities along similar lines.

Type 1 activities, Tudor notes, are 'based on the idea that an activity is likely to produce more relevant language and be more motivating if learners are allowed to invest it with a content which is "their own"' (p. 15). Example A in Appendix 8.1 falls into this category. Type 2 activities acknowledge the fact that most of the messages learners convey in their daily lives will be in the L1 and bring this communicative agenda into the classroom (see example B in Appendix 8.1). The third type of activity involves learners in the kinds of process that have traditionally fallen to the teacher, such as materials selection, explanation and diagnosis and evaluation during the checking of other students' work (see example C). This serves as a form of learning, Tudor suggests. The final category of activity (see, e.g. example D in Appendix 8.1) gives 'learners scope to use their imaginative skills, creativity and sense of fun' (p. 16).

5 CAVEATS

This chapter has presented the case for learner involvement in materials selection, design and presentation. The advantages of such involvement are summarised below. However, three points should be borne in mind.

1. It needs to be recognised that if the materials used are restricted to those produced by learners this will have an effect on their ability to cope with other types of text (Gadd 1998). A combination of teacher-selected and learner-generated texts is therefore likely to be preferable.

2. In some contexts, moreover, the attempt to transfer responsibility for classroom decision-making from teacher to learners may be seen as an abdication of responsibility. If learner-centred teaching is to work, learners must be willing to share in the decision-making process, and patient preparation may be necessary before they are ready for this and willing to legitimate less familiar types of activity. Even when this is possible, the teacher's responsibility remains undiminished. As Stevick observes:

> If we, in our zeal to be 'humanistic', become too 'learner-centered' with regard to 'control', we undermine the learner's most basic need, which is for security. We may find that we have imposed our own half-baked anarchy on the class. Absence of structure, or of focus on the teacher, may be all right in certain kinds of psychological training, but not in our classrooms. In a task-oriented group like a language class, the student's place is at the center of a space which the teacher has structured, with room left for him to grow into. In this kind of relationship, there are two essentials for the teacher: *faith* that the student will in fact grow into that space, and *understanding* of where the student is in that space at any given moment. When both these ingredients are present, there is the possibility of true 'humanism' in teaching.
>
> (Stevick 1980: 33; original emphases)

3. The relationship between the kinds of learner-centred teaching discussed in this chapter and learner autonomy, despite some of the more obvious points of contact (e.g. learners selecting learning materials; learners determining the focus of feedback), is not as direct as it might seem. Indeed, Benson and Voller (1997), writing of methods and materials in autonomous learning projects, point to a possible paradox: that these 'might tend to inhibit rather than promote autonomy unless they are able to accommodate more directive roles for their users' (p. 177). It is with this in mind that emphasis has been laid on a creative role for learners. (For further discussion of this point, see Littlejohn (1997) and Nunan (1997); for more general discussion of teacher–learner roles, see, e.g. Wright 1987 and Tudor 1993, 1996.)

6 SUMMARY

The focus in this chapter has been on learners producing materials for use in class by their classmates or other students. This has a number of positive effects as far as the learner is concerned, both in relation to motivation and learning. When learners are actively and creatively involved, motivation is increased; such activities as peer teaching (including correction) constitute a valuable and valued learning experience and can contribute to group solidarity. There are also benefits for the teacher. Monitoring learners as they discuss and prepare materials raises the teacher's awareness of individual or general difficulties. Some of the material is potentially re-usable with learners in other classes. Teacher-preparation time is reduced. And because there will always be an element of unpredictability, the classroom is a more interesting place for the teacher as well as learners.

While the use of most of the activity-types described here is likely to lead to increased motivation, one type of material – that is, spoken (and recorded) and written texts produced by learners – is likely to be the most relevant from a linguistic perspective. Careful in-class analysis of this type of material, which is as finely tuned to learner level as it could be, is sure to be helpful not only for those involved in producing that text, but for others in the same class.

Chapter 9

Evaluating effects

Evaluation revisited – in-use evaluation of published materials: objectives of in-use evaluation; data collection; learner involvement; collating data; meetings; the value of in-use evaluation – in-use evaluation of teacher-produced materials: the trialling of materials intended for publication and materials for internal use; revision; problems – post-use evaluation: evaluating outcomes; evaluation of the materials selection procedures

1 EVALUATION REVISITED

In this chapter, we close the circle that started with pre-use evaluation (see Figure 9.1, overleaf). In Chapter 1, it was suggested that the evaluation of materials prior to use, however rigorously this is carried out, should be only a first step in the evaluation of those materials. As a number of writers have pointed out, pre-use evaluation can merely indicate potential suitability (e.g. Brumfit 1979, Daoud and Celce-Murcia 1979, McDonough and Shaw 1993, Tomlinson 1999). To establish whether materials really are suitable (and in what ways and to what extent), two further stages of evaluation are necessary. The first, in-use evaluation, is conducted throughout the period that the materials are being used. The second, post-use evaluation, takes place at some point later.

Until recently, with the exception of pre-publication trialling (a rather special case), neither in-use nor post-use evaluation had received much attention in the literature – and what was said took the form of exhortation rather than concrete suggestions concerning method. There are a number of possible reasons for this neglect. Perhaps writers about materials evaluation have seen pre-use evaluation as more important; perhaps in-use and post-use evaluation simply do not happen because time is not available or has not been allocated for this; or perhaps those who make them happen are too busy making them happen to write about what they do. Ellis (1998) offers two further speculations: that either teachers know all they need to know about a book after using it day in and day out and therefore do not feel the need for any kind of formal evaluation or that they feel 'daunted' by what they see as the enormity of the task. Personal experience suggests that (1) teachers do evaluate materials as they use them, but this is not organised or formalised, (2) teachers also carry out post-use evaluation in order to determine whether to continue to use the same materials, but even when this is done in an organised fashion (i.e. in a group) it tends to rely on impressionistic holistic judgements rather than evidence. One of the purposes of this chapter is to demonstrate that in-use and post-use evaluation can be made much more systematic (by, among other things, making planned use of teachers' daily experience) without being daunting in scale. The chapter synthesises and builds on the ideas of a small number of writers who have made suggestions for the form that such evaluation might take. The evaluation of teacher-produced materials is also considered, with particular reference to the revision process.

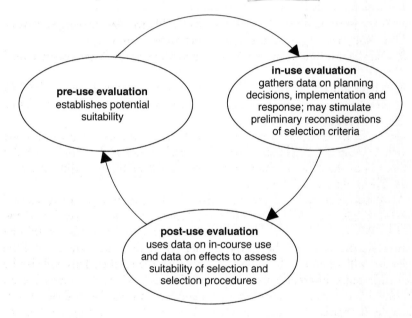

Figure 9.1 Closing the circle

2 IN-USE EVALUATION OF PUBLISHED MATERIALS

2.1 Objectives of in-use evaluation

The in-use evaluation of published materials is motivated by two objectives. The more obvious, as indicated above, is to revisit the decision taken at the selection stage. By planning lessons based on the materials, by teaching them and by observing the effects, the teacher is in a position to make almost a moment-by-moment assessment of whether the materials are standing up to the test of use. What normally happens is somewhat different. The kind of evaluation that we usually carry out, as we teach with materials, tends to be much more fragmentary. In planning a lesson, we will be balancing a number of externally-imposed or self-imposed requirements of which we will be more or less consciously aware: to do a little more work on something learners found difficult in the last lesson, for instance; to move a step further towards the fulfilment of the course aims; to ensure a learning experience that is coherent, varied, well balanced. In other words, our attention is on learning outcomes and our interest in the materials is limited to the contribution that they can make to these outcomes. Evaluation of the materials themselves thus tends to be *ad hoc* rather than planned.

If materials evaluation at this stage is to be more systematic it will have to be capable of answering questions such as the following:

1. What proportion of the materials was I able to use unchanged, that is, without needing to 'shape' (i.e. adapt) them in any way?
2. Did the unchanged materials appear to work well? What evidence do I have for this?
3. What spontaneous changes did I make as I taught with the materials? Did these improvisations work well? If not, what do I need to do differently?

In-use evaluation along these lines, which relies heavily on conscientious record-keeping and evidence-based reflection, is concerned not only with the evaluation of the original material, but also its adaptability to different contexts. The evaluator will be the teacher.

A second purpose of in-use evaluation is to investigate what teachers do with materials, the obvious inputs being reports by and observation of the teacher. When these are part of a formal teacher-appraisal system within an institution, the focus will be on the teacher rather than the materials and the evaluator will, of course, be someone other than the teacher. This will also be the case in quite differently motivated investigations, where the emphasis is on illuminative description rather than formative or summative evaluation. For example, Richards and Mahoney's (1996) study of textbook use by English teachers in Hong Kong, which used questionnaires and observation to discover what teachers believe and do, draws conclusions not about the materials but about teachers' autonomy from the textbook. We return to the topic of 'Materials and research' in the final chapter.

2.2 Data collection

Evaluation of the effects of programmes has traditionally taken the form of examining students' end-of-course test scores. While this single, quantitative measure will still speak loudly to all concerned, it has come to be recognised in recent years that test scores can only be a partial measure of course effects and that programme evaluation (and within that, materials evaluation) should draw on more sources of information. Such information needs to be gathered, as we have seen, at different stages; it should ideally come from learners as well as teachers; and if it is to answer the questions 'Why?', 'How?' and 'How well?' (and not simply 'What?' or 'When?'), it will need to be collected in a variety of ways, one of which will be observation. If we are careful, this data-gathering can be organised in such a way that triangulation (the comparison of different perspectives on the same event) is possible. This will make the data more reliable.

2.2.1 Records of use

In situations where in-use evaluation is not organised, it tends to be anecdotal, unfocused and occasional. A first step in the direction of more systematic evaluation is therefore to establish a record-keeping system. Masuhara's (1998) term 'records of use', helpful though it is, actually covers a range of possibilities. There is a scene in the film *Dead Poets' Society* when the dangerously inspirational teacher encourages students to tear out the introduction to the book they are using; this way of recording what has not been used may be a little drastic. At its most basic, a record of use would indicate which parts of a book had and had not been used (unchanged). This information could be in the form of ticks and crosses on the book itself or on a specially devised sheet listing all the components of a lesson or unit (the latter would obviously be more convenient for record-keeping purposes and comparison with other teachers). More detailed records might contain (1) brief explanations of *why particular sections had not been used* (2) notes on *the reasons for* and form of any adaptation and (3) notes on *the reasons for* and form of any supplementation. The time potentially involved in this more elaborate kind of record-keeping would not be inconsiderable, even if a record sheet were developed to simplify the process. It would make most sense in a situation where several teachers were using the same materials and if there were opportunities for regular comparison of records (e.g. a weekly meeting). We come back to meetings of staff under 'Collating data', below.

2.2.2 Observation

Experienced teachers 'observe' without needing to be advised to do this, but such observations tend to be neither recorded (in any sense) nor systematic. One way of making observation more systematic would be to include in the kinds of record of use described above a *process* dimension (i.e. notes on what actually happened when the materials were used) (Richards 1993, 1998). While such a record might include reference to what the teacher did (e.g. in making spontaneous changes of plan), what would be particularly important, as far as materials evaluation is concerned, would be an indication of how the learners responded. Again, such records might take a number of forms.

Teachers could annotate their lesson plan (if this exists as a detailed document) at points during the lesson when this is possible or make brief notes on the book itself. Brief notes of these kinds might form the basis for a more considered set of notes, written up after the lesson. Some teachers keep a regular journal in which they reflect on their teaching. While both of these forms of professional reflection on action have their virtues, as ways of evaluating materials they may be somewhat unfocused. A better alternative for this purpose would therefore seem to be 'observation sheets' (Tomlinson 1999) on which the teacher records, for example, the kinds of difficulties that learners appear to be having with the materials – instructions, questions or tasks.

A more developed form of this idea is represented by what Ellis (1997, 1998) calls 'micro-evaluation'. If macro-evaluation, as defined by Ellis, is an attempt to evaluate a programme (or project) in its entirety, then micro-evaluation focuses on a single aspect, administrative or curricular, of the programme. Within the area of curriculum, materials and their effectiveness would be an obvious interest. From the perspective of teachers involved in a programme, a focus on materials makes a good deal of sense. As Ellis (1998: 218) puts it, 'their attention is ... more on whether specific activities and techniques appear to "work" in the context of a particular lesson'. Moreover, when evaluation is related to the materials used in class, or some feature of these, it is more likely to seem 'less daunting' and 'more manageable' (p. 222).

While Ellis's (1998) wide-ranging paper provides a concise and clear introduction to evaluation procedures at a general level, his particular concern is to demonstrate how the same analytical framework can be applied at a micro-level – for example, that of a communicative task. The approach recommended, which is illustrated with reference to a listening task, involves the following steps:

1. description of the task (input to the learners, the procedures they will have to follow; whether they will be involved in receptive or productive language use; and what the outcomes will be) and its objectives;
2. planning the evaluation;
3. collecting information: (a) *before* the task is used (information on learners' present state of knowledge/competence – established through a pre-test; and previous experience of this kind of task); (b) *while* the task is being used (what happens, especially in relation to what is anticipated – this will require observation; recording may also be helpful); (c) *on completion* of the task (information on actual outcomes – established through, e.g., examination of learner products and post-test; and feedback on teacher's and learners' opinions);
4. analysis of the information;
5. conclusions and recommendations.

The obvious drawback of this approach, as Ellis acknowledges, is that it is 'costly in time and effort'; it should therefore be seen as 'an example of the kind of comprehensive evaluation that is possible and that might be undertaken occasionally' (p. 236). The justification for going to these lengths would no doubt be stronger if a teacher were experimenting with an activity prototype rather than just a one-off task and/or if more than one teacher stood to benefit from the findings of the evaluation.

The kind of observation suggested by Tomlinson and Ellis is, of course, a good deal easier when the teacher is not directly involved in the activity; in institutions where peer observation is well established it could prove an interesting alternative to a concentration on the teacher.

The value of recorded observations of material-in-use, whatever their form, is that they capture the teacher's or observer's perceptions of what is going on at the time. They also have obvious limitations. Even when the teacher is free to see, he or she sees selectively; and though an observer may see more, there is the same problem. The picture is incomplete without some insight into the learners' views.

2.3 Learner involvement

In Chapters 1 and 2, it was suggested that learners' reactions to materials might be elicited as part of the selection process. Learners can also contribute to in-use evaluation.

Task 9.1

1. What kinds of information could learners supply that would be helpful to a teacher wishing to carry out in-use evaluation of materials?

2. In what ways might the teacher use this information?

3. In what different ways could the information be elicited?

4. Do you have any experience of involving learners in in-use evaluation of materials? If so, how did you go about this and what did you find out? If not, how would you organise this? (Try to be as specific as possible.)

Let us assume that the materials are a given in the sense that the teacher cannot just abandon them if they seem unsuitable in certain respects. What the teacher needs to know, therefore, is whether the materials are perceived as intrinsically interesting and useful, for instance, and whether his or her way of mediating between the materials and the learners is seen as effective. As we have seen in Chapters 3–6, there are a number of ways in which this information can then be used. Any additional insights into how and to what extent learners use the materials out of class can also be helpful in indicating whether the teacher needs to provide more or clearer guidance.

The kinds of questions below, which are taken from a larger questionnaire designed to elicit learners' views on what helps them in their language learning, would be appropriate for this purpose:

What is good and not so good about the materials you are working with now? What do you think is missing from them? What changes would you make to them?

(Breen and Candlin 1987: 27)

Such questions might be used to initiate a discussion with the whole class or with a representative group of learners (a focus group) out of class. In relation to more narrowly targeted evaluation, the focus can be correspondingly sharper, as in the example below (Figure 9.2) of a questionnaire used during a micro-evaluation of a task. See also Appendix 2.2 and Wright (1987: 146–7).

Please answer these questions. There is no need to write your name.

1. How easily could you do this task?

   VERY   QUITE   ONLY WITH
   EASILY   EASILY   DIFFICULTY

2. How enjoyable did you find this task?

   VERY   QUITE   NOT
   ENJOYABLE   ENJOYABLE   ENJOYABLE

3. How much did this task help you to learn English?

   VERY   SOME   NOT VERY
   MUCH   MUCH

4. Can you write one thing you liked about the task?

   _____

5. Can you write one thing you did not like about the task?

   _____

Figure 9.2 Learner questionnaire (Ellis 1998: 235)

A very quick technique for collecting learner reactions concerning the interest and value of an activity is the rating slip illustrated in Figure 9.3, overleaf. This can be used to obtain feedback on any element of a lesson, for example a reading text, a discussion, a task. Learners first need to be told why they are being asked to evaluate the activity. The slips are then handed out, filled in immediately and collected. When students are used to the procedure, the whole process takes no more than a couple of minutes. Away from the hurly-burly of the classroom, the teacher adds all the ratings for 'value' together and subdivides the total by the number of respondents to give a mean score, repeating this process for 'interest'. If means fall below 3.5 on either measure, it is worth considering whether changes need to be made to the material itself or to the way in which it was handled. In smallish classes, means can, of course, be distorted in either direction by one or two individuals awarding very high or low ratings.

Please rank the task you have just completed. 5 = very valuable/very interesting; 1 = useless/boring. Give a brief explanation of any mark of 2 or 1.

	VALUE	INTEREST
I thought the task was . . .	5	5
	4	4
	3	3
	2	2
	1	1

because _____

_____

Figure 9.3 Rating slip (McGrath 1997)

If this procedure is used repeatedly, some learners might feel more involved – and be more willing to cooperate – if, once the calculations are complete, they are told what the group as a whole felt about the activity. In the case of a relatively unsuccessful activity, they might also be interested to know what changes the teacher intends to make as a result of the feedback, and be prepared to offer suggestions of their own. Such suggestions can be especially useful during the trialling of teacher-produced materials.

Learner diaries can also provide useful insights into individual reactions to materials. However, if these are to be more than just occasional or incidental, explicit prompts may be necessary, for example 'In your next entry, say something about . . .'. When learners are writing diaries regularly, they might from time to time be asked to share some of their reactions with classmates. One technique for doing this is the 'diary card'. Pieces of card are made available in two different colours (paper would be an alternative), with one colour (e.g. red) representing a negative feeling, and the other (yellow, say) a positive feeling. Each student chooses one comment from his or her diary, writes on a card of the appropriate colour and pins or sticks it up on the classroom wall, door or window. Students are encouraged to read their classmates' comments, during the lesson (the management of this may require some forethought) or during a break, and respond (agreeing, disagreeing, making different points) using white slips of paper and pinning/sticking these next to the cards to which they refer. The white slips may in turn attract further comments . . .

Student evaluation of materials might also take a less direct form. In the example below from a published coursebook, though learners' attitudes to the materials are elicited, they are also asked to evaluate their learning and their participation (not surprisingly the book is called *Team Player 4*). This is a regular feature of the book from which it is taken.

Figure 9.4 My learning diary (Spencer and Vaughan 1999)

Appendix 9 contains two further examples from published coursebooks *Copy Appendix 9* in which students are asked to evaluate their own abilities in relation to the performance objectives of the book. The first and earlier of these examples, which comes from an intermediate/upper-intermediate level coursebook, forms the basis of the penultimate lesson of the book. The implied message is that if students register a negative or doubtful rating against particular items, they should go back to the sections of the book where these are dealt with (hence, the lesson numbers on the right). This may seem perversely circular if the materials were the cause of the problem; however, class discussion after this activity would be a way of identifying the source of any problems (materials, learner, teaching) as well as establishing how widespread these are. The approach adopted in the second example, where the focus is on vocabulary, is similar, but this forms part of a regular end-of-unit check.

2.4 Collating data

guidance for your boss

Data collected by an individual teacher has a value for that individual; when confirmed by data on the use of the same materials by other staff, it takes on a very different status.

Since what is at stake is the management of learning within a particular section of the institution, the task of collating individual data sets is best handled by a coordinator (e.g. Head of Department, Course Director, Director of Studies). A summary can then be presented to a meeting of the teachers concerned for discussion.

2.5 Meetings

Teachers' meetings can be rather humdrum affairs in which nothing of real substance is discussed. And yet a weekly teachers' meeting would be an ideal forum for the discussion – perhaps in subgroups based on shared materials or classes – of materials evaluation in progress.

In institutions with a small language department, where teachers are using different coursebooks, the focus might be on features common to these books, such as the tasks accompanying written texts or the relevance of speaking activities, with each meeting examining a different feature (Rea-Dickens and Germaine 1992). This kind of shifting focus would be a way of ensuring coverage and depth. Extracts from instruments designed for pre-use materials evaluation might well be suitable for this purpose, with a little adaptation, perhaps (Rea-Dickens and Germaine 1992).

Task 9.2

1. Two possible foci for in-use evaluation suggested in the last paragraph are the tasks accompanying written texts and the relevance of speaking activities. List three further possible foci for in-use evaluation.

2. Choose one of these. Then devise a short list of questions (your own or adapted from a published instrument) to be used for structured observation and discussion.

Apart from their intended purpose – to monitor the effectiveness of the materials in use – such meetings would have a number of other benefits at both an individual and an institutional level. The opportunity to share ideas and supplementary materials, especially within a shared context, is highly valued by teachers, who spend much of their working lives 'alone' in a classroom –

an opportunity from which the experienced might gain as much as the inexperienced. Positive outcomes should also contribute to a cooperative and trusting atmosphere in which 'hidden needs and wants' (Masuhara 1988: 258) can be revealed. Teacher development groups (Head and Taylor 1997) have sprung from such beginnings. From the perspective of materials evaluation, however, one further likely effect should be noted. In the course of a detailed discussion of materials that have just been taught it quickly becomes apparent which assumptions about teaching and learning are shared, and this in turn provides a good basis for re-examination of the criteria used to select those materials.

Table 9.1, below, summarises the evaluation processes and techniques discussed thus far. All the techniques listed in Table 9.1 can also be used in the evaluation of teacher-produced materials, though – as with published materials – some will only be applicable where two or more teachers are using the same materials.

Table 9.1 Procedures and processes for in-use evaluation of materials

Stage	Evaluator	Procedure
in-use	teacher	• records of use • observation of learners
	observer	• observation of teacher and learners
	learners	• plenary questioning • focus group interview(s) • questionnaire • rating slips • diaries/diary cards • self-evaluation
	coordinator	• collation of data
	teachers' meeting	• exchange of experience and ideas

2.6 The value of in-use evaluation

Some of the benefits of in-use evaluation procedures of the type described above have already been referred to:

- Data is collected on the suitability or otherwise of the materials.
- Teachers are sensitised to learners' reactions to the materials.
- The opportunities for sharing and discussion generated by this kind of evaluation are valued by staff.

The conclusion to Ellis' (1997) paper on micro-evaluation makes two further points:

- Teachers think about evaluation as they plan lessons.
- Adopting a formalised procedure necessitates precise thinking about what and how.

Ellis also speculates that micro-evaluation may be an easier way in to action research (and the kind of reflection that is believed to be beneficial for teacher development) than identifying a 'problem'; and, more generally, and following Clarke (1994: 23), that the careful scrutiny by teachers of events in their own classrooms enables them to 'validate' their experience and leads to professional empowerment.

3 IN-USE EVALUATION OF TEACHER-PRODUCED MATERIALS

The context for which materials have been produced will normally affect how systematically in-use evaluation is carried out. For instance, in many situations, teachers produce materials just for use with their own classes. What they discover about the strengths and weaknesses of the materials through trying them out will usually be incidental rather than planned, and the materials will only be revised if this seems to be essential (for instance, because the same materials are to be used with another class) and time is available. When materials are being prepared for internal institution-wide use, on the other hand, many of the points made in the previous section will be relevant. Data is needed. This can come from learners and teachers using the material and from an observer; a similar response (positive and negative) from multiple users (or from the triangulation of learners, teacher and observer) will provide a sounder basis for judgement than a single-class trial, especially when the teacher in the latter is also the materials designer.

3.1 The trialling of materials intended for publication and materials for internal use

When it comes to trialling, there are at least three important differences between materials intended for publication and materials for internal use. First, there is the closeness of contact between the teacher/materials designers and the learners (and perhaps other teachers) for whom the materials are intended (which may lead materials designers to think they know what is needed). Second, teachers/materials designers potentially have much greater flexibility to make changes to the materials (which means that it is perhaps less important to get them 'right' first time). A further major difference will be the time and resources available; publication can involve a significant investment for the publisher, and many publishers have now understood that careful piloting (at least of major coursebook series) makes sound financial sense. Although the piloting of materials intended for publication lies outside the scope of this chapter, there are a number of papers that touch on this which are potentially relevant to teachers preparing materials for use within their own institutions.

One of the implicit recommendations that comes through such papers is that it is desirable to prepare a sample of the material, for example a prototype unit, before embarking on the preparation of a complete first draft (Rajan 1995, Richards 1995). This is typically the approach followed by would-be authors when they first submit their work to a publisher. The prototype materials then need to be field-tested (piloted). One of the general questions to which such piloting should provide an answer is the following: 'Do they [the materials] work successfully when they are taught by teachers who were not involved in the process of developing them?' (Richards 1995: 109). This question is perhaps particularly relevant in the case of ESP materials, where student (self-perceived) needs and teachers' knowledge of the specialist area are important considerations, and where the results of piloting may prompt reconsideration of a preliminary needs analysis or of the use made of subject specialists (Balarbar 1995). It will also be a relevant question when materials are being prepared for institution-wide use. For Rajan (1995: 203), who was developing English literacy and oracy materials for adult workers in Singapore, key questions were whether:

- situations and activities were appropriate and interesting to the learner
- the language used was too easy or too difficult or just right
- explanations in the mother tongue in the video, audio and print materials were adequate
- the assumed time-frame for the completion of activities was realistic.

As will be clear from the above set of questions, specific categories of material will prompt specific questions, but key questions should obviously relate to learner response (e.g. clarity, interest, value, level, support) and teacher response (e.g. appropriateness, ease of use, support, time needed). While learners and teachers thus have key feedback roles, an observer may be able not only to corroborate the feedback from these sources but also give a richer, more descriptive account of how the materials were used (e.g. exploited, adapted) and this may in turn suggest possible directions for further development.

Readers with an interest in piloting procedures are referred to Richards (1995) and Barnard and Randall (1995). Richards describes the stages of a textbook writing project in which a sample unit was piloted and expert reviews commissioned of the first draft of the first book; Appendix 5 of his paper illustrates the extent of the revisions made to the first version. Barnard and Randall compare approaches to the piloting of ELT textbooks in Oman at two different points in time; the conclusions they draw concerning the most effective methods might well be relevant for institutional materials trialling. Donovan (1998) offers a publisher's perspective.

3.2 Revision

For a writer, revision can mean one of three things: the self-directed redrafting familiar to anyone who cares about form, shape and effect; the modifications prompted by armchair feedback from others, including colleagues, co-authors, publisher's readers and editors; and the (often more radical) rewriting that follows the trialling of the materials. In this section we concentrate on the latter, making a distinction between review (an evaluation process) and revision (a design process). (For insights into the creative process itself, and relations with others, see, for example, Prowse 1998, and papers in Hidalgo et al. 1995.)

3.2.1 A search for principles

Lynch (1996) presents a detailed discussion of changes made over a ten-year period to an intensive university pre-sessional programme in English for Academic Purposes. The published text which initially formed the core of the programme was first supplemented, and then replaced (by another published text); finally, the course team developed their own materials. Preparing to revise these following a period of use, Lynch looked around for help. He observes:

> 'Revision' does not feature at all in the indexes of any of the most obvious EFL sources (Dubin and Olshtain 1986, Hutchinson and Waters 1987, Yalden 1987, Nunan 1989, Rea-Dickens and Germaine 1992). The verb 'revise' does occur in the text of several books, although I notice that Breen and Candlin, for example, preferred to use the verb 'refine'. Where it *is* used, 'revise' appears without any accompanying discussion of the precise process involved. In general, the implication of commentaries on the revision process amounts to this: revision – and other aspects of evaluation – is a matter of judgement.
>
> (Lynch 1996: 27)

Lacking more precise guidance, Lynch drew on a number of sources to create his own model of the revision process (see Figure 9.5, below). He comments on this:

> The starting point is Breen's (1989) division of evaluation into three stages: workplan, process and outcome. Outcome data would include such things as test scores and student reports. The process perspective would bring in insights from the 'course-in-action', which Johnson and Johnson (1970) characterise under five headings: clarity, level, action, attitude and time. Of

these, 'action' is glossed by Breen and Candlin (1987) in terms of five or six questions – 'Who?', 'What?', 'How?' and so on. So using the two sets of process and outcome data – noting that the term 'data' here covers not just empirical facts but also individual responses and attitudes – the course designer makes decisions about revision. If change is in fact required, then the revision options boil down to adding, deleting, moving or modifying (Nathenson and Henderson 1980).

(Lynch 1996: 33)

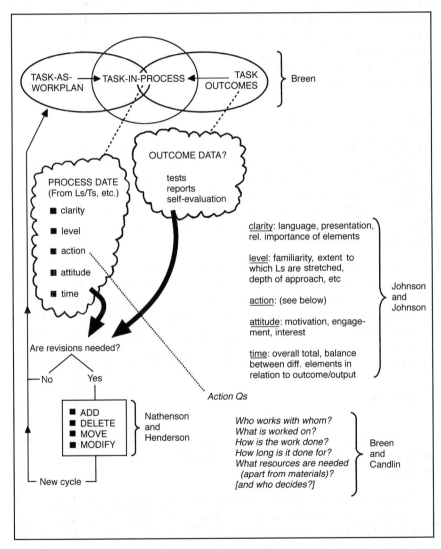

Figure 9.5 Influences on revision (Lynch 1996: 32)

Working through the revision process brought him to the following conclusion:

> I hoped that the literature on materials evaluation and design would provide guidance as to how to make revision decisions more systematic – though not automatic. The lesson that I draw from reflecting on the evolution of Course 3 is that the revision process does demand what Prabhu called 'the fresh exercise of discretion and decision' (1987: 102); the process can never be completely systematized, in the sense of being reduced to a straightforward flowchart or, looking ahead, to an expert system. There will always be a need for judgement and interpretation, no matter how 'hard' the information we are able to gather. For that reason I have drawn deliberately woolly clouds around the process and outcome data.
>
> (Lynch 1996: 34)

What is helpful about Lynch's proposal is that, like that of Ellis (1998) discussed earlier in this chapter, it brings together both process and outcome data and specifies the nature and (in the case of process data) the possible foci of this. It thus goes a long way towards answering the question: 'How can I know whether the materials are satisfactory?' Both forms of data will also shed light on specific features that may warrant revision.

3.2.2 The diagnosis of weakness

Jolly and Bolitho (1998), who are also concerned with revision, relate the diagnosis of weaknesses in teacher-produced material to specific steps in the design process. Chapter 5 reproduced a diagram (Figure 5.3) from their paper which represents in their words a 'simple', and indeed 'simplified', uni-directional set of steps that a materials writer is likely to go through. Pointing out that though this may reflect what occurs when one is writing for publication, they argue that materials writing should actually be a 'dynamic and self-adjusting process'. It is the failure to understand that materials need to be 'tuned', they suggest, that explains why so many materials 'lack that final touch of excellence' (p. 96). In Figure 9.6, p. 195, an elaborated version of Figure 5.3, there is an additional step in the downward sequence that is responsible for keeping the whole system in motion. This trigger is evaluation. On the basis of his or her evaluation or learner feedback, the teacher reconsiders any one of the previous steps and makes adjustments to the materials as they are being used or after the event. And the process is potentially cyclical.

The focus in this diagram on the process by which the materials were conceived provides us with a rather different perspective on revision. One possible implication of the feedback loops in the diagram is that if teacher-produced materials do not work as well as expected, we can attempt to locate the source of the problem by retracing our steps up the action sequence. Thus, we might first consider what happened at the stage the learners used the materials. Were the materials used as intended? If so, what happened that was unexpected? What, according to the teacher or learners, was the problem? (Note that what the teacher or learners point to may only be a symptom of the real problem – see K. Richards 1995.) Answers to such questions at the first stage may indicate that we need to give further thought to earlier steps in the design sequence – the pedagogical realisation, for example, or the initial analysis of need. Something approximating to this approach is exemplified in Jolly and Bolitho's paper, where two sets of materials are evaluated in terms of the various stages in the diagram, though not in sequence. (Appendix 5.2 contains a worksheet which formed part of these materials.)

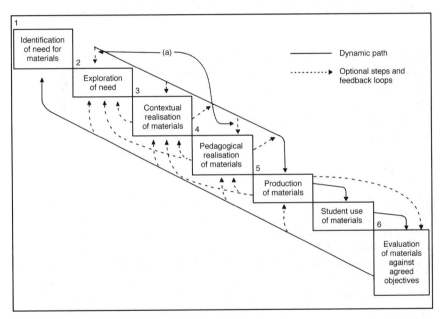

Figure 9.6 A teacher's path through the production of new or adapted materials (Jolly and Bolitho 1998: 98)

Task 9.3

1. Before reading on, turn to Appendix 5.2 and evaluate the worksheet. Can you predict any problems?

2. How would you tackle these problems?

Now read on ... Jolly and Bolitho's evaluation is shown in Figure 9.7, over-leaf.

| EVALUATION | Student comments on difficulties with worksheet, e.g. |

1. 'In Step one there is a fact and a hypothesis in the sentences. It's confusing.' [This sent the teacher back to 'Pedagogical Realisation' and led to the changed instructions and underlinings in Version 2.]*

2. 'Can't the "if" sentences also be positive, do they only express regret?' [This student had noticed an important oversight which took the teacher back to the exploration stage and led to the inclusion of two further examples in Step two of the revised version of the worksheet.]

3. Teacher noted problems with 'I wish you would finish . . .' vs. 'I wish you had finished . . .' [Further exploration led the teacher to production of follow-up worksheet on 'possible vs. impossible wishes'.]

4. The class liked Step three and enjoyed making up similar sentences about other members of the group.

* Space did not permit the inclusion of Version 2, the revised worksheet.

Figure 9.7 Evaluation of worksheet from Appendix 5.2 (Jolly and Bolitho, 1998: 99–100)

3.3 Problems

One of the problems noted by Lynch is that the literature provides no explicit principles on which revision can be based. Lynch's own proposal, Jolly and Bolitho's design and evaluation model, and Ellis' evaluation framework are helpful in this respect in that each suggests a set of organised, ordered procedures which can be justified theoretically and/or empirically. However, one of the tactics on which this or any evaluation depends – to obtain as much feedback as possible from others – may backfire if this results in conflicting views. How is one to prioritise the feedback? Whose view is the more important? Tickoo (1995), who gives a fascinating account of the trials of piloting a textbook series for younger learners in India, notes that some writers in the writing team wanted to disregard views which conflicted with their own: 'responding to the views of untrained teachers and first generation readers would amount to unprincipled and unacceptable compromises' (p. 36). The textbook team also found themselves in conflict with the press and public opinion over the role of a textbook: the team wished to present Indian society as they saw it; others thought they should depict 'what should be', that is, a more desirable society. In an institutional context, the question might present itself as an opposition between the views of learners and teachers, between subgroups of learners or, as in the Tickoo example, between subgroups of teachers.

All writers know that it is difficult to make cuts in material that they have painstakingly produced. There may even be a proportional relationship between the pain of production and the reluctance to jettison. We have to be able to separate the two, of course, and we have to be capable of reviewing the evidence objectively. Jolly and Bolitho (1998), who offer advice on the contents of 'a materials writer's kitbag', include the following: 'phials containing small doses of courage and honesty enabling writer to throw away materials that do not work or cease to enchant' (p. 115).

A key question in all this is: 'When to stop revising?' At what point does one decide to settle for what one has and stop tinkering? A commercial publisher might well want to draw the line after just one round of piloting if this has been reasonably successful (but what are the criteria for determining what 'reasonably successful' means?). In an institutional context, teachers who are asked to trial successive versions of the material may eventually lose patience (and if the materials are still unsatisfactory, even press for their abandonment); individual teachers trialling their own materials can obviously go on refining for as long as they have interest and time.

Ultimately, there is probably no answer to dilemmas such as these. Lynch (1996), following Prabhu (1987), concluded that revision is basically a matter of judgement. This seems a wholly logical conclusion if we recognise that, as discussed above, revision can be divided into two stages. Stage one might more accurately be called evaluation or *review*. If this is positive, no further action is taken; if it is not, the decision may be taken to proceed to stage two and make certain changes (i.e. *revise*). Stage two, it should be noted, involves not only potentially simple decisions such as (following Nathensen and Henderson 1980) deleting or moving but also the more complex operations of adding and modifying – in other words, creating and crafting. Materials *writing*, which is what is involved at this second stage in the revision process, is a craft (Dubin 1995) and, as such, can be guided but probably not bound by principles.

Principles are, however, necessary in relation to the use within institutions of materials prepared by other teachers. In part, this is a matter of record-keeping, but agreement on what is and is not permissible is also important. In situations where it is common practice for teacher-produced (in-house) materials to be shared (Block 1991), it is likely that individual teachers will want to make small changes even before re-using the material produced by a colleague. In these situations, certain groundrules are desirable: for example (1) each version of the material carries the name of its originator, the date when it was produced, and the learners with whom it was used; (2) no version of the material is destroyed without the consent of its originator; (3) a careful record is kept of how the material was used and with what effect. In time, the decision may be taken to replace all earlier versions with a single version with which everyone is content, but this should be by consensus.

4 POST-USE EVALUATION

If in-use evaluation has been carried out seriously, it will provide two enormously valuable inputs to post-use evaluation. First, there is the data that has been generated, which will clearly indicate the extent to which the materials have been used in their original form and how much has been rejected. Second, and probably more important, the process of data-gathering (and discussion, if more than one teacher has been involved) will have had the effect of sharpening and organising the teacher-user's (or users') awareness of the strengths and weaknesses of the materials. Doubts which started to surface will have either disappeared or been strengthened to the point that they can now be articulated and supported with evidence.

As indicated in the previous section, however, the information that comes out of in-use evaluation will relate to such questions as interest, linguistic level, cognitive level and sufficiency of practice material. What is now needed is information on cumulative effects. After all, the materials were selected or designed in order to aid learners to achieve particular learning outcomes.

4.1 Evaluating outcomes

Seen in a narrow sense, the evaluation of outcomes is fraught with difficulty during both in- and post-use evaluation. As Tomlinson (1999) notes, students' ability to produce an item that has only just been taught or their failure to produce the same item can be equally misleading. In the first case, they may be retrieving the item from short-term memory; in the second, they may simply need more time to 'digest' what has been taught. Instances of students being able to use a language correctly in very controlled situations, such as an oral drill or a grammar exercise, yet failing to use the item correctly in free conversation are a common phenomenon. (Ellis' (1998) suggestion that one measure of outcomes might be the learner's ability to transfer the knowledge/skill acquired to a parallel situation without continuing support would be one way of building in this kind of check.)

We could try to compare the results in tests or examinations of the current cohort of students with those (in a previous year or a parallel class) taught using other materials. Comparisons of this kind are, however, notably unreliable (*pace* Tomlinson 1998e: 263) since so many variables are involved.

Task 9.4

1. What are the variables that would make the results obtained in such a comparison unreliable?

2. Are there any ways of controlling these?

Classrooms are not laboratories. Learners have lives outside classrooms, lives that interact in different ways with what is taught in the classroom, reinforcing that learning (a study group, the help of a parent, sibling, private tutor), supplementing it (interaction with the language outside the classroom) or inhibiting it (e.g. commitments that limit the time available for review – and therefore have a knock-on effect on understanding and long-term retention). In contexts where learners have easy access to English outside the classroom it will be difficult to separate classroom effects from out-of-class exposure. Moreover, learners differ in a great many ways. Teachers and teaching styles also differ (Katz 1996), and even if two classes using different materials were taught by the same teacher, the teacher's own preferences might lean towards one set of materials rather than the other. The very fact that they were, unusually, in the spotlight might well affect the attitudes of learners and teacher.

Problems such as these notwithstanding, it is possible to chart specific learning gains of individuals and a whole class by comparing recorded (spoken or written) instances of use at different points in time. Foci might include: phoneme acquisition; structural accuracy or range; lexical repertoire; length or complexity of sentences; spoken or written fluency (measured quantitatively). Analysis of this kind of data is likely to indicate that, contrary to one's impressionistic judgements, and allowing for normal backsliding, there have been developmental gains.

Other kinds of learning may also be assessable, if not measurable. The increasing self-confidence that is one result of the kinds of practice opportunities offered by a coursebook may be a matter of self-report but are also observable in such changes of behaviour as a greater willingness to ask questions or take turns in group discussion, and lessening dependence on notes during oral presentation. Learners may also report an increased interest in language learning, and this may manifest itself in a change of attitude in class (and less frequent absence, perhaps). 'Softer' measures such as these, where the teacher's own enthusiasm for the materials may have as much an effect as the materials themselves, are clearly not in themselves evidence for or against the superiority of one coursebook (or set of teacher-produced materials) over another. Taken cumulatively, however, they represent a strong argument for the greater suitability of X rather than Y.

As has been indicated at several points in this book, learners' views on the materials they have been using need to be taken seriously. A number of suggestions for how this might be done in relation to self-access materials were made in Chapter 7 and an example given earlier in this chapter of a coursebook which invites learners to comment on the materials they are using at regular intervals. What other approaches are there to the elicitation of learner feedback that would not only reveal their views of the specific materials they have been using but would also inform the selection of future materials by giving some insight into their priorities?

Though a questionnaire or plenary discussion would be obvious elicitation techniques, activities which combine individual commitment (i.e. personal evaluation) with the possibility of group interaction might be preferable.

Having an opportunity to hear others' views has the dual advantage that it is a possible corrective to the adoption of over-hasty and therefore unthinking positions; the requirement to justify one's views in the face of a challenge can also lead to a better thought-through rationale for the position one has adopted. One technique which could be used for this purpose is the pyramid activity. Pyramid activities can be organised in different ways, but if the starting instructions at the first (individual) stage of a pyramid discussion were, for example:

- List up to 3 things that *you liked* about the book.
- List up to 3 things that you *didn't like* about the book.
- List up to 3 reasons why you thought the book was *useful*.

and these instructions remained unchanged throughout pair and group stages so that the ideas brought to each stage had to be whittled down to just three, this could lead to extremely valuable insights not just into learners' views of the particular materials they have been using but also into the criteria by which they make judgements *and how they prioritise these criteria*. This would be yet another potential measure of the appropriateness of the criteria used to select the materials.

In the Delphi technique (as described by Weir and Roberts (1994)), there are also a number of stages. (1) Individuals first write down their views in response to a specific prompt (which in this case might be, for instance, 'What do you want from a textbook? List the things that are important to you.'). (2) The lists are collected, summarised, and recirculated. (3) Each individual then ranks each of the items on the cumulative list according to his or her own priorities. (4) The lists are collected again, and the rankings collated to provide a prioritised collective view. (5) Individuals are given a copy, together with a record of their own rankings, and asked if they wish to modify these. Explanations are encouraged in the event of anyone wishing to maintain a divergent stance. As Weir and Roberts note, the technique is intended to establish consensus within a group, and the written format permits this consensus to be reached even without the members of the group being present in the same room. In a classroom context, it would of course be possible for the whole procedure to be conducted orally (perhaps after the first stage, to ensure individual commitment as far as possible) and to use the board to record the responses. If, as in this case, the objective is merely to elicit views and the extent to which these are representative of the class as a whole, the final stage of asking learners to reconsider their rankings can also be skipped.

Table 9.2, below, summarises the procedures suggested in this section for post-use materials evaluation, and incorporates processes and procedures discussed in relation to in-use evaluation that would also be applicable to this stage.

Table 9.2 Procedures and processes for post-use evaluation of materials

Stage	Evaluator	Procedure
post-use	teacher	• assessment of measurable learning gains • use of 'softer' measures, such as gains in confidence or interest
	learners	• plenary discussion (including pyramid activities and Delphi technique) • focus group interview(s) • questionnaire • diaries • self-evaluation
	coordinator	• collation of data
	teachers' meeting	• discussion of collated data on in-course use and effects • re-examination of procedures and criteria for textbook selection

4.2 Evaluation of the materials selection procedures

From the perspective taken here, the central questions to which in-use and post-use evaluation can provide answers are the following:

- How suitable are the materials?
- How good were the selection procedures?

The two questions are separable in that, though the materials may have turned out to be generally suitable, the nature of that suitability and/or certain key deficiencies were not identified during the selection process.

Key elements in the selection process, though not the only ones, are the criteria used and the format adopted. One simple way of evaluating the instrument used for selection would be to use it again, perhaps in an adapted form, to check whether the same results are obtained following experience. Figure 9.8a, overleaf, contains *edited* sections from a published checklist; Figure 9.8b shows the further simple adaptations needed to make this suitable for post-use evaluation.

Other aspects of the process would include the number of people involved and the steps taken to ensure that the criteria were applied consistently. One of the key tasks following post-use evaluation is therefore to re-examine the selection procedures to consider whether any modifications are necessary. If not, or when these modifications have been made, the circle is closed – temporarily; for when there is a change in one or more of the key features of the teaching–learning environment, re-evaluation will be needed.

Aims and approaches	
❑ Is the coursebook suited to the learning/teaching situation?	❑ Was the coursebook suited to the learning/teaching situation?
❑ How comprehensive is the coursebook?	❑ How comprehensive was the coursebook?
Does it cover most or all of what is needed?	Did it cover most or all of what is needed/
Is it a good resource for students and teachers?	Was it a good resource for students and teachers?
❑ Is the coursebook flexible?	❑ Was the coursebook flexible?
Does it allow different teaching and learning styles?	Did it allow different teaching and learning styles?
Design and organisation	
❑ Is the grading and progression suitable for the learners?	❑ Was the grading and progression suitable for the learners?
Does it allow them to complete the work needed to meet any external syllabus requirements.	Did it allow them to complete the work needed to meet any external syllabus requirements?
❑ Is there adequate recycling and revision?	❑ Was there adequate recycling and revision?
❑ Is it easy to find your way around the textbook?	❑ Was it easy to find your way around the textbook?
Is the layout clear?	Was the layout clear?

Figure 9.8a: Cunningsworth (1995: 3, edited)   Figure 9.8b: adapted version

End-of-course evaluation (of learners or of a course itself) tends to be seen as the end of the affair. The attention of teachers and administrators then turns to holidays or, only too often, preparations for the next course without any pause for reflection. And yet in some ways the period immediately after post-course (or in this case, post-use) evaluation is the key stage, the point at which action needs to be taken to make the kinds of changes which – on the basis of the evidence – appear to be desirable. Elsewhere in this book reference has been made to the importance of institutional support. This applies particularly to the facilitation of in-use and post-use evaluation, both of which require advance planning and time.

5 SUMMARY

This chapter has reiterated the need to see the evaluation of published materials as a process that continues beyond the stage of initial selection. In-use evaluation requires systematic record-keeping, and, if more than one teacher is using the same material, the regular sharing of experiences. Post-use evaluation necessitates the consideration of effects. Learners can be involved in both stages. The results of this process will shed light not only on the suitability of the materials but also the suitability of the criteria used in their selection.

The chapter has also drawn attention to the importance of evaluating teacher-produced materials and the relative paucity of guidance concerning the revision of these. It has suggested that revision may be thought of as a two-stage process, the first stage in which is evaluative and can be relatively systematic, whereas the second (design) stage may rest more on personal judgement.

Chapter 10

Materials and . . .

This chapter is rather different from those that have preceded it. It is concerned with the relationship between materials and . . .

- learning
- ideology
- culture
- syllabus
- method
- research.

The intention is to provide an opportunity for consideration of a number of special topics that could not easily be incorporated within the framework adopted for the previous chapters, but also, and this is much more important, to illustrate the absolute centrality of materials in language education. In formal (e.g. state-school) systems, materials, mediated by teachers, are a key link in the externally-determined design chain which potentially runs from curriculum to syllabus and leads to public examinations. In any language-learning setting, materials – published, teacher-produced or learner-produced – provide much of the content of the teaching–learning encounter. They are an in-class resource for learners and teachers – what learners learn with, and an out-of-class resource for learners – what they learn from. Published textbooks also link teachers and learners to the outside world. They are a means to access not only the target language and possibly its culture(s) but also the accumulated knowledge and experience – of language, learning, learners, teaching and teachers – of those involved in making the books, all of whom have striven to produce materials that are perceived as relevant, interesting and useful. It is this centrality which argues strongly for the inclusion of a 'materials' component in pre-service and in-service teacher education programmes. The same centrality makes the study of language learning–teaching materials, and their development, classroom use and evaluation, not only a legitimate but also a hugely important focus of research for teachers and teacher educators.

1 MATERIALS AND LEARNING

Learners can learn more than language from the materials used in language-learning classes. What is learnt – or there to be learnt – is most obviously embodied in the materials as content, but certain other types of learning may also result. Some of these outcomes will be intended and positive; others may be negative. A particularly useful introductory reading on this topic is Littlejohn and Windeatt (1989).

1.1 Learning from content

In the global 'structural' (audiolingual) textbooks of the late 1960s and early 1970s, lessons typically began with specially written dialogues and stories about fictional people. While these texts were sometimes interesting and occasionally amusing, for the most part they were content-less. They were no more than *language*-teaching texts. In some countries, however, there were, and still are, locally produced textbooks containing texts – such as literary extracts and historic speeches, familiar tales, and stories about local heroes – which have clearly been selected for their content. The specific reasons for the inclusion of particular texts or text-types may be as varied as the texts themselves: for instance, 'great literature' and speeches may be justified on cultural or inspirational grounds while local content can offer some security in a sea of unfamiliar language and reinforce a sense of cultural identity. Nowadays, of course, when there is so much emphasis on the use of authentic texts, one of the key criteria for the choice of one text rather than another is its intrinsic interest, and one of the features that makes a text potentially interesting is its content, that is, the fact that it is informative.

Cook (1983, cited in Littlejohn and Windeatt 1989: 157) lists six forms of 'real content' in materials: (1) content from another academic (school) subject; (2) student-contributed content (see Chapter 8), which would presumably include students talking about themselves; (3) the language itself, i.e. as an object of analysis; (4) literature; (5) culture; (6) 'interesting facts'. Littlejohn and Windeatt suggest two further forms of 'carrier content': (7) learning to learn (see below) and (8) specialist (i.e. ESP) material in a student's own discipline.

1.2 Learning from process

Learners learn not only from what they read (or hear), they also learn from interaction with others and from the process of carrying out tasks. This learning goes beyond the merely linguistic (e.g. negotiating meaning; arguing a point of view). One of the arguments for group tasks is that they encourage socialisation and teamwork; they also make possible learning by observation of others. Moreover, specific types of task can provide practice in such 'transferrable skills' as, for example, collecting and classifying information, reasoning, critical thinking, creativity and problem-solving.

Littlejohn and Windeatt's (1989) incisive discussion of the 'hidden curriculum' in language-learning materials draws attention to a number of other less benign possible results of the classroom procedures embedded in materials. One of these has to do with power relations in the classroom, as reflected in a choral substitution drill:

> [P]upils will hear the 'model sentence' and each substitution somewhere between 15 to 20 times, depending on the way the class is grouped . . . For the pupils, the experience of simply repeating sentences after the teacher's prompts would appear to demonstrate clearly that their role in the classroom is largely a powerless one in which they mechanically follow instructions. The fact that this is done in chorus adds the sense of anonymity and being 'one of the mass' upon which much social control – inside and outside the classroom – seems to rest.
>
> (Littlejohn and Windeatt 1989: 167)

Now while this could be dismissed as a rather jaundiced view of a single procedure which has certain (limited) linguistic and psychological justifications, other examples are more convincing. For instance, their analysis of one set of materials leads to the following conclusions:

> At its simplest level, the picture that may be presented by the above sequence of sections is that learning English involves reading texts in detail, attending to items of vocabulary, rules of grammar and punctuation, and writing isolated sentences. At a deeper level, however, it can be seen that each time the learners are required to do something, the activity involves closely following a model or referring back to a text. One can say, therefore, that an underlying message being transmitted to the learners is that to learn English one must complete a series of short, controlled exercises that require reproduction of already presented linguistic facts with little in the way of personal creativity, expression or interpretation.
>
> (p. 163)

Commenting on a functionally-oriented set of materials, they suggest that the absence of any explicit reference to grammar, vocabulary and punctuation may give learners the impression that 'learning English essentially involves learning fixed phrases into which one can slot different items . . . The material may distinguish itself from the first course book by its emphasis on pairwork throughout, but underlying the series of exercises we have a similar view of language learning' (ibid.).

They conclude: 'Depending on the prior experience of the individual learner, the view of language learning projected by material can be of central importance since it may shape learners' perceptions of their own abilities and of the steps they need to take to progress further' (p. 164).

1.3 Learning to learn

Many coursebooks these days include specific sections designed to raise learners' awareness of what they can do to become more effective learners. Such sections may take the form of suggestions on how to organise one's learning; they may encourage self-assessment (e.g. of progress, learning difficulties or learning preferences) or reflection on attitudes (see Appendix 9). Alternatively, this 'teaching' may be much less explicit and be woven into tasks. One assumption behind skimming and scanning activities, for instance, is that learners who are accustomed to reading word by word and sentence by sentence will eventually learn to adjust their reading strategy to their reading purpose.

1.4 Attitudes and values

Littlejohn and Windeatt' s examples of how attitudes and values can be represented in materials include the following:

1. A coursebook contains hundreds of photographs of people in different roles. Only two of these photographs are of black people. One is a muscular athlete and the other a manual worker.
2. In the first 25 pages of another coursebook there are more than 30 references to smoking and drinking.

What we have here are not a couple of isolated instances but undeniable *patterns*, reinforcing a stereotype in the first example and apparently endorsing certain behaviours in the second. As evidence that this might have an effect, Littlejohn and Windeatt refer to a survey of studies on sexism in materials by Porreca (1984: 172):

> In one study, Jenkins (cited in Nilsen 1977) found a direct correlation between the length of time spent using Alpha One Reading Program (which apparently portrayed girls as 'stupid, dependent, whining and tearful' and boys as 'active and aggressive') and the degree to which pupils' attitudes matched those in the materials.

To judge only from the few details provided of the study, learners' age might have been one factor in their susceptibility.

Drawing on the educational literature on outcomes, Littlejohn and Windeatt make a distinction between referential learning (i.e. learning from content) and experiential learning (learning through doing), suggesting that of the two experiential learning may exert a more powerful influence. If this is the case, concerns about content in materials may be a little exaggerated. Littlejohn and Windeatt' s own conclusion is as follows:

> In order to begin to argue that such features of materials may bring about particular kinds of learning outcomes ... one needs to show that specific values or attitudes are *pervasive* throughout the text (Gordon, 1984) ... Without this evidence, one may simply object to the inclusion of certain items on the grounds that they offend our moral sensibilities.
>
> (p. 173; original emphasis)

Task 10.1

1. Do you think it is important that materials should offer opportunities for learning more than language? Can you think of any other forms of positive non-linguistic learning that might result from working with published materials? Select a lesson in the coursebook you are using or any other coursebook that is available. Is there any evidence that the author intended to provide for the learning of more than just language? If not, and if you are in favour of material serving more than one learning purpose, how could you adapt the lesson so that it can fulfil more purposes?

2. Do you agree with the view that experiential learning is likely to have a more powerful effect than referential learning, and that referential learning would only have any effect if it pervaded the materials? Do you have any evidence to support your view?

2 MATERIALS AND IDEOLOGY

Ideology, like culture, can be built into materials by design, as when a country wishes to promote a particular set of national values. It may also be less conscious, but no less manifest, in the nature of the reality depicted visually and verbally in materials, in the relationships and roles envisaged for teacher and learner, and perhaps most subtly in the language selected for inclusion.

The following quotations indicate some of the concerns that have been expressed. Dendrinos's (1992) book on *The EFL Textbook and Ideology* draws attention to the extent that ideological positions, conscious or unconscious, underlie every aspect of textbook writing and design:

> [T]he EFL textbook ... will contain material whose purpose will be the linguistic acculturation of learners and therefore their subjugation to social conventions. (p. 152)

Themes, topics and titles of units, and how these are articulated, are in themselves revealing in relation to the social reality to be constructed for textbook users. (p. 175)

[P]ictures, illustrations, photographs, etc. are social constructs and they ideologically position their addressees towards realities. (p. 165)

[T]he selection of language functions to be transmitted and acquired is arbitrarily and ideologically loaded. (p. 165)

[. . . and this selection will] contribute to the development of different conceptions of social reality and determine how the pupil as a social and institutional subject will interact with that reality. (p. 170)

Littlejohn and Windeatt's discussion of values and attitudes has been referred to in the section on 'Materials and learning'. In a later paper, Littlejohn (1997) turns his attention to 'ideological encodings' in self-access tasks. Taking as a reference point Lum and Brown's (1994) list of twenty exercise/activity-types, he analyses these with respect to the role that they imply for the learner, using three questions for this purpose:

1. What role in the discourse is proposed for the learner: initiate, respond or none?
2. What mental operation is to be engaged?
3. Where does the content for the task come from? From within the task itself, from the teacher or from the students?

(Littlejohn 1997: 186)

His conclusions are: (1) with one or two exceptions, the exercises offer very little scope for learners to initiate, that is, to use their own words; (2) only a fairly narrow range of mainly low-level mental processes is involved; (3) in most cases, there is no opportunity for learners to be creative, that is, to express their own ideas. This leads him to the paradox that 'in ideological terms, there is, thus, a clear tension apparent here in the ostensible aim in the provision of self-access facilities and its realization in practice' (Littlejohn 1997: 188).

So how might a teacher respond to the concerns expressed above? In relation to the problem of self-access tasks, Littlejohn suggests a number of changes in the way self-access is organised that would give the learner more freedom. These include a shift in activity-types towards activities which encourage learner initiation and creativity; the use of 'example' answers rather than keys; the possibility of peer feedback; and involving learners in the preparation of exercises (as suggested in Chapter 7). (For further suggestions and examples of alternative exercise-types, see Tomlinson 1998f.)

As for the values and attitudes represented in materials, Littlejohn and Windeatt (1989) offer the interesting idea that materials might themselves be made an object of 'critical focus' (p. 175). Learners might, for instance, be encouraged to comment on the attitudes or values that seem to lie behind the selection of texts, topics or visuals or, more broadly, on the way in which the materials influence what they do in the classroom.

For Dendrinos, the questions are linguistic and the answers lie in linguistic research:

> Questions . . . which could serve as a point of departure for the investigation of one or more textbooks are questions such as: what categories of verbs (mental, action, feeling, process verbs) are selected to define and delimit the behaviours, attitudes, feelings, relationships of the people presented in the textbook? What nouns and adjectives are selected to describe people as institutional subjects (as men and women, parents and children, employers and employees, teachers and pupils, etc?). What type of comparative/contrastive statements are made in relation to what, and which are the entities being compared and ultimately favoured? In what kind of communicative encounters are strongly or weakly directive statements made and who uses what type of modalized statements? For what communicative purposes are transitives used instead of intransitives and vice-versa, and in what circumstances are agent-focusing mechanisms used or avoided?
>
> (Dendrinos 1992: 181–2)

Questions such as these, she hopes, will 'serve as stimuli for those responsible for the evaluation of textbooks to assess them not only as teaching aids but also as media for pupil pedagogization' (p. 182).

Task 10.2

1. Do you feel that Dendrinos' concerns are justified? Choose a textbook, one that you use normally or whatever is available. Examine it for evidence to support or counter her comments.

2. What do you think of the suggestion that materials might be made an object of critical focus? Look through a textbook for one or more features on which you would like learners to reflect critically. Discuss these with your colleagues.

3 MATERIALS AND CULTURE

It has been suggested that knowing a language is inseparable from understanding the culture in which the language is spoken – that is, that without cultural knowledge of fairly specific kinds, one cannot fully understand what is said or written (Brown 1990b). This view raises a number of issues in relation to the selection and development of materials:

- what one means by 'culture' and 'cultural knowledge';
- the extent to which it is possible to generalise about the culture of, say, a number of countries in which the target language is spoken;
- what cultural knowledge is likely to be needed by a particular category of students in a particular context.

Faced with the challenge of designing an English course for Moroccan secondary schools, where English is a second foreign language and studied only in the final three years, Adaskou, Britten and Fahsi (1990: 3–4) were obliged to confront all these issues. They distinguish between four senses of culture:

1. The aesthetic: 'Culture with a capital C: the media, the cinema, music (whether serious or popular) and, above all, literature'.
2. The sociological: 'Culture with a small c: the organisation and nature of family, of home life, of interpersonal relations, material conditions, work and leisure, customs and institutions'.
3. The semantic: 'The conceptual system embodied in the language... Many semantic areas (e.g. food, clothes, institutions) are culturally distinctive because they relate to a particular way of life.'
4. The pragmatic (or sociolinguistic): 'The background knowledge, social skills, and paralinguistic skills that, in addition to mastery of the language code, make possible successful communication.'

Adaskou et al. could see the need for a cultural component in senses 3 and 4, but were dubious about the relevance of 1 and 2, given the likely needs of the learners and the lack of any explicit reference in the official syllabus to this kind of cultural knowledge. However, they saw it as important to consult teachers, teacher trainers and inspectors. From the resulting discussions with groups of teachers, and questionnaires to and structured interviews with all three groups, a clear consensus emerged. Most English teachers felt that the use in coursebooks of foreign milieux would invite cultural comparisons and lead to discontent with students' own material culture; and that the patterns of behaviour normal in an English-speaking social context would not be desirable models for young Moroccans. The informants also felt that the learners would be no less motivated to learn English if the language were not presented in the context of an English-speaking country. Field-trials and subsequent feedback not only confirmed this view but indicated that learners were more motivated to learn English when the language was presented in contexts with which they could identify. The writers' conclusion suggests, however, that teacher attitudes may be even more important than learner attitudes: 'Students use a particular course only once, but teachers will use it many times. And it is cultural content, more than any other single aspect, that in our opinion influences teachers' attitudes' (p. 10).

In other situations, where learners are more likely to travel to Britain or another English-speaking country, it is conceivable that a different view might prevail. After all, words conjure up concepts or images. 'Breakfast' represents a meal that may vary in both its content and the time at which it is taken. 'Home', 'school', 'polite', 'big', may all be translatable, but still be understood in distinctively different ways by speaker and hearer. Anyone who knows another language well will be able to supply examples of words for which there is no exact translation equivalent. We can therefore say that in this sense materials embody cultural content, and that knowledge of this content is essential if one is to understand the language. Language-learning materials, as has been suggested in a previous section, can also be made to carry cultural content. This may be about some culturally neutral aspect of real life (insofar as anything can be culturally neutral), some exotic culture, or about specific cultural features present in the world of the learner or that of the speech communities in which the target language is the mother tongue.

How such speech communities are represented is, of course, a matter of concern:

> EFL books whose aim is to present reality in today's Britain over-represent the white middle-class population with their concerns about holidays abroad and leisure time, home decoration and dining out, their preoccupation with success, achievement and material wealth. Absent, or nearly absent, are the great variety of minorities, people of African, Indian, Pakistanese descent who make up a considerable part of the population; and the problems of the homeless and the unemployed, of the socially underprivileged, of the illiterate masses are rarely or never mentioned . . . Generally, an idealized version of the dominant English culture is drawn, frequently leading populations of other societies to arrive at distorted conclusions based on the comparison between a false reality and their own lived experience in their culture.
>
> (Dendrinos 1992: 153)

One argument against a bicultural approach is that, taken to an extreme, it may be seen as a form of cultural imperialism (Alptekin and Alptekin 1984), as a result of which one culture is overwhelmed by the flow of potentially misleading information from the other. Alternatively, when learners see no possibility of travelling to an English-speaking country or even interacting directly with native speakers of English, it may be perceived as an irrelevance (Altan 1995). In a world in which English has assumed a global importance, it has been argued, a multicultural approach would be more appropriate (Prodromou 1992a); Altan's (1995) suggestion is that what might be thought of as international culture (human rights, interactive media, Japanese business practice, the ecu being his examples) or general knowledge should be used as the content for practice in the receptive skills of listening and speaking but that practice in the productive skills should relate to the learner's own socio-cultural context. Underlying this distinction between 'input' culture and 'output' culture is the belief that language learning is complexified by the introduction of a cultural component and that in any form other than the kind of general knowledge an educated person might be expected to have about the world he or she lives in, this is unnecessary.

The need to relate these arguments to specific contexts is underlined by Prodromou's (1992a) survey of the interests of 300 Greek students of English, mostly young adults. This revealed that alongside a very strong linguistic orientation (84 per cent said they wanted lessons to be 'about the English language'), there was an interest in 'facts about science and society' and, among intermediate- and advanced-level students, social problems. British life and institutions was preferred to the American equivalent (60 per cent and 26 per cent respectively), a finding explicable, Prodromou suggests, by the high standing of the Cambridge examinations and the 'bad press' accorded to America in the post-war period. What is also of interest is the generally low value given to 'local' topics. Prodromou speculates that this can be explained by 'the highly charged nature of Greek political life . . . Discussions of political or semi-political topics (such as Greek newspapers) can be unexpectedly divisive' (p. 46).

Nunan (1991: 211) comments: 'Learners have an infinite capacity to surprise, and there is a danger that the claim of cultural inappropriacy may be used as an excuse for refraining from action. It may also block classroom initiatives which the learners themselves might welcome.' Rather than making assumptions about learners' views, further context-specific research of the kinds reported in this section is obviously needed.

Task 10.3

1. '"Globally" designed coursebooks have continued to be stubbornly Anglo-centric' (Altan 1995: 59). Is this true of the materials you use? If so, do you see it as a problem?

2. Altan goes on:

> There is no such thing as culturally-neutral language teaching. ELT coursebooks convey cultural biases and implicitly communicate attitudes concerning the culture of the target language and indirectly the learners' native culture. Passages and units with foreign cultural themes and topics not only cause difficulties in comprehension, but actually seem to increase misunderstanding and confusion about the non-native culture, leading to a lack of production and of success. When both the materials we use and the way we use them are culturally adverse, then inevitably learners switch off and retreat into their inner world to defend their own integrity. (ibid.)

Do you think that Altan's comments on the effects on learners of materials containing foreign cultural themes and topics have relevance for the learners you teach?

4 MATERIALS AND SYLLABUS

There are two basic ways of representing the relationship between materials and syllabus. In the first and still more common, the syllabus determines if not the selection of materials at least the way in which they will be exploited for teaching purposes. This was referred to as a syllabus-driven approach in Chapter 5. In the second, materials are selected first, for their intrinsic interest and general linguistic appropriateness, and a specific linguistic syllabus is then derived from them. We called this a concept-driven approach in Chapter 5, but in a more restricted sense it has also been termed a text-driven approach (see, e.g., Tomlinson 1998d: 147). In creating materials for the occasional lesson the individual teacher may start from either of these positions, but for the teacher who is devising a whole course and for the professional materials writer this is an issue that requires serious thought. The first part of this section assumes a syllabus-driven approach. In the second part, we consider some of the pros and cons of a concept-driven approach.

4.1 Syllabuses and teachers

Teachers and materials writers require an organisational framework for their work. A syllabus fulfils this function. At its narrowest, it is no more than an inventory of items to be taught; in broader conceptions, these items will be logically derived from a statement of aims and objectives, related to a time-frame, and sequenced. In the broadest (most prescriptive?) form of syllabus specification, teaching procedures and perhaps aids will also be indicated. (For an early discussion of syllabus content, see the various contributions to Brumfit (1984); for further discussion of syllabus-types, see, for example, Nunan (1988c) and White (1988).)

This syllabus-first view is economically described by Nunan (1991: 208):

> [M]aterials, whether commercially developed or teacher-produced, are an important element within the curriculum, and are often the most tangible and visible aspect of it. While the syllabus defines the goals and objectives, the linguistic and experiential content, instructional materials can put flesh on the bones of these specifications.

When there exists an official syllabus which teachers are expected to follow, this will be an important factor in materials selection. In some contexts, teachers are only permitted to use 'authorised' textbooks (i.e. those which have passed official scrutiny); in other cases, it falls to the teacher to check the coverage of a textbook against the syllabus. If no official syllabus exists to pre-scribe or to guide, textbooks are sometimes allowed to take over this function: the textbook syllabus becomes the course syllabus by default, as it were.

The reason why this should not be allowed to happen is that decisions concerning syllabus need to be taken before a textbook is selected. As Cunningsworth (1984: 1) has remarked, 'coursebooks are good servants but poor masters'. In other words, coursebooks should not dictate what is done but be selected for what they can do to help. Logically, therefore, the selection of a textbook would take place only after some preliminary assessment of needs in the broad sense. As noted previously, while there may be a rough match between a coursebook syllabus and the needs of a particular group of learners, the match will not be a perfect one (this applies to any kind of external syllabus). It follows that even when there is an official teaching syllabus (or an end-of-course public examination which may serve a similar purpose), a teacher still has a responsibility to establish aims and objectives for the course which also take other contextual factors and known learner needs into account. Where no syllabus exists, teachers need to give thought (again, before selecting a textbook) to what kind of syllabus(es) would be appropriate and how the syllabus(es) might be specified.

It is one thing to specify what is to be taught; it is quite another to design an instructional plan. The following quotation from Rossner (1988: 141) indicates some of the problems:

> For the modern language teacher, the task seems endlessly complex: How does one reconcile the need to get the elements of the new language sorted out with the need to get used to hearing and understanding, speaking, reading, and writing it? And on top of that, how does one gradually plan for learners to become adept at matching form to function? And having done that, how does one plan for learners to accommodate the language in use to situational constraints imposed by channels of communication, location, surrounding events, and the participants?

This is one reason why teachers tend to base their teaching on textbooks, of course.

The argument advanced thus far in this section is that materials have been selected because they embody a syllabus that has been determined at least in part by the teacher. Richards and Rodgers (1986) appear to take a rather different view. They make three points about the potential relationship between syllabus and materials, suggesting that:

> The instructional materials . . . specify subject matter content, even where no syllabus exists, and define or suggest the intensity of coverage for syllabus items, allocating the amount of time, attention and detail particular syllabus items or tasks require. Instructional materials also define or imply the day-to-day learning objectives that collectively constitute the syllabus.
>
> (Richards and Rodgers 1986: 25)

While the first point may seem little more than a restatement of Nunan's view of syllabus and materials quoted at the beginning of this section, the inclusion of the phrase beginning 'even' in the first sentence introduces a very different perspective. Although partially mitigated by words such as 'suggest', and later 'imply', this view seems to assign to materials the role of teacher's partner rather than servant. In certain circumstances, as when teachers are inexperienced or a new approach is being introduced, support is of course needed and is probably most valued in the form of appropriate materials. In other situations, a less equal partnership would be desirable, as argued above.

4.2 Materials writers and syllabuses

Tomlinson (1998d: 147) makes the argument for a text-driven approach:

> [O]ne of the things we know about language acquisition is that most learners only learn what they need or want to learn. Providing opportunities to learn the language needed to participate in an interesting activity is much more likely to be profitable than teaching something because it is the next teaching point in the syllabus. And deriving learning points from an engaging text or activity is much easier and more valuable than finding or constructing a text which illustrates a pre-determined teaching point . . . If the written and spoken texts are selected for their richness and diversity of language as well as for their potential to achieve engagement then a wide syllabus will evolve which will achieve natural and sufficient coverage.

One of several assertions in the above quotation is that a text-driven approach 'will achieve natural and sufficient coverage'. However, one of the potential limitations of a text-driven approach is precisely that it does not yield a syllabus with sufficient coverage. As if recognising this, Tomlinson cites Prowse's (1998) suggestion that this problem can be overcome if a checklist is used to monitor coverage.

  The point should perhaps be made that while the reference to a checklist is a tacit admission that some form of external syllabus or self-generated list of learning items can be helpful, it is not an abandonment of the principle of a text-driven approach. Whether or not a checklist is used, there is value in materials designers preparing a grid which shows when specific items are introduced and recycled and the attention paid at different points to skill development. Since a grid of this kind should reveal gaps and imbalances, it can function as a monitoring device even without reference to any external categories.

Task 10.4

1. 'Materials design exists at the interface of syllabus design and methodology' (Nunan 1991: 214). What does this mean? Is it true?

2. Most teachers are familiar with language form syllabuses, whether they relate to grammatical structures, functions or phonological features, and can make judgements about the adequacy and appropriateness of these for their own teaching context. However, most modern textbooks will also include skill syllabuses and these can only be evaluated if the teacher has a clear understanding of what constitutes skilled behaviour and how this can be developed. This task consists of two steps.

    (a) Think of a specific group of learners and a single skill (e.g. speaking) that is important for all the members of the group. Now try to write down in as much detail as possible the various things they need to be able to do in that skill area. You may also be able to identify enabling knowledge and skills that feed into the main skills that you have noted.

    (b) Analyse your coursebook (or any other relevant book that is available) to see how this skill is dealt with in the book. Is there evidence that the writer has adopted a systematic approach to skill development (i.e. that the materials have been based on what can reasonably be called a skill syllabus)?

5 MATERIALS AND METHOD

In a carefully designed approach to language teaching (see, e.g., Stern 1983, Richards and Rodgers 1986) we might expect a high degree of consistency between aims, objectives, syllabus, materials and method. Thus, materials will embody syllabus content and the method that is used to facilitate the learning of that content will be congruent with overall aims and objectives and with the beliefs about language and language learning that lie behind these.

Method, normally understood as a coherent set of procedures, can be said to exist at three levels: (1) the theoretical level, or what is supposed to happen; (2) the level of materials, insofar as these prescribe what teachers/learners are to do; and (3) the classroom level. Levels (2) and (3) represent successive stages in interpretation or approximation.

This section focuses on the relationship between levels (1) and (2) and (2) and (3). It first raises a number of questions concerning the realism (and, indeed, the desirability) of the interlocking framework described above. It then turns to the relationship between materials and teacher and the teacher's role in realising the intentions of the materials designer.

5.1 Materials as the realisation of principles

Materials represent the first stage in which principles are turned into practice. Here we consider the extent to which materials really do (and, in the case of communicative materials, can) reflect the beliefs that supposedly lie behind them.

Rossner's (1988: 161) random survey of materials published between 1981 and 1987 found that:

> [F]ew authors have yet found ways to make available to teachers and learners resources which can provide a basis for tasks and activities in the EFL classroom that truly reflect the ideals of communicative approaches as articulated by applied linguists ... Probably truly 'communicative' tasks and activities can only be evolved by teachers who know their learners' needs and wants well, and who are used to working within the constraints surrounding particular teaching and learning situations ... it goes without saying that successful classroom language development depends on the ability of teachers to put together coherent sequences of activities which may be based on published or other materials, but which have been adapted, reformulated and supplemented to respond to the particular needs of those students in that situation.

Clarke (1989a), writing just one year later and with a similar purpose, comments on the 'considerable dichotomy between what is theoretically recommended as desirable and what in fact gets published and used on a wide scale' (p. 73). His helpfully detailed survey of the literature on communicative principles, and in particular authenticity, can be summarised as follows:

1. There are two schools of thought on text authenticity, with one group insisting on the real and another arguing that the primary criterion for decisions concerning the selection of materials should be appropriateness for the learners. One argument put forward by the latter group is that real materials which are inappropriate in terms of level or perceived relevance to learners can be just as alienating as meaningless form-focused activities.
2. There is agreement that authentic texts should be processed in relation to the writer's communicative purpose (i.e. that tasks should be focused on the writer's meaning and a response to that meaning).
3. There is concern about context both in relation to the wider context from which an authentic text has been taken and the sequence of activities within a lesson.
4. There is an acceptance of information-gap activities and role play and simulation as communication tasks.

In a survey of materials published between the mid-1970s and the late 1980s, he finds that:

1. The principle of authenticity in relation to texts has been widely adopted (he dubs this 'the "realia" explosion' (p. 79)), but photographs and even texts appear in some cases to have been included for largely cosmetic

reasons. 'Simulated realia' or 'pseudo authenticity' takes the form of simulated newspaper headlines and graphic devices such as notepads and handwriting. Listening texts are frequently at least semi-scripted. Original materials are adapted, sometimes without this being made explicit.

2. Despite widespread acceptance of the principle of authentic response, there is a continuing reliance on comprehension questions, which in some cases focus on points of detail. Authentic materials are sometimes used only to make a linguistic point. 'Form (whether in the sense of grammatical structure or function) thus still maintains ascendancy over meaning, a situation which is only partly concealed by the creation of an aura of authenticity' (p. 82).

3. A concern for context is evident in materials with a thematic- or topic-based structure; in other materials text selection seems 'random' or the contexts linked only by the linguistic feature that binds them together.

4. Although there is little evidence of the use of the information-gap principle in coursebooks, there are attempts to create a purpose for communication by inviting the learner to make a personal response to, e.g., a questionnaire, a topic, a poem. Role play is also used. Whether these materials, and indeed many of the texts included, will seem relevant to learners is questionable.

In short, 'modern materials tend not to exemplify the communicative principles they purport to embody' (p. 84).

5.2 Method in books and classrooms

The potential gap between principles and materials is even wider when it comes to the classroom use of materials, since teachers may or may not use the materials in ways that correspond to the intentions of the materials designer.

In an attempt to ensure this consistency, materials designers have sometimes produced materials in which procedures are laid down in great detail. The intention is to ensure that the materials are 'teacher proof', that is, that the materials are used as intended. There are certain situations, as when a new approach is being introduced or when the teachers who will use the materials have little teaching experience, when explicit and detailed instructions on what to do will be appreciated as support. But there comes a time when the unfamiliar becomes familiar and the inexperienced more experienced. If the instructions are written into student materials in such a way that the teacher has virtually no freedom to deviate from them, it is at this point that frustration may start to set in.

After all, most teachers like variety as much as learners. This is why they prefer materials that can be exploited in different ways (Nunan 1988a), and why they will from time to time voluntarily cease to use a textbook that has served them reasonably well in favour of something novel. Teachers also understand that one of their roles is that of mediator, between materials and learners (interpreter) and between learners and materials/syllabus (adapter, supplementer), and when they recognise that there is a gap between learners and materials (in either direction), they will want to do something to bridge that gap. Making what appears to be a rather different point, Jolly and Bolitho (1998: 112) have commented on the fact that teaching 'against the grain' (i.e. using materials with which one feels uncomfortable) 'leads to dissatisfaction, loss of confidence and learning failure'. Because teachers have preferred ways of teaching (styles that reflect their classroom personalities), they will want to make adjustments to materials – as one might with clothes – until they feel comfortable with them. One result is that even when teachers are ostensibly following the same method (i.e. an organised set of procedures), that method will be realised in potentially very different ways. (See, e.g., Katz's (1996) analysis of three teachers using the same set of writing materials.)

There is another side to this. The designer of the materials with which the teacher is making merry might feel distinctly uneasy at any radical deviations from his or her well-laid plans. The basic question when there is a difference between the procedures laid down in materials and a teacher's view of how learning is best facilitated is whether the teacher should adapt the materials or adapt to the materials. The obvious answer – and many materials designers would also concede this – is that teachers should follow their instincts and adapt the materials, but this raises much larger issues, such as how learners will react, whether the teacher is competent to take such a decision, and whether the change will have any longer term consequences in terms of learner outcomes. Nunan (1988a) provides extracts from two lessons to demonstrate that though teachers may be using materials based on communicative principles, interactions between teacher and learners may be 'non communicative'. In the teacher-fronted sections of both lessons, 'the teacher nominates the topics as well as who is to speak, and the questions are almost exclusively of the display type (questions to which the questioner already knows the answer)' (p. 139). Though Nunan is careful not to make a judgement of the teachers, the implication is that the approach adopted by the teachers perhaps unwittingly subverted the intention of the materials designer and presumably resulted in learning outcomes different from what was intended.

Nunan (1988a, 1991: 211–12) also reports on a study to determine whether experienced and inexperienced teachers used materials in different ways. Twenty-six teachers, differentiated according to length of experience, were given an authentic listening text and a set of worksheets, and asked to plan and teach a unit of work based on the materials. No procedures were prescribed. One of the most striking findings of the study was that the more experienced teachers (more than eight years' experience) spent considerably more time teaching the materials than the less experienced (less than four years' experience); however, the less experienced group used a greater variety of learner configurations than their more experienced counterparts. Possible reasons for the latter finding, Nunan suggests, may be that because the materials were novel the experienced teachers judged that they 'needed more teacher mediation, explanation and support' or that the less experienced teachers had been influenced by an emphasis in their teacher education programmes on groupwork and pairwork. No details are given of learner response or learning outcomes.

Task 10.5

1. Rossner's (1988) review of a range of published materials contains the following conclusion: 'few authors have yet found ways to make available to teachers and learners resources which can provide a basis for tasks and activities in the EFL classroom that truly reflect the ideals of communicative approaches as articulated by applied linguists' (p. 161). Is this still the case?

2. Richards and Rodgers (1986: 25–6) state that within different instructional designs the roles envisaged for materials will differ, illustrating this with reference to materials within a functional/communicative methodology and materials within an individualised instructional system. Take a close look at a set of materials. What roles were envisaged for them by the writer(s)?

6 MATERIALS AND RESEARCH

In relation to language learning–teaching materials, we can pose three rather different questions about research. Questions 1 and 2 both refer to a specific set of materials, but might lead on to more general considerations.

6.1 What is the research or theoretical basis for these materials?

If teachers are the mediators between materials and learners, then materials writers, according to one perception, are the mediators between 'the output of scholars/researchers ("theorists") and teachers/learners' (Dubin 1995: 14). They are, in other words, applied linguists bringing their knowledge and experience to bear on a particular set of problems. Although Dubin's characterisation of the classroom teacher ('Just give us engaging classroom scripts that will hold the interest of our learners') verges on caricature, and ignores the growing number of teacher-researchers, she does draw attention to a potential difference between those who take on the responsibility for providing others with teaching materials and those who make use of those materials: 'The writer must have a thorough grasp of developments in the field, but also must have the ability to embody abstract theory in concrete practice' (ibid.). She adds: 'One important element of craft knowledge is the utilization of relevant research that bears on materials writing' (ibid.). Similarly, Byrd (1995b: 6), who sees materials as a testing-ground for theory, states: 'At our most professional, materials writers are attempting to give classroom realization to ideas about language learning and language teaching that derive from varying theoretical sources' (note the careful prefatory phrase). For Tomlinson (1998c), a key source would be the findings of second-language acquisition research.

This is not to imply that the materials writer is simply an uncritical interpreter of the ideas of others. As Dubin and Olshtain (1986: 123) recognise, the writer whose materials deal with socio-cultural awareness, for instance, must be familiar with the output of socio-linguistic research but must also be able to make judgements about the relevance of this research for a particular group of learners, its appropriateness to the topics being treated and so on. They make the further point that in cases where writers have used research findings as the primary input, the resulting materials were 'too narrow for the needs of most programs' (ibid.).

If we accept the view that materials should rest on a research base of some kind, this raises questions in relation to a particular set of materials such as 'What kinds of research/theories appear to underpin the materials?' 'To what extent did the writer make conscious research-based decisions, and in relation to what features of the work?' In order to determine the research/theoretical basis for materials we would obviously need to interrogate the materials themselves (e.g. the tasks, as Littlejohn (1998) and Ellis (1997, 1998) suggest, the introduction, the teacher's book) and, if we can get personal access to them, the writer(s), publisher's editor and the designer. In order to make judgements such as whether the underpinning research base is sound or the theories current, we would also need to be well informed ourselves. McDonough and Shaw (1993: Chapters 6–10) provide useful summaries of research in each of the main skill areas, and integrated skills, and look at how this research is reflected in teaching materials.

A particular theory or body of research could, of course, inform very different sets of materials. The comparison of materials within the same category, for example supplementary skills materials focusing on listening, might not only prompt questions to do with what theoretical assumptions the materials have in common but also the nature of their surface variation – and the effects that this has on users. This line of questioning raises the issue in relation to successful/less successful materials of the relative importance of specific theoretical underpinnings on the one hand and the skill and experience of the materials writer on the other.

6.2 What research processes were involved in the writing of the materials?

Question 1, above, is concerned with one kind of input to materials design:

previous research into language, learning and teaching, and the way in which this is used. This question asks about the research specifically conducted in relation to the particular set of materials under consideration. It would be most relevant in the context of materials evaluation. What kinds of research by author and/or publisher preceded the writing? What was the nature and extent of any piloting and/or other forms of feedback on the materials? Suggested readings: Barnard and Randall (1995), Richards (1995), Donovan (1998).

6.3 What research has there been into materials selection and use and what remains to be done?

This is clearly a more general question. Byrd (1995a: 6) claims that 'materials writing and publication has developed into a professional track within the professional field of teaching ESL', but acknowledges that the body of knowledge on which practitioners within a profession typically base their work remains ill-defined. Her list of 'fundamental questions' requiring study is as follows:

- How can study of written text in textbook format result in language learning?
- How do students use text and/or textbooks in their study?
- Do students from different cultures use text and/or textbooks in different ways?
- How do language teachers use text and/or textbooks?
- Are there better and worse ways of using text and/or textbooks?
- How is learning content from text and/or textbooks different from learning communication in language through study of text and/or textbooks?

(Byrd 1995b: 6)

To these we might add a number of other questions:

- How are textbooks selected (and related to this, how are textbook evaluation instruments designed, validated and checked for reliability?)?
- How are textbooks evaluated once they have been selected?
- In what ways does/can research into the classroom use of materials feed into textbook design (a general question to which the specific answers under question 2 can contribute)? How does such research influence and how is it influenced by teacher education?

Suggested references for further reading in some of these areas can be found in Chapters 2, 3 and 9 – see, for example, Chambers (1997), Torres (1993), Richards and Mahoney (1996) and Richards (1998). Rea-Dickins (1994) includes a useful short survey of research on materials evaluation, including work in modern languages. This includes Mitchell, Parkinson and Johnstone (1981), a mainly observational study of the use of a French audiolingual textbook; see also Parkinson, Mitchell and McIntyre (1982), an evaluation study of the piloting in more than forty schools of a 'communicative' French course. The two papers by Richards referred to above contain references to research outside the area of languages.

Task 10.6

1. Look back at question 1, above. Choose a language skill that is important for the kinds of students you teach. Summarise the conclusions of the research that you are familiar with in relation to this skill. Decide what the pedagogic implications of these are and the relevance for the learners you have in mind. Design an instrument which will allow you to analyse the treatment of this skill in a set of published materials. Choose either a supplementary skills book or a coursebook that appears to give reasonable prominence to the skill. Analyse the materials to determine how far they appear to be based on linguistic research.

2. A distinction is sometimes made between educational research and evaluation (see, e.g., Rea-Dickens 1994, Ellis 1998). While these two forms of enquiry typically make use of the same data-gathering techniques, there will normally be differences in their purposes (e.g. to contribute to theory-building versus to contribute to pedagogy), their outcomes and perhaps their design. How might this distinction be applied to question 2, above? What kinds of enquiry would you see as research rather than evaluation?

3. Choose one of the possible areas of research suggested under question 3, above, that you would be interested in exploring and would be feasible in your situation. Carry out a literature review to find out what has already been done in this area. Then design a research plan which includes hypotheses or research questions and an indication of method. Talk through your plan with your colleagues.

Appendices

Join In

Günter Gerngross and Herbert Puchta
BEGINNER TO INTERMEDIATE

Join In is a complete new course for children offering a motivating and enjoyable start to learning English.

The course is written by the highly successful author team of Günter Gerngross and Herbert Puchta, who together have many years' experience of teaching and writing for young learners. Their materials draw on important findings in the fields of Neurolinguistic Programming and Multiple Intelligences – the result is a course through which children learn easily and quickly.

Join In is available in three levels plus an optional Starter level. At levels 1–3, each **Pupil's Book** is accompanied by an **Activity Book** for extra language practice, and an **Audio Cassette/CD** which contains all the listening texts, songs and stories.

There is an attractive range of optional extras to go with the course: a **video** containing all the songs and stories in the Pupil's Book; colourful **flashcards** to present and practise vocabulary; a **CD-ROM** full of lively games and activities and a **Holiday Pack** with puzzles and games for children to do in the holidays (these can be used independently).

A By permission of Cambridge University Press

Putting children first

DAVID PAUL

The *Finding Out* series has gained great popularity throughout Asia.

This motivating five-level course

- ◆ uses 'The Questioning Approach' in which children are encouraged to learn by using their innate curiosity, and to ask questions to find out answers

- ◆ contains more than 75 games for active learning

- ◆ takes a simple approach to phonics enabling children to make rapid progress

- ◆ has easy to use **Teacher's Books** with photocopiable games

- ◆ has **Cassettes** presenting models of pronunciation with extended songs, chants and dialogs

Working in English

Leo Jones

INTERMEDIATE

Student's Book	77684 8
Teacher's Book	77683 X
Student's Book Audio Cassette	77682 1
Student's Book Audio CD	77681 3
Personal Study Book	77685 6
Video	77679 1

Working In English is a comprehensive new course for Business English learners from Leo Jones, co-author of the immensely successful *International* and *New International Business English* courses.

40 one hour units are organised into 7 modules providing the core course. This is supplemented by extra activities from the Teacher's Guide to offer maximum flexibility. The units focus on the practical day-to-day functions that all business people – whatever their level or experience – have to carry out.

The accompanying Video contains specially filmed documentary sequences made in Europe and the USA that relate to the themes of the modules and provide authentic input to the course.

The Personal Study Book offers useful reference material and fun practice activities to do out of class. It is sold with a free audio CD to provide extra self-study listening practice.

The course offers:

- a flexible approach, making the course very teacher-friendly
- content that is suitable for a broad range of Business English students
- a comprehensive package of supplementary materials.

Working together to learn English

AMERICAN ENGLISH

D. SPENCER AND D. VAUGHAN
S. SALABERRI AND L. GONZALEZ
E. CRESTA AND D. HOWARD-WILLIAMS
P. DOMINGUEZ AND R. TUÑAS

Team Player

A stimulating six-part learning program for teenagers, **Team Player**

◆ provides personal development for the student through co-operative learning activities and cross-cultural comparisons

◆ takes a communicative approach to learning grammar, vocabulary and functions

◆ encourages learners to discover for themselves how English works through **Investigating English**

◆ integrates all four skills

◆ allows for mixed-ability classes through **Extra Assignments**

◆ combines the color-student book with practice book pages in one volume per level

◆ has a comprehensive **Teacher's Guide** which is a complete resource including tests, answer keys and photocopiable Resource pages as well as notes on American culture

D By permission of Macmillan Heinemann

Go!

Steve Elsworth and Jim Rose
with Olivia Date and Patricia Mugglestone

BEGINNERS - PRE-INTERMEDIATE

The fresh young course with 'green' themes and an outdoor spirit!

Go! is a bright and exciting three-level course for lower secondary students. Bursting with energy and filled with activities and topics your students will enjoy, Go! tackles the key interests and concerns of today's young learners - in particular, the environment.

Students can identify with the young 'Sea Watch' explorers in their adventures around Britain and Australia, while the serialised cartoon stories - Snowboy, Gorilla Mountain and Rain Maker - encourage students to read for pleasure.

- Short, achievable teaching units
- Opportunities for systematic skills practice and new language development
- 'Grammar Check' revision pages and learner training
- Each Teacher's Book includes teaching notes, photocopiable tests and ideas for additional activities
- Practical and user-friendly

Go! is also available in special editions for Italy, Portugal, Spain, Greece, Poland and Argentina. For more information contact your local Longman representative or agent, or write to Pearson Education in the United Kingdom.

British English Courses: Lower Secondary

E   By permission of Pearson Education Ltd.

Give yourself a treat!

Reward **is a multi-level, multi-component course, taking learners from beginner to upper-intermediate level.** *Reward* **offers**

◆ a grammar syllabus covering the essential structures at each level

◆ extensive vocabulary development

◆ integrated skills work

◆ regular progress checks

◆ cross-cultural focus provides stimulating input and encourages discussion

◆ **Practice Book** with **Cassette** for self-study and extension work

◆ interleaved **Teacher's Book** for ease of use

PLUS

Grammar and Vocabulary Workbooks provide extra practice in these key areas

Photocopiable **Resource packs** (plus **Business Resource packs** for the higher levels)

Customizable **Tests** on diskette are a flexible tool for the busy teacher

CD-ROMs from elementary to upper-intermediate levels offer extra activities

At four levels the **Video** combines drama and documentary to engage all students

 By permission of Macmillan Heinemann

World Class

Michael Harris and David Mower with
Paul McCann and Olivia Date

FALSE BEGINNERS - INTERMEDIATE

World Class is a four-level course with a strong educational and cross-curricular approach. Fast-paced, it builds on students' natural curiosity and combines fun and fantasy with amazing facts about the world.

- 90 - 100 classroom lessons per level
- Revises and recycles vocabulary and structures
- Encourages learner independence with study tips and regular self-assessment checks
- Active language sections help students work out grammar rules
- Photocopiable assessment tests in each Teacher's Book

Also available

World Class is available in an edition for Arab learners entitled The World through English.

G   By permission of Pearson Education Ltd.

Longman English Works

Robert O'Neill

BEGINNERS - INTERMEDIATE

Longman English Works is a two-level general English course for people at work, or preparing for work. Designed for learners who want to make rapid progress, each level is short, intensive and challenging.

The emphasis is on core structures and functions needed for work-related tasks. All language areas are treated thoroughly, and practised and recycled in different contexts. The clear layout of the units makes the books ideal for self-access and revision.

H By permission of Pearson Education Ltd.

Compact

Debra Powell, Madeline McHugh and Alice Lester

ELEMENTARY - UPPER INTERMEDIATE

Compact is specifically designed for intensive courses. Each of the four levels contains approximately 40 hours' classroom work. A carefully structured syllabus gives comprehensive coverage of language and skills, and practical exercises encourage students to explore the language fully. The international appeal and stimulating topics make the course suitable for all types of groups.

The Teacher's Books provide useful advice for teachers of short courses, projects and suggestions on how to extend or reduce the length of the course.

I By permission of Pearson Education Ltd.

Academic Encounters
Content focus: Human behavior
Reading, study skills and writing
Bernard Seal
UPPER-INTERMEDIATE TO ADVANCED

Student's Book	47658 5
Teacher's Manual	47660 7

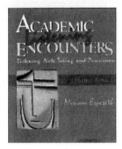

Academic Listening Encounters
Content focus: Human behavior
Listening, note taking, and discussion
Miriam Espeseth
UPPER-INTERMEDIATE TO ADVANCED

Student's Book	57821 3
Teacher's Manual	57820 5
Set of 5 Cassettes	57819 1
Set of 4 Audio CDs	78357 7
Audio Sampler	65935 3

These two books use a content-based approach to help students develop the skills they need to meet the demands of college courses in an English-speaking environment. At the same time, both books enable students to build a strong foundation in the content area of the course – human behavior. The two books can be used together, but they function equally well as stand-alone texts.

Academic Encounters introduces students to topics such as stress and health, non-verbal communication, and love, using authentic readings from university-level textbooks that engage students in the topic while exposing them to academic discourse.

Academic Listening Encounters explores the same topics using a variety of taped materials, including listening exercises, interviews, and classroom lectures.

Both books provide students with many opportunities to practice their writing.

APPENDIX 2.2
Interview prompts (interviews with learners/teachers)

Eliciting teachers' views on coursebooks

1. Do you think coursebooks are important?
2. What are your criteria for choosing a coursebook?
3. Which part(s) of the coursebook do you frequently use and which part(s) do you seldom use?
4. When, why and how do you supplement the coursebook?
5. What kind of help would you like to have from the coursebook in teaching grammar or any other aspects of the language?

Eliciting learners' views on coursebooks

1. How often do you use your coursebook?
2. Which part(s) of it do you use most frequently and which part(s) do you seldom use?
3. Which part of the book do you like best and which part do you like least?
4. Is the coursebook important to you?
5. What kind of coursebook would you like to have?
6. Do you like the coursebook you have now?

Source: Tang (2001)

APPENDIX 2.3
Extract from textbook analysis

Title: *Cambridge English for Schools SB 1* **Author:** *Littlejohn and Hicks*
Publisher: *CUP*

A. BOOK AS A WHOLE

1 *Type*: 'General', 'main course', class use for post beginners
2 *Intended audience*
   age-range: 12–16   school: secondary schools   location: world-wide
3 *Extent*
   a. *Components*: durable 'Student's Book' and consumable 'Workbook'
      Student's cassette. Teacher's Book, Class cassette, video
   b. *Total estimated time* 1 school year
4 *Design and Layout*
   4 colour SBk, 160pp; 2 colour WBk, 96pp; 2 colour Teacher's Bk 176pp
5 *Distribution*

a. *Material*	teacher	learners
cassettes	[X]	[X]
tapescript	[X]	[ ]
answer key	[X]	[ ]
guidance on use of class material	[X]	[ ]
b. *Access*		
index/wordlist	[X]	[X]
detailed content list	[X]	[X]
section objective	[X]	[X]

6 *Route through material*

specified	[X]	
user determined	[ ]	

7 *Subdivision*
   6 'Themes' of 5 'units' each: with some standardised components according to type:
   Topic: Tasks about the topic, song, 'Decide. . .' exercise, Time to Spare?, Language Record
   Language Focus: Language tasks, 'Out and About' social English, Time to Spare? Language Record, Revision Box
   Activity: steps of an activity, evaluation
   Culture Matters: no recurring pattern
   Revision and Evaluation: self-assessment, revision exercise/practice test and test design; evaluation on learning process

B. OVERVIEW OF AN EXTRACT

1 *Length*: 1 'Theme' out of 6, 16.5% of the Student's Book
2 *Sequence of activity*
   Topic Unit: 1 class discussion, 2 listening to sounds, 3 brainstorming and reading, 4 brainstorming 5 poster design, 6 song, 7 reading, 8 Decide. . . (exercise choice), 9 Poster work, 10 Language Record
   Language Focus: 1 Discussion, 2 listening, 3 grammar discovery and practice, 4 grammar discovery and practice, 5 Out and About, 6 Language Record
   Activity: 1 research at home, 2 writing (family tree), 3 writing about family, 4 comparing work, 5 evaluation of work done.
   Culture Matters: 1 discussion, 2 reading, 3 reading, 4 comprehension and discussion
   Revision and evaluation: 1 self-assessment, 2 test, 3 designing own test, 4 evaluation of learning process

Source: Littlejohn (1998: 197)

APPENDIX 2.4
Extracts from published evaluation checklists

VS		CRITERIA	MS	VMP
		PRONUNCIATION CRITERIA		
5		1. Completeness of presentation	1.5	7.5
5		2. Appropriateness of presentation	1.5	7.5
4		3. Adequacy of practice	2	8
		GRAMMAR CRITERIA		
5		4. Adequacy of pattern inventory	3	15
4		5. Appropriate sequencing	2.5	10
4		6. Adequacy of drill model & pattern display	3	12
4		7. Adequacy of practice	3	12
		CONTENT CRITERIA		
4		8. Functional load	3	12
4		9. Rate & manner of entry & re-entry	2.5	10
4		10. Appropriate of contexts & situations	2	8
		GENERAL CRITERIA		
5		11. Authenticity of language	2	10
3		12. Availability of supplementary materials	4	12
3		13. Adequate guidance for non-native teachers	1	3
3		14. Competence of the author	2	6
2		15. Appropriate level for integration	3	6
1		16. Durability	2.5	2.5
1		17. Quality of editing & publishing	3.5	3.5
1		18. Price & value	3.5	3.5

Title _____ Author _____ Evaluated by _____

VS—Value Scale   Range 0–5   MS—Merit Scale   Range 0–4   VMP—Value Merit Product

 Source: Tucker (1975: 360–1)

Weight	GENERAL	Rating 4 3 2 1 0
____	takes into account currently accepted methods of ESL/EFL teaching	— — — — —
____	gives guidance in the presentation of language items	— — — — —
____	caters for individual differences in home language background	— — — — —
____	relates content to the learners' culture and environment	— — — — —
	SPEECH	
____	is based on a contrastive analysis of English and L1 sound systems	— — — — —
____	suggests ways of demonstrating and practising speech items	— — — — —
____	includes speech situations relevant to the pupils' background	— — — — —
____	allows for variation in the accents of non-native speakers of English	— — — — —
	GRAMMAR	
____	stresses communicative competence in teaching structural items	— — — — —
____	provides adequate models featuring the structures to be taught	— — — — —
____	shows clearly the kinds of responses required in drills (e.g. substitution)	— — — — —

(etc)

B Source: Williams (1983: 255)

FACTUAL DETAILS

Title: _____
Author(s): _____
Publisher: _____ Price: _____
ISBN: _____ No. of Pages: _____
Components: SB/TB/WB/Tests/Cassettes/Video/CALL/Other _____
Level: _____ Physical size: _____
Length: _____ Units: _____ Lessons/sections _____ Hours: _____
Target skills: _____
Target learners: _____
Target teachers: _____

ASSESSMENT (* Poor ** Fair *** Good **** Excellent)

Factor	Rating and comments
Rationale	
Availability	
User definition	
Layout/graphics	
Accessibility	
Linkage	
Selection/grading	
Physical characteristics	
Appropriacy	
Authenticity	
Sufficiency	
Cultural bias	
Educational validity	
Stimulus/practice/revision	
Flexibility	
Guidance	
Overall value for money	

C Source: Sheldon (1988: 242)

C – Activities

1   Do the materials provide a balance of activities that is appropriate for
    your students? (See 4.4, 12.1 and 12.4(a).)

    Yes ☐ *No* ☐ *Comment* _____

    _____

    (You may also want to refer to Exercise 1 on page 275.)

2   Is there a sufficient amount of communicative output in the materials
    under consideration? (See 4.3 and 5.3 for a description of what this
    means, and Chapter 8 for a large number of examples of this type of
    activity, both speaking and writing.)

    Yes ☐ *No* ☐ *Comment* _____

    _____

3   Do the materials provide enough roughly-tuned input for your students?
    (See 4.3.)

    Yes ☐ *No* ☐ *Comment* _____

    _____

D   Source: Harmer (1991: 281)

Language content

☐ Does the coursebook cover the main grammar items appropriate to each level, taking learners' needs into account?

☐ Is material for vocabulary teaching adequate in terms of quantity and range of vocabulary, emphasis placed on vocabulary development, strategies for individual learning?

☐ Does the coursebook include material for pronunciation work? If so what is covered: individual sounds, word stress, sentence stress, intonation?

☐ Does the coursebook deal with the structuring and conventions of language use above sentence level, eg how to take part in conversations, how to structure a piece of extended writing, how to identify the main points in a reading passage? (More relevant at intermediate and advanced levels.)

☐ Are style and appropriacy dealt with? If so, is language style matched to social situation?

Skills

☐ Are all four skills adequately covered, bearing in mind your course aims and syllabus requirements?

☐ Is there material for integrated skills work?

☐ Are reading passages and associated activities suitable for your students' levels, interests, etc? Is there sufficient reading material?

☐ Is listening material well recorded, as authentic as possible, accompanied by background information, questions and activities which help comprehension?

☐ Is material for spoken English (dialogues, roleplays, etc) well designed to equip learners for real-life interactions?

☐ Are writing activities suitable in terms of amount of guidance/control, degree of accuracy, organization of longer pieces of writing (eg paragraphing) and use of appropriate styles?

Topic

☐ Is there sufficient material of genuine interest to learners?

☐ Is there enough variety and range of topic?

☐ Will the topics help expand students' awareness and enrich their experience?

☐ Are the topics sophisticated enough in content, yet within the learners' language level?

☐ Will your students be able to relate to the social and cultural contexts presented in the coursebook?

☐ Are women portrayed and represented equally with men?

☐ Are other groups represented, with reference to ethnic origin, occupation, disability, etc?

Methodology

☐ What approach/approaches to language learning are taken by the coursebook? Is this appropriate to the learning/teaching situation?

☐ What level of active learner involvement can be expected? Does this match your students' learning styles and expectations?

☐ What techniques are used for presenting/practising new language items? Are they suitable for the learners?

☐ How are the different skills taught?

☐ How are communicative abilities developed?

☐ Does the material include any advice/help to students on study skills and learning strategies?

☐ Are students expected to take a degree of responsibility for their own learning (eg by setting their own individual targets)?

E   Source: Cunningsworth (1995: 3–4)

APPENDIX 3.1 Extracts from an evaluation checklist

Choosing a textbook

Does the book suit your students?

1. Is it attractive? Given the average age of your students, would they enjoy using it?	YES	PARTLY	NO
2. Is it culturally acceptable?	YES	PARTLY	NO
5. Is it about the right length?	YES	PARTLY	NO
9. Does it achieve an acceptable balance between the relevant language skills, and integrate them so that work in one skill area helps the others?	YES	PARTLY	NO

Does the book suit the teacher?

2. Is there a good, clear teacher's guide with answers and help on additional activities?	YES	PARTLY	NO
4. Are the recommended methods and approaches suitable for you, your students and your classroom?	YES	PARTLY	NO
5. Are the approaches easily adaptable if necessary?	YES	PARTLY	NO
9. Does the book use a 'spiral' approach, so that items are regularly revised and used again in different contexts?	YES	PARTLY	NO

Does the book suit the syllabus and the examination?

1. Has the book been recommended or approved by the authorities?	YES	PARTLY	NO
4. If it does more than the syllabus requires, is the result an improvement?	YES	PARTLY	NO
8. Is there a good balance between what the examination requires and what the students need?	YES	PARTLY	NO

Score: 2 points for every YES answer, 1 point for every PARTLY answer, 0 for every NO answer.

Source: Grant (1987: 122–6)

APPENDIX 3.2 Analysis of selected evaluation checklists

Author	Date	Main categories		Format/special features	Comments
Bruder	1978	level objectives style lang. background	age time convictions competency	3-point assessment scale for student's and teacher's book. Plus sign (+) indicates good match between materials and learner/teacher needs, minus (–) a mismatch, and zero (0) that the text can be adapted.	This is not simply a proposal. Bruder (1978: 210) claims that 'the system has been found to result in reliable inter-rater judgements of given texts for specified situations'. A full discussion of the categories is provided.
Cunningsworth	1995	aims, approaches design, organisation lang. content skills	topic methodology teacher's books practical considerations	Yes/No questions with boxes for ticking	Presented as 'a basic quick reference checklist' containing 'some of the most important general criteria' (Cunningsworth 1995: 3). More narrowly focused checklists are provided elsewhere in the book.
Daoud and Celce-Murcia	1979	subject matter (topics, contexts) exercises physical make-up	linguistic coverage (structures, vocab.) illustrations	5-point numerical rating scale for both student's book and teacher's book.	Suggests 3-stage process in which selection is progressively narrowed down, with main categories being used during second (data-recording) stage.
Harmer	1991	practical considerations layout, design activities skills	language type subject, context guidance	Yes/No questions with boxes for ticking plus space for comment	Included as Appendix in general methodology book; contains cross references to discussion in earlier sections of the book.
Skierso	1991	bibliographical data aims, goals subject matter layout, physical makeup	vocab, structures exercises and activities	Categories with amplifying (clarifying) questions; rating and weighting scales. Categories included for evaluation of Teacher's book.	Expansion of Daoud and Celce-Murcia (1979). Extremely detailed. Indicates 65 (!) sources for checklist items. Preceding discussion includes additional prompts to guide evaluation.
Tucker	1975	pronunciation grammar	content general	Incorporates two rating scales, one for value (importance in context) and one for merit (quality). Scores are multiplied to produce not only an arithmetical total (the value-merit product) but also a graph in which the actual and ideal profiles can be displayed.	The focus on pronunciation and grammar reflect the period in which the checklist was designed. A full discussion of the categories is provided. Tucker points out that the evaluations of different evaluators can be plotted on the same graph, e.g. using different coloured lines.
Williams	1983	general speech grammar vocabulary	reading writing technical	Includes column for weighting and a 5-point numerical rating scale	Presented as example of how a checklist can be generated for a specific context. The starting-point is a set of explicitly stated assumptions about language teaching which are used to generate general, linguistic, pedagogical and technical criteria. Different assumptions or modifications to the categories of criteria would produce different specific criteria.

APPENDIX 3.3 Extracts from published materials

It's Pablo's turn to do the housework.
Look at the picture and complete the list of things to do.

Do the housework!

1. Wash the dishes

2.

3.

4.

5.

A Source: Gershon and Mares (1995)

tips

* *express*
means *going*
very fast.

Peter is now visiting Singapore with his family. Complete his postcard to Kate. Use the notes below to help you.

- arrived yesterday evening
- from Kuala Lumpur
- by *express coach
- staying at Harbour Hotel
- 200 m from the sea; near a big shopping centre
- visited Jurong Bird Park today; very beautiful; saw many kinds of birds
- want to visit Sentosa Island tomorrow

20 September

Dear Kate

Hi. We arrived here (1) _____

We travelled (2) _____

_____, and now we are staying (3) _____

_____. It is only (4) _____

_____. Today, (5) _____

_____. Tomorrow, we want to

(6) _____.

Best wishes

Peter

Kate Baker
Flat B, 32/F
465 King's Road
North Point
Hong Kong

B   Source: Etherton et al. (1997)

Today is Monday. Look at Anita's diary for last weekend and complete her conversation with Peter.

Saturday

9:30 go swimming ✗
12:00 go shopping ✓
2:00 meet Sally, Jane, and Karen ✗
3:30 eat at Ronnie's Burger Cafe ✗
7:15 go to the movies with David ✓

Sunday

1:30 Granny's house for lunch ✓

Did you have a good weekend, Anita? — Yes, I did.

Did you go to the Burger Cafe? — No, I didn't.

Did you go shopping? — _____

And did you meet your friends on Saturday? — _____

And did you go swimming? — _____

Oh boy! Did you see your grandmother? — _____

And did you go to the movies? — _____

And, umm ... did you go with David? — _____

Oohh ...

C   Source: Spencer and Vaughan (1999)

∩ Solo Would you like to...?

Renee sent e-mail to Lori inviting her to a concert.

1. Read Renee's message. Fill in the spaces. Use these words. There is one extra.

come	eat
~~concert~~	band
play	starts
ticket	have

Hi, Lori.

I'm going to the Burning Roses ___*concert*___ this Saturday and

_____ an extra _____. Would you like to _____?

They're a great _____. The concert _____ at 8:00 at

Meadowlands Arena. We can go out to _____ after the concert, if

you like. Please let me know.

Renee

Now listen and check your answers.

2. Write an invitation to a concert or another event.

It can be a real event, one you make up, or one on page 77.

Use these words and expressions:

  going   this_____   would you....   at _____

3. Follow-up. Exchange invitations with a partner. Decide if you can or can't go.

Answer the invitation.

Dear Renee,

Thanks for your invitation. I'd love to go. Why

don't we meet at the station at 7:30?

Lori

Dear Renee,

Thanks for your invitation. I'd really like to go,

but I have other plans that night. Maybe some

other time.

Lori

D   Source: Helgesen et al. (1999)

WRITING

Tourist brochure

1   Which of the following customs and manners are true in your country?

- Punctuality is not important.
- It is normal to bargain in shops.
- You mustn't cross your legs in the presence of a superior.
- Smoking is forbidden in public places.
- It is usual to have a siesta after lunch.
- People say 'Sorry, sorry' when something goes wrong, even though it's not their fault.
- Queueing is not usual.

2   Work with someone else of your nationality if possible and make notes about your country, or one you know well, under the following headings: *Customs, Good manners, Bad manners, Advice to visitors*. Example:

3   You are going to write an entry for the *Local customs* section of a tourist brochure, talking about the customs and manners of people in your country and giving advice to visitors (e.g. *If possible visitors should . . . ; Take care to . . . ; Make sure you . . . ; Visitors should be careful not to . . . ; It is unwise to . . . ; It is never a good idea to . . .*). Include at least two examples of bad advice but pretend it is good advice (e.g. *Never tip taxi drivers; Feel free to smoke downstairs on buses.*) Divide your notes into paragraphs and write a draft.

4   Show your draft to other students (preferably students of the same nationality). Ask them to identify the bad advice and to suggest improvements.

5   Rewrite your entry paying particular attention to the use of *-ing* and *to* + base form.

6   Discuss the customs and manners mentioned. Do you know the reasons for any of them? Are they changing in any way in the modern world?

E   Source: Bell and Gower (1992)

Preparation for task

1 Look at the map and pictures of Thailand. What do you know about Thailand? Can you imagine how social customs there differ from those in your country?

2 Below is an extract from a travel guide to Thailand which gives 'tips' to foreign visitors about social behaviour and customs. Read the extract and answer the following questions.

a   Which social situations are mentioned?

b   Some of the tips have two alternatives – can you guess which is the correct one?

3 🖭 [7.4] Nikam Nipotam was born in Thailand, but was brought up in England. You are going to hear him talking about customs to a colleague who is going to Thailand. Listen and underline the correct alternatives in the extract below.

4 Compare your answers with a partner. Were you surprised by anything Nikam Nipotam said?

Tips for foreign visitors to Thailand

Thailand is famous for its hospitality, and the average visitor will have no difficulty in adapting to local customs. The following tips are mostly common sense, but to avoid giving offence, foreign visitors may find them useful.

1.   When addressing a Thai person it is polite to use just *their first name / their surname*.

2.   In more formal situations you should use the word 'Khun'. This is like 'Mr' and is used for addressing *men / both men and women*.

3.   It is not usual to shake hands when you meet a Thai person. Instead you do a 'wai' – you put your hands together as if you are saying a prayer, and bow your head slightly. You should always use this greeting when you meet *older people / your friends*.

4.   Couples should be careful about how they behave. You don't see Thai couples *holding hands / kissing in public*.

5.   The head is very important in Thai culture. It is *very respectful / not respectful* to touch another person's head.

6.   If you're invited to someone's home, you should *always take off your shoes / never take off your shoes*. It's very important to remember this!

7.   When eating a meal with Thai people, you should expect the food to be served in large bowls in the centre of the table. Everyone helps themselves, using *chopsticks / a spoon and fork*.

8.   Finally, you should never insult the Thai royal family. Thais always show respect towards their royalty, and they expect visitors to do the same.

Task

1 Imagine that a visitor from a different culture is coming to your country (a British or American tourist, a Thai person like Nikam Nipotam or one of your fellow students). You are going to draw up a list of eight tips about social behaviour, like the ones in the extract. Make a list of ideas under the following headings:

- addressing people
- meeting and greeting
- gestures
- public behaviour
- an invitation to someone's house
- at a meal
- dress code
- other important 'dos' and 'don'ts'

Ask your teacher about any words or phrases you need and write them in the *Personal vocabulary* box.

2 When you have finished, you can:

Either: listen to the other students' lists to see if they included any useful tips that you didn't think of. Then work with a partner and act out a conversation like Nikam Nipotam's. Imagine your partner is either:
- a foreign guest staying with your family.
- a foreign business associate.

or: give a talk to the rest of the class about social customs in your country. Listen to the tips that other students give you about their countries and note down any customs that are very different from those in your country. Discuss the ones that you find most interesting / surprising and ask questions about anything that you do not understand.

Look at the phrases in the *Useful language* box.

Optional writing

Write up the tips for foreign visitors to your country, as in the extract for people visiting Thailand.

F   Source: Cunningham and Moor (1998), *Cutting Edge Intermediate*, reproduced by permission of Pearson Education Ltd

APPENDIX 3.4A
Materials analysis: phase one

I What do the materials aim to do and what do they contain?

1. When they finish their course, what should your learners know *of* and *about* the target language?
2. What should they be able to do *in* and *with* the language?
3. What knowledge about language and what guidance for using language appropriately for different purposes in various situations is offered in the materials?
4. What do the materials offer which your learners will need to *know*?
5. What do the materials offer which your learners will be able to *do*?
6. What is *missing* from the materials?

II What do the materials make your learners do while they are learning?

7. How do you think you *best* learn a language? What is most useful for learners to *do* to help them to learn?
8. What procedure or sequence of work does the learner have to follow in order to be successful at the task?
9. Which types of task seem to be most conducive to *learning*?
10. Which helpful ways of learning seem to be *missing* from the tasks provided in the materials?

III How do the materials expect you to teach your learners in the classroom?

11. What can I do as a teacher which can best help my learners to learn a new language?
12. What are you expected to do to help your learners work successfully through the materials?
13. Do [the] materials give you enough freedom to adopt those roles which for you are the most *helpful* to learners discovering a new language?
14. Are you asked to take on roles you do not regard as appropriate?
15. Do the materials *limit* what you want to do as a teacher in using them with your learners?

(based on Breen and Chandlin 1987: 14–16; original emphases)

APPENDIX 3.4B
Materials analysis: phase two

I Are the materials appropriate to your learners' needs and interests?

19. How and to what extent do the materials fit your learners' long-term goals in learning the language and/or following your course?
20. How far do the materials directly call on what your learners already know of and about the language, and extend what they can already do with and in the language?
21. How far do the materials meet the immediate language learning needs of your learners as you perceive them?
22. What subject-matter (topics, themes, ideas) in the materials is likely to be interesting and relevant to your learners?
23. In what ways do the materials involve your learners' values, attitudes and feelings?
24. Which skills do the materials highlight and what kinds of opportunity are provided to develop them?
25. How much time and space, proportionately, is devoted to each skill?
26. How is your learner expected to make use of his/her skills?
27. How are the learners required to communicate when working with the materials?
28. How much time and space, proportionately, is devoted to your learners *interpreting* meaning?
29. How much time and space, proportionately, is devoted to your learners *expressing* meaning?
30. How and how far can your materials meet the desire of individual learners to focus at certain moments on the development of a particular skill or ability use?

II Are the materials appropriate to your learners' own approaches to language learning?

31. On what basis is the content of the material *sequenced*?
32. On what basis are the different parts of the materials *divided* into 'units' or 'lessons', and into different sub-parts of units/lessons?
33. On what basis do the materials offer *continuity*? How are relationships made between earlier and later parts?
34. To what extent and in what ways can your learners impose *their own* sequencing, dividing up and continuity on the materials as they work with them?

(based on Breen and Chandlin 1987: 18–23; original emphases)

APPENDIX 4.1
Extracts from published materials

Read the ads. Compare the CD players. (5 points)

SALE! **CD Players**
Electra Compact Disc Player
- New model
- 3-Disc Changer
- 3 kg
- 35 cm x 30 cm x 10 cm

ONLY

$159.98

Special Discount

Sonic Portable Discguy

last year's model

$119⁹⁹

-Shock Protection
- 1 kg
- 14 cm x 14 cm x 3 cm

1. The Electra is ___*bigger*___ than the Sonic.
   (big)
2. The Sonic is _____ .
   (expensive)
3. _____ .
   (heavy)
4. _____ .
   (new)
5. _____ .
   (small)
6. Which would you buy?
   _____

A   Helgesen et al. (1999), *English Firsthand 1*

Do the following activities in pairs

a) Take turns to ask and answer the following questions. Respond using either *I think so* or *I don't think so*.

- Is Sydney the capital of Australia?
- Is it going to rain tomorrow?
- Can ducks swim under water?
- Does your teacher speak Chinese?
- Is there going to be a test next week?

B   Source: Cunningham and Moor (1998), *Cutting Edge Intermediate*, reproduced by permission of Pearson Education Ltd.

1. Role-play.

You are interviewing a new TV star named Lupe. Check your information about her, using tag questions.

Example: **A:** Hello, Lupe. You're Mexican, aren't you?

             B: Yes, I am.

             A: And you can ...

~~Mercedes Martinez~~

Lupe Garcia

GARCIA, G

Full name:	GARCIA, Guadalupe (Lupe)
Nationality:	Mexican
Languages:	Speaks Spanish, French, and English fluently.
Parents:	Mother Mexican. Father French. Both work for a Mexican television station.
Home town:	Mexico City
Acting experience:	Played a leading part in the TV series "Texas."

C   Source: Abbs et al. (1998), *Take Off 4*

B   A survey about after-school courses

In this section we are talking about after-school courses in subjects such as music, sports, health, first aid, photography, scouting, or other hobbies or interests (but not normal school subjects).

B1   *First, practise reading this dialogue with a partner.*

S1 Have you ever studied any course outside of school?
S2 Yes, I have.
S1 What type of course was it?
S2 It was a course with St John Ambulance.
S1 Who was your teacher?
S2 She was called Mrs Tam.
S1 How long was your course?
S2 It was one evening a week, for six weeks.
S1 How much did it cost?
S2 It cost only $200 for the whole course.
S1 Would you recommend it to other people?
S2 Yes, I would recommend it. It's a very good course.

B2   *Next, in pairs, talk about the two courses below. S1 asks questions, using the survey form (and the dialogue on page 89) to help him/her. S2 uses the notes to help with his/her answers.*

SURVEY FORM		
1 Any course outside school?	**Guitar lessons**	**Computer classes**
2 Type of course?	YMCA — Mr Romero	Ram-Rom College — Mr Mario
3 Teacher?	Twice a week, 8–9 p.m.	6 weeks, Sat., 9–11 a.m.
4 Length of course?	$75 an hour	$1,500
5 Cost?	Very good course	Poor teacher, old computers
6 Recommend?		

B3   *Now work with a partner, and ask each other about any real courses you have taken outside school. Use the survey form above to help you. Write brief notes of your partner's answers. Report some of the most interesting courses to the whole class.*

 D   Source: Etherton and Kingston (1999), *Oxford Certificate English 4*

Read about bonsai trees. Answer the questions. Color the picture.

Some trees are naturally small, but this is not the case with bonsai trees. Bonsai trees are naturally large trees, but in Japan (and now anywhere in the world) people can make naturally large trees grow very small indeed. The word "bonsai" means small in Japanese. People grow bonsai trees in small pots. They cut the leaves, shoots and roots of the tree in the pot very often, so that the tree stays small. A bonsai tree which is 150 years old, can be only 60–70 centimeters high. But everything about the tree is perfect. Tiny leaves grow on miniature branches, and the miniature branches grow from perfect little trunks. People all over the world collect bonsai trees.

1 Are bonsai trees naturally small?

_____

2 What does the word "bonsai" mean?

_____

3 What do people plant bonsai trees in?

_____

4 What do people do so that the trees stay small?

_____

5 How tall do bonsai trees grow?

_____

6 Which parts of bonsai trees stay very small?

_____

E   Source: Kniveton and Llanas (1995), *Kid's Club 4 (Activity Book)*

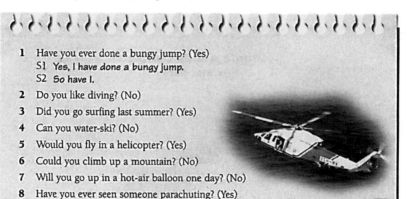

C1 *Practise in pairs. S1 is Sandra. Read the question aloud, and then answer it. S2 is Chris. S2 must agree with S1, using* **So** *or* **Neither**.

1 Have you ever done a bungy jump? (Yes)
  S1 Yes, I have done a bungy jump.
  S2 So have I.
2 Do you like diving? (No)
3 Did you go surfing last summer? (Yes)
4 Can you water-ski? (No)
5 Would you fly in a helicopter? (Yes)
6 Could you climb up a mountain? (No)
7 Will you go up in a hot-air balloon one day? (No)
8 Have you ever seen someone parachuting? (Yes)

F Source: Etherton and Kingston (1999), *Oxford Certificate English 4*

Listening

Our physical appearance is determined by a combination of the genes inherited from our parents and the environment and conditions in which we grow up.
With a partner, note down one or two ways in which the following factors influence our physical appearance.

a nutrition and diet
b health care – availability and quality of doctors, dentists, hospitals etc.
c climate
d economic and social background
e any other factors you think are important

⌨ Now listen to the extract from a radio programme called *Pause For Thought* and answer questions 1 – 5.

1 What do the low doors in medieval castles illustrate?
2 What was the effect of a lack of calcium?
3 What has happened to the Japanese recently?
4 Why did pale skin have social importance in earlier times?
5 What does the condition of Elizabeth I's teeth show us?

Did any of the speaker's points match yours?
Do you agree that the environment is the main influence on our appearance?

G Source: Foley and Hall (1993), *Distinction*

APPENDIX 5.1 Teacher's notes

Day one

1 Warmer: describing people
Quick diagnostic test of students' knowledge, get them to each write five sentences, describing someone in the class without mentioning their name. They should think about the following areas: height/build/age/face/eyes/hair/clothes. Teacher reads out descriptions, students guess who is being described.

2 Vocabulary: build adjectives
a) Students match 'build' adjectives in exercise two to definitions.
b) Bring in large visuals of famous people for students to describe using target language.

3 Listening: descriptions for picture recognition (build + age)
Home-made listening: people of different ages describing people in the large visuals. Students firstly decide which visual each person is describing. Then listen again and decide on the approximate age of each person speaking. Feed in language in exercise three and check meaning.

4 Reading poems
Bring in poems on the theme of 'old age'. Check comprehension and sentence stress.

5 Writing poems
Students write their own poems about different times of life.

Day two

1 Lead-in
Do exercise four with the whole class as a lead-in activity.

2 Vocabulary: hair and eyes
Put two columns on the board headed 1. *Hair* and 2. *Eyes*. Write various target adjectives (from exercises five and six) scattered over the board, e.g. *large, straight, round*. In pairs, students decide which adjectives go under each column. Get open-class feedback. As a meaning check ask students to do the word-order task in exercise five and the matching task in exercise six.

3 Writing descriptions of family
Ask students to write their descriptions focusing on face, eyes and hair. Go round and check that all is OK, feeding in extra vocabulary where necessary.

4 Speaking role-play
Get students to pretend to phone one another up, to ask their partner to go and meet a member of their family (who they have just written about) at the airport. For some reason, the student him/herself can't go. The students must give a full description of their relative to their partner.

Day three

1 Warmer: clothes vocabulary
Ask students to brainstorm all the clothes vocabulary they know. Write a list on the board, and encourage student to student explanations of unknown words. Bring in various items of clothing to prompt students.

2 Writing/Speaking: clothes survey
The students conduct surveys about what kinds of clothes people would wear in different situations, e.g. to dinner at a friend's house, to a wedding, to work in the garden, to a job interview.

3 Vocabulary: describing clothes
The students match the words to the definitions in exercise seven.

Then, in pairs, they think of occasions when the words might be applied to them!

4 Listening
Give students a homemade listening activity. Interviewers are discussing applicants after the interviews, including reference to how they were dressed. Who got the job? Did style of dress matter?

5 Class discussion
How much does the way people dress affect what we think about them? What else affects the way we think about them? (Prioritise.)

text by R. Acklam first published in *Practical English Teaching*, 1994.
© Mary Glasgow Publications/Scholastic

APPENDIX 5.2 Worksheet (Jolly and Bolitho)

HYPOTHETICAL MEANING: WORKSHEET

STEP ONE

a) Fact or hypothesis? Tick the right box for each statement

	FACT	HYPOTHESIS
1 I'm pleased that you've finished the work		
2 I wish you would finish the work		
3 It's time you finished the work		
4 I wish you had finished the work		
5 If only you had finished the work		
6 I see that you've finished the work		
7 If you had more time you would soon finish the work		
8 I'm surprised that you've finished the work		

b) Now underline the verb forms of 'finish' in each sentence. What do the <u>facts</u> have in common? What do the <u>hypotheses</u> have in common? What is the <u>paradox</u> about some of these verb forms?

Here are some more examples, from the press, to help you with the answers to these questions.

1 It 's time the Americans substituted action for words.
2 If I were the Prime Minister I'd think hard before trying to impose Conservative policies in Scotland.
3 Many Alliance politicians wish the parties had gone into the election united under one leader.
4 Economic experts are puzzled to see that the pound has not risen on world markets.
5 If only England had a player of Maradona's calibre.

STEP TWO

There is an idea 'behind' many of these sentences with hypothetical meaning. Look at these examples:

It's time you had your hair cut. (It's too long)
I wish my brother were here with me. (But he isn't)
If only I had worked harder. (But I didn't)

a) Now provide the ideas behind each of these statements.

1 I wish you didn't smoke so heavily. (   )
2 It's time we went home. (   )
3 Just suppose you had dropped the bottle. (   )
4 If only you had listened to your mother. (   )
5 I'd have bought the car if it hadn't been yellow. (   )
6 It's high time you got rid of that old jacket. (   )
7 If I were you I'd catch the early train. (   )
8 He looked as though he'd seen a ghost. (   )

Which of the above examples expresses (a) regret?
(b) advice?
(c) strong suggestion?
(d) a wish?
(e) reproach?

b) Now try to explain the difference <u>in the speakers' minds</u> between these pairs of statements:

    I (a) 'It's time to leave.   II (a) 'It's time to get up.'
        (b) 'It's time we left.'   (b) 'It's time you got up.'
   III (a) 'It's time for us to take a break.'
       (b) 'It's high time we took a break.'

STEP THREE

Make statements to respond to or develop these situations, using the instructions in brackets in each case.

1 It's 9.30 and René still hasn't arrived in class. (Comment reproachfully on this.)
2 Adrian's hair is rather long. (Advise him to have it cut.)
3 Nathalie hasn't done her homework. (Advise her to do it next time.)
4 You haven't worked very hard during the course. (Express regret.)
5 Pauline is still teaching at 12.45. (Reproach her.)
6 Thomas asks to borrow your rubber for the tenth time. (Make a strong suggestion.)
7 You went out last night and Robert de Niro was on TV. (Express regret or relief.)
8 It's 8 pm and your landlady still hasn't put dinner on the table. In fact, she's painting her toenails. (Use a question to make a strong suggestion.)

REFERENCES

Look at:
Murphy, R. 1996, *English Grammar in Use* (new edn.) Units 37 and 38. Cambridge: Cambridge University Press.
Swan, M. 1996, *Practical English Usage* (new edn.) 606 and 632.2, Oxford: Oxford University Press

APPENDIX 5.3 Grammar exercises

Complete the sentences with a gerund using the following verbs.

practise	~~take~~	go	become	pass
get	~~travel~~	do	teach	save

1   I'm worried about ...*taking*... my exams.
2   I've often dreamed of ...*travelling*... round the world.
3   We talked about .... married one day.
4   I bought some new clothes before .... to the interview.
5   They believe in .... children to look after themselves.

A   Source: Walker and Elsworth (2000), *Grammar Practice for Elementary Students*

Complete the sentences, putting the verbs into the gerund or the ***to***-infinitive.

1   .*Eating*... too many sweets is bad for you. (eat)
2   Do you want .*to stay*.. here tonight? (stay)
3   Daisy suggested .... a day at the beach. (spend)
4   I always enjoy .... at night. (read)
5   She's decided .... him a new watch for his birthday. (buy)

B   Source: Walker and Elsworth (2000), *Grammar Practice for Elementary Students*

Exercise D

Make true sentences using these words:
never sometimes often usually always
Example:
I have a drink before going to bed.
I <u>usually</u> have a drink before going to bed.

1 I wake up without an alarm. _____
2 I have a shower in the morning. _____
3 I have tea for breakfast. _____
4 I read the newspaper in the morning. _____
5 I walk to school / university / work / the shops. _____

C   Source: McGrath and Prowse (1993), *Intermediate Grammar Helpline*

What do you usually do in the mornings? Finish these sentences.

I always _____

I often _____

I sometimes _____

I hardly ever _____

I never _____

D   Source: Gershon and Mares (1995), *On Line (Workbook)*

Match these problems with the best advice.

1. I can't sleep at night.   Why don't you take some aspirin?
2. I have trouble meeting people.   You shouldn't drink so much coffee.
3. I have a headache and a fever.   You ought to drive more slowly.
4. I was late again for work.   You should get an alarm clock.
5. I got another speeding ticket.   Maybe you should join a club.

E   Source: Gershon and Mares (1995), *On Line (Workbook)*

Reply to these people and give advice. Use should/shouldn't.

1 I'm tired.   4 I feel sick.
2 I've got toothache.   5 I've got a cold.
3 My back hurts.   6 I've got a cough.

F   Source: Greenall (1997), *Reward Elementary*

Unscramble these questions, then answer them in complete sentences with your own information.

Questions	Answers
1. classical music like you do?	
_____ ?	**Yes, I really like it.**
2. kind you like of do movies what?	
_____ ?	_____
3. in you are computers interested?	
_____ ?	_____

G   Source: Gershon and Mares (1995), *On Line (Workbook)*

Most of these sentences have an error. Correct the errors you find.

1. Do you know when does the flight arrive?

2. Masako is not sure how long can she be away.

3. I wonder how long does the ship take to reach Shanghai.

4. Tell me where you want to go in Italy.

5. I don't know how much does a membership cost.

6. The travel agent asked me what kind of vacation I want to take.

H   Source: Ellis and Gaies (1999), *Impact Grammar*

---

1. Complete the table with sentences from the conversation.

sentence starts with a WH question	WH question is embedded in a statement
• *How can you get more value for your travel dollar?*	• *...what the All-Continent Travel Club has for you.*
•	•
•	•

2. Study the word order in the questions and the statements. How is it different?

3. Can you say what is wrong with this sentence?
   He wants to know what country am I visiting.

I   Source: Ellis and Gaies (1999), *Impact Grammar*

Exercise D

You are attending an international conference at which such issues as racial conflict, youth unemployment and the drought in Africa are being discussed. You want to comment on some of the points made by the various speakers. Choose the verb you would use. (In some cases, more than one answer may be correct.)

Example:
1d

The speaker said:	*You say:*
Young blacks have a new sense of identity. They feel they are black first and British second.	**1** You _____ that young blacks feel they are black first and British second. In my country . . . **(a)** put forward **(b)** implied **(c)** told **(d)** claimed
Racial conflict – and there is worse to come – is an inevitable result of racial discrimination.	**2** You _____ that there is more racial conflict to come. My impression is that . . . **(a)** argued **(b)** warned **(c)** expressed **(d)** commented
The politicians would like us to believe that the unemployed are the victims of economic forces. We know better. They are victims, all right, victims of political decisions.	**3** You _____ that the unemployed are the victims of political decisions. Could you . . . **(a)** suggested **(b)** mentioned **(c)** felt **(d)** persuaded

J   Source: McGrath and Prowse (1993), *Intermediate Grammar Helpline*

Pretend you are Amy. Tell your mother about some of the conversations you had today. (These dialogues contain statements, instructions and questions. Change them into reported speech. Use any suitable reporting verbs.)

1 Amy: Why are you so excited?
   May: I won $5,000 in a lottery yesterday!
   Amy: Are you going to spend all the money?
   May: No, I'm going to put it in a bank.

   I asked May why she was so excited. She said that she had won $5,000 in a lottery the previous day. I asked her whether she was going to spend all the money. She replied that she was going to put it in a bank.

2 Amy: Are you our new neighbour?
   Des: Yes, I am.
   Amy: We are having a party tomorrow. Can you come to it?
   Des: I'm not sure. I may come.
   Amy: You have to come! You will enjoy it!

K   Source: Etherton and Kingston (1999), *Oxford Certificate English 4*

Read these texts, then do the exercise below.

EXPERTS are trying to trace the source of salmonella poisoning which has killed two elderly patients and affected three more at Bradwell Hospital, Chesterton, Staffordshire.

Ticket collector Arthur Spicer, 25, was recovering in hospital yesterday after being stabbed in the chest and beaten about the head at Baldock Station, Hertfordshire.

PENSIONERS Jim and Lilian Barbery enjoy colourful breakfasts at their home in Trefullock Moor, Cornwall . . . their hen Goldie has started laying bright blue eggs.

Police are investigating the theft of a necklace belonging to Lady Howe, wife of a former Chancellor of the Exchequer, from a hotel room in Newcastle upon Tyne on May 24.

In which of these sentences is the agent really necessary? _____

1 Two elderly patients at Bradwell Hospital have been killed (by food poisoning).
2 Three other patients have also been affected (by food poisoning).
3 Ticket collector Arthur Spicer, 25, was recovering in hospital yesterday after being stabbed in the chest (by someone).
4 A man is being questioned (by the police).
5 Blue eggs have been laid (by a Cornish hen).
6 The hen, formerly known as Goldie, has been renamed Bluebird (by her owners).
7 A necklace belonging to Lady Howe was stolen (by thieves) on May 24.
8 It had just been insured (by her husband) for £2,000.

L Source: McGrath and Prowse (1993), *Intermediate Grammar Helpline*

Rewrite these sentences in the passive.
1 Michelangelo painted the Sistine Chapel.
2 They grow cotton in Egypt.
3 They make Mercedes cars in Germany.
4 Hemingway wrote *The Old Man and the Sea*.
5 Verdi composed *Aida*.
6 William I built the Tower of London.

M Source: Greenall (1997), *Reward Elementary*

B2 *Complete these news items by changing the verbs **either** into the active **or** into the passive form of the present perfect tense. Think carefully about the present perfect tense.*

A school in America (**a**) _ _ _ _ (introduce) a new computer-assisted phone system so that parents can call in and find out what homework their children should be studying. The system (**b**) _ _ _ _ (use) a lot by the parents since it was introduced. The school says that students' work (**c**) _ _ _ _ (improve) since the new system started. This new idea (**d**) _ _ _ _ (welcome) by the parents. 'We (**e**) _ _ _ _ (learn) a lot more about the school recently,' said one parent.

N Source: Etherton and Kingston (1999), *Oxford Certificate English 4*

APPENDIX 5.4 Vocabulary exercises

Draw lines from each verb to one or two words in the circle.

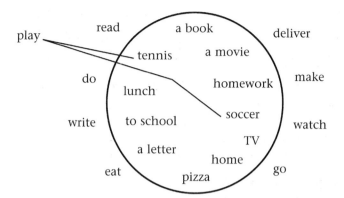

A Source: Maurer and Schonberg (1999), *True Colours*.
Reprinted by permission of Pearson Education, Inc.

1 Which of the following is usually found in the classroom?
   (a) subjects   (b) wall chart   (c) caption   (d) horoscope
2 She hated school, so she often ————————.
   (a) played truant   (b) expelled   (c) failed   (d) broke out
3 What's this?

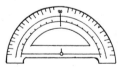

   (a) a pencil sharpener
   (b) a set square
   (c) a ruler
   (d) a protractor
4 Which of the following is not a state school?
   (a) a primary school   (b) a prep school
   (c) a comprehensive school   (d) a Sixth-Form College
5 She's in her first year at university. She's ————————.
   (a) a pupil   (b) an apprentice   (c) a scholar   (d) an undergraduate

B Source: Watcyn-Jones (1994), *Target Vocabulary 2*

Show the difference in meaning between these sets of adjectives by placing them in the correct positions on the scales. Look at the example.

Example
common, rare, unique, unusual

ONE ◄────────► MANY

| | | | |
|a|b|c|d|

Answer
a unique   b rare   c unusual   d common

1 damp, dry, humid, moist, soaked, wet

WET ◄────────► DRY

| | | | | | |
|a|b|c|d|e|f|

2 gigantic, huge, large, sizeable, small, tiny

LITTLE ◄────────► BIG

| | | | | | |
|a|b|c|d|e|f|

C   Source: McGrath and Prowse (1987), *Extensions*

Put the foods under the correct supermarket sections.

potatoes	shrimp	duck	spaghetti	cheese
apples	tomatoes	butter	salmon	cherries
	cornflakes		pork chops	

Fruit and vegetables — *Dairy products* — *Cereals and pasta* — *Meat and poultry* — *Fish and seafood*

D   Source: Taylor et al. (1994), *Reflections (Workbook 1)*

1) Can you complete these expressions? Use a dictionary for any you don't know.

Example: .(d) sentence..   someone to ten years in prison

a) give	1)	a crime
b) release	2)	someone's fingerprints
c) be found	3)	someone with murder
d) sentence	4)	evidence
e) charge		
f) commit	5)	guilty
g) take	6)	a parking fine
h) put	7)	someone on probation
i) pay	8)	someone on bail

2) Match the words with the definitions and make sentences. You may use your dictionary.

Example: A *defendant* is a person accused of a crime.

a) witness	1) defends people accused of serious crimes
b) barrister	2) where a trial is held
c) magistrate	3) decides whether a person is innocent or guilty of a serious crime
d) jury	4) gives evidence during a case
e) court	5) tries people accused of minor offences

E   Source: Prowse and McGrath (1984), *Advances*

We expect a piece of written English to be more or less consistent: it can be a mixture of *informal and neutral* expressions or it can mix *formal and neutral* expressions; but it should not mix informal and formal expressions.

Use the expressions given below to write out *two* versions of this text. The first version should be suitable for a magazine for young teenagers and the second for older readers.

(1)_____ somebody (2)_____ something (3)_____. You (4)_____ expect the (5)_____ to (6)_____ it (7)_____ (8)_____ this (9)_____ quite as easy as it (10)_____. For (11)_____, (12)_____ people in the street, (13)_____ them questions, and (14)_____ them to (15)_____ their pockets.

(1) What if/Suppose   (2) stole/nicked   (3) of yours/that belonged to you   (4) would almost certainly/'d (5) cops/police   (6) get/retrieve   (7) for you./back for you, wouldn't you?   (8) However,/But   (9) isn't/is not   (10) may seem/sounds   (11) one thing/instance   (12) it might involve stopping/they'd probably have to stop   (13) ask/asking (14) get/obliging   (15) empty/turn out
Examples:
TEXT 1   *What if somebody nicked something...*
TEXT 2   *Suppose somebody stole something...*

    Source: Prowse and McGrath (1984), *Advances*

A   Use the definitions below to build words beginning *un-* or *in-* and ending *-able* or *-ible*. In some cases, you will need to omit the *e* at the end of the verb. Check the meanings of any words you don't know in your dictionary.

Example   *Word*
You can't pronounce it: un/pronounce/able (not/able to be/
                                             pronounced)

1 You can't bear it: ....
2 You can't believe it: ....
3 You can't tolerate it: ....
4 You can't define it: ....
5 You can't forgive it: ....
6 You can't forget it: ....

G   Source: McGrath and Prowse (1987), *Extensions*

Write the missing words in the sentences below. Choose from the following:

bed and breakfast	chalet	motel
boarding house	guest house	self-catering
campsite	holiday camp	spa
caravan	hotel	youth hostel

1 If you have a tent, you can always stay at a _____.
2 A _____ is a place with a spring of mineral water, where people go for their health — usually to try to cure various diseases.
3 In Britain you can stay the night at a _____ place. This is usually a private home and is fairly cheap. It is sometimes called a _____.
4 The Ritz is a famous _____ in London. So is the Dorchester.
5 A _____ is a large private home where you can pay to stay and have meals. These are very common at seaside resorts.

H   Source: Watcyn-Jones (1994), *Target Vocabulary 2*

A   The human body is made up of a number of components which can be grouped according to various criteria. Copy the word map on to a piece of paper.

Now, working with a partner, use the words below to complete the boxes in the word map.

calves	*muscles*	*joints*
shoulder	*bones*	*heart*
liver	*organs*	*knee*
skull	*soft tissues*	

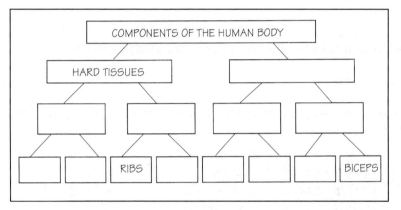

COMPONENTS OF THE HUMAN BODY

HARD TISSUES

RIBS   BICEPS

I   Source: Foley and Hall (1993), *Distinction*

Match the answers to the questions.

1. What might you *put off* doing?   a. Bad teeth.
2. If you eat too much, what might you *put on*?   b. Your friend's little brother.
3. Who might you *put up* with?   c. 16 hours a day.
4. What might *put you off* someone?   d. Weight.
5. If you were self-employed, what might you *put in*?   e. Homework.

J   Source: McGrath and Prowse (1987), *Extensions*

APPENDIX 6.1 Extracts from published materials

Ask and answer about Martin Luther King, Jr.'s life.

> When was he born?

> What did his father do?

> How old was he when he won the Nobel Peace Prize?

Martin Luther King, Jr.

I HAVE A DREAM

... I have a dream that my four little children will one day live in a nation where they will not be judged by the color of their skin but by the content of their character...

EARLY LIFE

Born:	January 15, 1929
Place of birth:	Atlanta, GA
Father's job:	Baptist minister
Mother's job:	Musician
Family:	1 brother, 1 sister
Martin:	Happy, intelligent, popular

CAREER

1954: Pastor of Baptist Church, Montgomery, AL

1960: Co-pastor (with Martin Luther King, Sr.) of Ebenezer Baptist Church, Atlanta

1960: President of Southern Christian Leadership Conference

1963: Made "I have a dream" speech in Washington, DC

1964: *Time* Magazine (January) "Man of the Year"

1964: Won Nobel Peace Prize (youngest winner)

1968: Assassinated in Memphis, TN (April 4th)

> **1957**: Visit to India convinced King that Gandhi's philosophy of "non-violent civil disobedience" was the right course to follow.

> **1983**: January 15th declared Martin Luther King Day (national holiday) in the United States.

EDUCATION AND FAMILY

Primary and high school:	Atlanta
Moorhouse College:	BS (sociology); graduated 1948
Crozer Theological Seminary:	BD (divinity); graduated 1951
Boston University:	Ph.D. (theology); graduated 1955

Married: Coretta Scott (1953); 4 children

Group work: Each student should take the information for one aspect of Martin Luther King, Jr.'s life and write a paragraph.

A   Source: Taylor et al. (1994), *Reflections*

Take the Money and *RUN*

Paulo Umberto is one of the world's best soccer players. Read the story and find out: Why is he thinking of moving to a new team?

Paulo Umberto is a lucky man. He is married to a wonderful woman and they have three healthy, happy children. He is also the best soccer player in his country. This past season he led his team, the Eagles, to the championship of his country.

The sportswriters say that the Eagles are the best team in the history of the country, and probably one of the best teams in the world. The Eagles do everything well—defense, passing and scoring. **Most everyone believes Paulo Umberto is the main reason for the success of the Eagles.**

But Paulo is thinking of leaving. His contract with the Eagles will end soon. So Paulo has been talking with the four owners of the team about a new contract. The four owners, all brothers whose family is very famous in the country, want very much to keep Paulo on the Eagles.

At the same time, **the owner of a famous English football team wants Paulo to play with his team.** He has offered Paulo a lot of money— much more than he earns now. If he signs with the English team, in five years he would make more money than he would earn in his lifetime playing in his country. He would be so rich that he would never have to worry about money again.

Paulo wants to continue to play for the Eagles and live in his own country. He really doesn't want to change his lifestyle and move to England. He doesn't speak English. His wife and his children want to stay in their country. He likes his teammates and the owners. He knows that they have offered him the best contract they can afford. No one is very wealthy in his country.

But the contract with the English team is very attractive. Paulo could help make that team the best in Europe, and maybe the world. And he would be very, very rich.

WHAT DO YOU THINK?

Do you think Paulo should 'go for the money'? Check the opinions you agree with.

❑ When there's a big chance, you should take it. Don't hesitate. You may never have a second big chance!

❑ Money and fame are exciting. If you can get them both, why not!

❑ I think you have to go for the money. You can never have too much money.

❑ Happiness is more important than money. You can't buy that with money.

❑ Peace and harmony are the most important things in life. If you have peace and harmony in your life, don't change, even for money.

Now exchange your ideas with a classmate.

TURN TO PAGE 81 FOR AN INTERACTION TIP.

LOOKING AT THE ISSUE

If you received a lot of money, what would you do? List three things.

1.	2.	3.

If you became very famous, how would you feel or what would you do? List three things.

1.	2.	3.

Are there things money can't buy? List three things.

1.	2.	3.

B Source: Day and Yamanaka (1996), *Impact Issues*

APPENDIX 6.2 Web addresses

Cable in the Classroom: www.ciconline.org

Commonwealth of Learning: www.col.org/cense

Global School/Net Foundation: www.gsn.org

International Education and Resource Network: www.iearn.org

University of Nebraska: http://class.unl.edu

Nick Nack's Telecollaborate site: http://www1.minn.net

North Carolina Center for International Understanding:
www.ga.unc.edu/NCCIU

University of Texas: www.en.utexas.edu/uv

www.worldwide.edu

Exemplary projects carried out as part of the Star Schools Project's focus on IT can be found at www.ed.gov/prog_info/StarSchools

Source: Shive (1999: 19)

APPENDIX 7.1 Text-based lesson plan

The learners and the lesson

Young adults (18–25), mixed nationality, upper intermediate, following a
General English course.
Time available: 1½ hours.

The text

the difficulty's also like stereotypes
the secretary's always got that image
of sitting on the boss's knee
and the man is the er breadwinner
of the family that's gotta be
and these all the sort of like prejudices
which come into the family
from the father and the mother
and reach into school life as well
once that sort of feeling
starts to ease off a bit
then obviously girls and boys are like
going to get more opportunities as well

[transcription of recorded interview (BBC)]

The planning stages

1. Choose your text: a text or picture in a coursebook or any other material
   you feel will interest your students.

2. Draw and label a nine-cell 'Ideas Grid' like the one illustrated. Give
   yourself plenty of space – an A4 sheet rather than the back of an envelope.

3. Brainstorm ways in which the material could be used to develop your
   students' competence in as many of the cell areas as possible, and write the ideas
   in the appropriate cell. Be specific, but don't spend time thinking about details.
   The idea is to generate as many ideas as possible in a short time – including
   different ideas for the same cell.

continued overleaf

Listening	Phonology
gist: what speaker says about stereotypes	stressed syllables: e.g. image, secretary, prejudice
Speaking	Grammar
personal reactions to speaker's ideas (could be written instead)	? the difficulty's = ? the secretary's = ?
Reading	Vocabulary
	stereotypes (opener) vocabulary building (e.g. parts of the body)
Writing	Discourse
transcribing tape spelling, punct. sentence formation	Spoken utterances → written discourse
Other (e.g. culture, study skills, etc.)	
Clues to the speaker's age, level of education, etc. Using recordings for self-study	

4. Select the ideas that you feel will be most relevant for the specific group of learners you have in mind. Don't discard the others. They may come in useful later (see Step 9, below).

5. Order the ideas you have selected in a rough sequence, and use this as the basis for a lesson plan.

Example of a plan based on the text and using ideas generated by the grid

1. Put key word on board: STEREOTYPES. Elicit associations, anecdotes, etc.

2. Set listening task (listening for gist): 'What does the speaker say about stereotypes?'

3. Play tape once and elicit answers. Use these to build up on board as much of the text as possible.

4. Ask students to work individually to transcribe extract, then play it once more, stopping at natural pauses.

5. Get individuals to come up to the board and write up information chunks of 5–8 words each. Other students check and offer suggestions for improvement. Replay tape to check final version.

6. Ask students to mark on their own (revised) transcriptions the stressed syllables in the following items without listening to the tape again:

difficulty, stereotypes, secretary, image, breadwinner, prejudice, obviously, opportunities

7. Comparison of answers (students read aloud). Encourage checking of any disputed answers by playing recording again.
8. Elicit conclusions concerning speaker: e.g. sex, age, educational background. Draw attention to vague fillers ('like', 'sort of') and regional pronunciation features if these are not mentioned.

Note: these eight steps do not constitute eight separate activities. Up to this stage, the plan really consists of five activities. Steps 2/3, 4/5 and 6/7 are all two-stage activities, each of which corresponds to only one of the cells in the grid (listening, writing – in the form of 'dictation' and therefore practising only spelling, and phonology). Step 1 practises speaking and Step 8 falls within the 'other' cell.

At this point in the lesson sequence, one possibility would be plenary discussion of the speaker's ideas. On the grounds that the practice would be more intensive (and therefore probably more useful) if done in pairs or small groups, this is offered as one of a number of 'free-choice activities' at Step 9.

9. Encourage the formation of pairs/small groups for work on one of the following tasks:

   a. Split the text into information chunks. Produce a correct written sentence for each. Add conjunctions as necessary. [rewriting/grammar/discourse]
   b. Respond to the views expressed by the speaker. Make notes on what you would say. Then find a partner to practise with. [speaking]
   c. Choose one of the categories below and write down as many English words in that category as you can:

OCCUPATIONS	PARTS OF THE BODY	FAMILY ROLES
secretary	knee	breadwinner (*earns money*)

   Can you think of any more words in these categories in your own language? Find out the English equivalents. [vocabulary/study skills]

For social as well as pedagogic reasons, the final stage in the lesson was planned as a whole-class activity.

10. Ask: 'If you had a suitable recording, which of the things that we've done today could you do on your own?'

Source: McGrath (1992)

APPENDIX 7.2 Standard reading exercise

Standard reading exercise

Before reading

1. Look at the title of your text. What do you already know about the topic? In note form write down at least five facts.

2. Write down six key words which you expect to find in the text.

3. Now write down as many associations as you can think of for each of the words you wrote in (2) above. Make 'word stars'.

4. Look at the first and last paragraphs of the text. Write a sentence which you think will describe the general idea of the text.

5. Write down five things which you would like to find out from the text. Write these in the form of questions.

Now read the text once. Do not stop at words or sentences which you do not understand. If you want to, time yourself.

Reading the text the first time

1. Was your general idea in (4) above correct?

2. Were your questions in (5) above answered? Mark the place in the text where you found the answers.

3. Find ten words which you did not understand and which you think are key words. Check their meanings in a dictionary.

Now read the text again from beginning to end.

Reading the text the second time

1. Look at each paragraph and underline the sentence(s) and/or phrase(s) which contain the broadest generalization in the paragraph.

2. Look at the remaining sentences in each paragraph: are they related to the parts you have underlined? If so, how?

3. Were there any parts of the text which you found very difficult? Look at these again. Try and decide why they are difficult. Ask for help if necessary.

4. Draw a diagram or flowchart to show how the text is organized.

5. Find as many of these as you can:

definitions	classifications
statements of aims	statements of scope

comparisons or contrasts	opinions
sentences containing causes	reasons for opinions
sentences containing results	examples
a line of argument	possible explanations
sentences in which a conclusion is drawn	reporting what other people have said
descriptions of people, things or concepts	descriptions of events, systems or processes

How did you recognize these types of sentences? Which of these helped you:

a. the overall meaning;
b. the position of the sentence in the paragraph or whole text;
c. certain words or phrases.
    Underline any words or phrases which helped you.

6. Can you say whom the author is writing for?

7. What is the author's intention: to inform? to persuade? or what?

8. Write a summary of the passage in about 200 words.

Source: Walker (1987: 48–9)

APPENDIX 7.3 Book review

3.6 Book review

CLASSIFICATION	R.RE/1 = Reading. Review writing/1
LEVEL	Intermediate
AGE	Young adult/adult
ACTIVITY TYPE	Reading and review writing
AIM	To encourage reflection on what has been read and to provide a record of reading achieved. To practise evaluative writing.
PREPARATION	Read a novel or short story that interests you.
INSTRUCTIONS	Use the review sheet below as a guide to writing a review of what you have read. For each novel or short story you read, complete one of these review sheets so that you build up a record of what you have read in English.

REVIEW SHEET

Title: -

Author: -

Publisher: -

Category: ªTick one)

Romance ☐   Historical ☐

Horror ☐   Science fiction ☐

Crime ☐   Other (describe) ☐

Spy ☐

The most important characters: -

- -

- -

Summary of the story: -

- -

What I liked: -

- -

What I disliked: -

- -

I do/do not recommend this book: -

- -

- -

FOLLOW-UP   File your review alphabetically by the title of the book in the 'review file' so that other students can read it. Look at other reviews in the file. You may find a review of a book you would like to read.

Source: Sheerin (1989), *Self-Access*

APPENDIX 7.4 Standard exercise

BEFORE VIEWING
What do you think will be in the news today?

WHILE VIEWING
1. How many headlines are there today?
2. Number the topics covered by the news items.

—— Politics: home	—— The Arts
—— Politics: abroad	—— Sport and Leisure
—— Crime	—— Gossip
—— Disaster/accidents	—— Public information
—— Natural world	—— Human interest
—— Science and technology	—— Weather

3. Write in the appropriate keywords from the news items.

	1	2	3	4	5	6
Who						
What						
Where						
When						

4. With your partner discuss the programme. Tell about the news item you found most interesting. Does your partner agree with you? What do you think will happen?

EXTENSION
Your group is now going to prepare a news programme. Choose a producer to coordinate the programme and also to introduce each item.

The rest of the group will form pairs and together prepare an item. One of you is the reporter and the other the person in the news.

You must be ready for the start of the programme, so work quickly!

Source: Kissinger (1990)

APPENDIX 7.5 Standard exercise example

The worksheet below is based on a text about education in the UK (the text itself is not reproduced).

BEFORE YOU READ
1. What do you think the title will tell you?
>   Look at the title, introduction, captions and headings.
>   How is the text organised? Does it have several sections?
>   Where does the text come from? Do you know or can you guess?
2. What do you already know about this subject? Make a list.
3. What would you like to know? Write your questions.

READ THE TEXT QUICKLY
DO NOT STOP AT WORDS OR SENTENCES YOU DO NOT UNDERSTAND
4. Can you find the answers to any of your questions?
5. What is the text about?
>   Which of these topics are mentioned? Add others not listed below.

state education	learning problems
private education	teaching methods
primary school	curriculum
secondary school	discipline
college/university	particular people
examinations	particular issues
....	....

READ THE TEXT AGAIN
6. Do you understand the main points?
>   For each of the topics you have ticked, write two or three words to remind you of the main points.
7. Are there many words you don't understand?
>   Write down up to six new words which you think are important.
>   Can you guess their meanings? Can you ask someone?
>   Do you want to look them up in a dictionary now or later?
8. What is the writer's purpose? Who is he/she writing for?
>   Does the writer give an opinion as well as giving information?
>   If so, where in the text?
>   What kind of people might read this text?

AFTER READING
9. What is your opinion?
>   What did you learn that you did not know before?
>   What did you find most interesting?
>   What happens in your country? What do you think about this?
10. Did you find any parts of the text difficult?
>   What made it difficult for you?
>   lack of knowledge about people, places or ideas mentioned
>   vocabulary – too many new words
>   grammar – sentences too long or complicated
>   organisation – too long, confusing

Source: Axbey (1989)

APPENDIX 7.6 Self-access tasks

3.4 Superman versus smoking

CLASSIFICATION   R.IT/1 = Reading. Information transfer/1

LEVEL   Intermediate

AGE   Adolescent/young adult

ACTIVITY TYPE   Information transfer

AIM   To extract and recognize relevant information from a reading text.

PREPARATION   Think about the problem of children smoking. How can they be persuaded not to start? Do you think the problem is a serious one? Make a list of three ways in which children could be prevented from trying cigarettes.

INSTRUCTIONS   Read the following text and use the information to complete the questionnaire below. Write the information on a separate piece of paper. Do not write on this card.

TASK SHEET

Over 100,000 primary school children wrote supporting Superman in his fight against smoking during the first four weeks of the Health Education Council's recent £500,000 campaign.

The campaign, which began just after Christmas, uses the Superman character to persuade 7- to 11-year-olds that they should 'crush the evil Nick O'Teen' and never say yes to a cigarette.

Most of the budget has been spent on producing and showing a cartoon television commercial, which features Superman in conflict with the arch-enemy Nick O'Teen.

The campaign, which is seen as a long-term project, is based on careful research. This showed that one in three adult smokers started before they were nine and that 80 per cent of children who smoke regularly grow up to be smokers. For boys, the average age for starting to smoke was found to be 9.7 years while for girls, it was 11.2 years.

continued overleaf

QUESTIONNAIRE

Country: __Britain_____   Intended public (age, sex . . .) _____

Budget: _____

Media used — television ☐
— radio ☐
— posters ☐
— magazines/comics/
newspapers ☐
— other ☐

Opening date: _____

Closing date   _____

Slogans _____

Estimated success — high ☐
— average ☐
— low ☐

KEY

Country _Britain_____   Intended public (age, sex . . .) boys + girls
aged 7-11___

Budget: £500,000____

Media used — television ☑
— radio ☐
— posters ☐
— magazines/comics/
newspapers ☑
— other ☐

Opening date: December_

Closing date: ? 'long term'

Slogans 'Crush the evil Nick O Teen',
'Never say yes to a cigarette'
☑ (over 100.000 children wrote)

Estimated success — high ☑
— average ☐
— low ☐

Comments to the teacher

1 Almost any informative text and some fictional ones can be reorganized in this way. Look carefully at the information contained in the text and sort the information into categories which can then be represented in schematic, tabular form.

2 As a variation, students can use the information contained in a text to draw or complete a diagram, a chart, a map, a plan, etc.

A   Source: Sheerin (1989)

4.10 Wartime agriculture

CLASSIFICATION   W.SC/1 = Writing. Sentence combining/1

LEVEL   Upper intermediate to Advanced

AGE   Adult

ACTIVITY TYPE   Sentence combining

AIM   To practise text organization by combining individual sentences in such a way that they form a logical connected text.

PREPARATION   Find a short text and read it carefully. Find as many different ways as you can by which connecting words link the sentences together to form a piece of continuous writing. Words which act as connectors in this way are:

__ All words which would not give you any information if they stood by themselves without the text, e.g. pronouns such as *he, they;* relative pronouns such as *who, which, that;* demonstrative pronouns such as *this, that;* words which point to a time or place such as *now, here, there,* etc.
__ Words which show the logical relationship between one part of the text and another such as *and, however, in spite of that,* etc.

INSTRUCTIONS   Using appropriate connecting words, link the sentences below together to make a connected text. Although there is a model text in the key, there is not just one right answer and you should combine the sentences in the best way you can. You may choose to combine two or more sentences together. The first two sentences have been linked in one possible way as an example.

TASK SHEET   1 Farming is the oldest industry of all.
2 Farming enjoyed a brief period of prosperity during the First World War.
3 There were submarine boat attacks on merchant shipping.
4 Britain imported about two-thirds of its food.
5 It was essential to increase home food production.
6 The Government encouraged the ploughing-up of grasslands.
7 The reason for the ploughing-up of grasslands was to grow more cereals.
8 The Government gained the co-operation of farmers in 1917.
9 The farmers co-operated because the Government gave them guaranteed prices in 1917.
10 In 1917 agricultural workers were given a reasonable minimum wage.
11 The wheat harvest was increased by sixty per cent.
12 There was a large rise in the production of potatoes, barley, and oats.

EXAMPLE   Farming, the oldest industry of all, enjoyed a brief period of prosperity during the First World War. (Sentences 1 & 2)

KEY   **Original text**
Farming, the oldest industry of all, enjoyed a brief period of prosperity during the First World War. Submarine boat attacks on merchant shipping, at a time when Britain imported about two-thirds of its food, made it essential to increase home food production. The Government encouraged the ploughing-up of grassland in order to grow more cereals, and gained the co-operation of farmers by giving them guaranteed prices in 1917. In the same year, agricultural workers were given a reasonable minimum wage. The wheat harvest was increased by sixty per cent, and there was a large rise in the production of potatoes, barley, and oats.
Adapted from *Britain since 1700* by R J Cootes & L E Snellgrove.

1.5 Character building

Elementary

20–30 minutes

Simple present

1 Draw a circle on the board.
2 Tell the learners they are going to build this into a character.
3 Ask them first of all whether it's a man or a woman.
4 Continue to ask questions to build up the physical representation on the board. For example, *Does he have a moustache? Is he fat? Does she have a big nose?*

5 Continue to ask questions (but without adding to the drawing) about where the person lives, their job, interests, family, and so on, and point out any apparent contradictions, for example, *Well, if he's so interested in sport, how come he's fat? She's only 28 and she's got ten children?*

Reverse the roles. Now learners ask you questions enabling you to build up a character. Ask a student to do the drawing on the blackboard so you have an opportunity to introduce or revise comparisons, for example, *No, he's not that tall,* or *Her hair's longer than that.*

The drawing on the board helps to suggest a character and serves as the basis for the subsequent work. As learners come up with suggestions, the pace increases and the learners themselves point our contradictions and suggest alternatives.

A Source: Campbell and Kryszewska (1992), *Learner-based Teaching*

5.3 My story?

LEVEL
Lower-intermediate and above

TIME
45–60 minutes

LANGUAGE
Giving the gist

PROCEDURE
1 Learners recall something really exciting that has happened to them or somebody in their family, or a particularly happy moment in their lives.

2 They describe this event in writing, in their own language, in a specified number of words. The stories should be written in a dramatic and gripping way.

3 Redistribute the texts and give each student five minutes to read the story and memorize it.

4 Collect the texts and ask each student to write in English the story they have just read, trying to preserve the character and drama of the original. You can make the original versions available on request for a short time, but the learners should not have them in front of them all the time.

5 Display all the stories. Learners mill around, read the stories, and look for their own.

6 Give out the native-language versions at random and ask learners to pair the originals with the translations.

7 Translators take the original version and their own translation and underline, in the original, phrases or words which they did not know, or would not know, how to translate. Discuss these with the whole class.

SAMPLE PRODUCT

Marek is a doctor and works in the hospital A few days ago, ~~he was a witness of witnessed the installation of~~ ~~installing~~/a special kind of telephone in his hospital. It was connected with George Bush's visit to Gdansk Using this telephone it was possible to get ~~the~~ a connection to Washington in 3 seconds by satellite This telephone was ~~set~~ installed by a 16-year-old boy, who had a few technical problems, because of differences between Polish and American standards

B Source: Campbell and Kryszewska (1992), *Learner-based Teaching*

1.10 My grammar problem

LEVEL
: Lower-intermediate and above

TIME
: 45–60 minutes

LANGUAGE
: Learners' problems

PROCEDURE
: 1 Ask each student to identify a grammar problem they have or think they have. To make the task easier tell the learners they may browse through their exercise books and recent homework.
2 Check that every student has got at least one problem.
3 Ask learners to mill around to see if they can find anyone with a similar problem or problems. The idea is that they should form pairs with related grammar problems. For example, various conditionals and mixed conditionals could pair up, or reported statements and questions, or passive and 'have something done' constructions.
4 Ask each pair to write down their problem on a piece of paper, for example 'conditionals'. They should write the grammatical term and also one example sentence. The problems are then displayed.
5 Each pair then chooses from this selection a problem they think they understand—a different problem for each pair.
6 Using reference books, grammar books, and the teacher, they prepare an explanation or mini-lecture on the problem. The teacher can answer specific questions but should not offer a complete explanation of the problem.
7 Each pair presents their lecture to the whole class. Others may challenge or ask for clarification. If the students cannot agree, or if the explanations are inaccurate or incomplete, add to or amend what they have said.

VARIATION 1
: If it is a large class, instead of forming pairs at stage 3, form groups of three or four, so that there will be fewer presentations in the last stage.

VARIATION 2
: For stage 7 split the pairs and ask the learners to form two big circles. Working clockwise, learners present their lecture to their neighbour, who passes it on. The activity ends when the explanations come full circle and the originator sees if the lecture has been simplified too much or misunderstood. If so, they may have to explain their reservations to their circle.

VARIATION 3
: After stage 3 ask each pair or group to write a sentence containing the problem. They write the sentence in the middle of a sheet of paper. Redistribute the sheets. Another pair then has to write a short story, the central part of which is the problem sentence. Remove the problem sentence by cutting it out or erasing it. The stories circulate and each pair has to try to reconstruct the missing sentence. The stories, the original problem sentence, and the suggested sentences are displayed. Discuss the outcome with the class.

VARIATION 4
: If students cannot find partners in stage 3, they should form pairs with any other student and try to incorporate both the problems in one sentence.

C Source: Campbell and Kryszewska (1992), *Learner-based Teaching*

3.3 GROUP CHAIN STORIES

LEVEL
Lower
intermediate –

TIME
60 minutes

MATERIALS
One piece of paper,
about A4 size, per
student

NUUMBERS
At least 2 groups of
about 6 per group

Procedure

1 Put groups round a table, each student with a piece of A4 paper and a pen.

2 Each group decides on the first line of a story. Encourage them to make this as open as possible, as in Stage 2 of the previous activity.

3 Everybody in the group writes this first line at the top of their piece of paper. Then individually they add the next sentence. The papers are then passed round to the person on the left. Each person then writes the sentence to follow the previous one on their new paper. This continues until the pages get back to where they began so that the first and last sentences of the stories are written by the same person.

4 Everybody checks their story for mistakes or improvements. If they want to change or correct anything they must consult the student who wrote it before doing so. If necessary they can ask you to arbitrate or advise. Check as many as possible yourself.

5 In their groups they each read out their final versions and vote on the one they want to present to the other group(s). I always check at least this one myself.

6 They rehearse their presentations. I use the word 'present' the story to the rest of the class in my instructions as it is open to a wide interpretation. Different groups will choose different formats, e.g. each person reads the line they wrote: one person narrates while the others mime: the group act out the story (with or without a narrator). I always suggest that as many of them should be involved as possible. In practice, I have usually found that they all take part, but that is their choice.

FOLLOW-ONS

The same as for Mutual Dictation Stories, Activity 3.2

NOTES

a Some of the best role plays I have seen have resulted from this activity. Even the more inhibited students seem happy and relaxed performing materials that they have been partially, but not wholly, responsible for. On one notable occasion the sketches that evolved were later performed in an end-of-course revue, totally unprompted by me.

b Another bonus of a group chain story is that in Stage 5 everybody listens to every story enthusiastically. We all have an egocentric streak which motivates us to listen to find out what happened to our contributions.

VARIATIONS

1 The technique could be used to generate dialogues.

2 Business or ESP application Students could focus on their particular area of interest, e.g. the opening line could be 'There are a number of stages involved in launching a new product'.

3 Teacher training application Teachers could focus on a particular teaching point, e.g. they could choose to write about different ways of using stories in the classroom.

ACKNOWLEDGEMENTS

I first saw Stages 1–3 of this activity done by Roger Woodham on a training workshop in Poland.

 Source: Deller (1990), *Lessons from the Learner*

APPENDIX 9
Student self-evaluation as materials evaluation

Communication Activity: Questionnaire

Complete this questionnaire for yourself and for another student. Write your own name above the first column and your partner's name above the second column. Indicate your answers like this:

VERY WELL ✓✓
WELL   ✓
NOT SURE? ? } Look up the lesson indicated.
CAN'T   ✗

TALKING
How well can you . . .

			Lesson
talk about past events?			1
talk about things you regret?			1
describe experiences which were important to you?			2
report simple conversations?			3
summarise newspaper reports?			4
give an account of an event?			5
compare life in different parts of the world?			7
describe the political and economic organisation of a country?			7
consider the causes of world poverty?			8
discuss attitudes to other countries?			8
talk about changes in society this century?			9
describe customs and festivals?			10
describe religious beliefs?			10
argue a point of view?			11
discuss courses of action?			11
argue about prices and bookings?			13
make introductions and talk to strangers?			14
give and reply to invitations?			15
be polite, pay compliments, and make excuses?			15
keep a conversation going?			16
insist and get your way?			17

			Lesson
argue about controversial issues?			17
define and describe objects?			19
give simple explanations of processes?			20.21
give simple explanations of how things work?			22
give accurate descriptions?			23
compare solutions to problems?			23
give advice?			25
give simple instructions?			26.30
explain the rules of a game?			27.29
explain the laws of a country?			28
discuss abstract issues?			29
discuss causes of past events?			31
argue about theories?			32
consider possible explanations?			33
discuss possible future events?			34
consider different possibilities?			35

LISTENING
In addition to understanding* what is said to you in Talking, how well can you understand . . .

			Lesson
someone describing a personal experience?			2
brief remarks at a party?			3
sports results?			4
descriptions of festivals?			10
airport announcements?			13
requests and enquiries from strangers?			14
polite conversations between strangers?			15
programme announcements?			16
requests to explain or repeat?			16
'phone-in' radio programmes?			25
children's questions about the world?			20

A   Source: Prowse and McGrath (1984), *Advances*

Learning summary

Grammar check: Using adjectives to describe people

She	has	curly, black	hair.
He	is	overweight	and has a dark mustache.
They	are		hardworking.

Vocabulary

Nouns
beard 20
mustache 20
glasses 20

Family relationships
mother 26
father 26
husband 26
wife 26
daughter 26
son 26
sister 22
brother 26
child 26
children 26
uncle 26
aunt 26
grandfather 26
grandmother 26
grandson 26
granddaughter 26
niece 26
nephew 26
cousin 26
mother-in-law 26
father-in-law 26
brother-in-law 26
sister-in-law 26

Adjectives
good-looking 20
plaid 22

for hair
bald 20
black 20
blond 20
curly 20
gray 20
long 20
shoulder-length 20
straight 20
wavy 20

for body/face type
about __ centimeters (tall) 20
average build 20
fat 20
heavyset 20
medium height 20
overweight 20
round 20
short 20
stocky 20
thin 20
well-built 20

for personality
crazy 26
friendly 20
funny 26
hard-working 26
intelligent 26
kind 26
outgoing 22
quiet 26

serious 26
shy 22
smart 22

Clarification language
Excuse me? 23

Functions and phrases

Asking about people
What's she like? 22
What color is his hair? 23

It's up to you

Look at the words and phrases. How well do you know them? Write a symbol next to each one.

○ = I remember this and can use it.

△ = I remember it but it's difficult to use.

? = I don't remember this at all.

If you don't remember, find the word in the book. Look at the page number. Look at the words. Choose 4 or 5 new words that you want to remember. Try to use the words every day for the next week.

B   Source: Helgesen et al. (1999), *English Firsthand 1*

TASKS: Keys and Commentaries

This section contains answers or possible answers to questions in certain tasks and commentaries on certain other tasks. Contexts vary widely, of course, and in cases where you are asked to reflect on or discuss your own teaching contexts or carry out a practical task, there is normally neither an answer nor a commentary.

TASK 3.5

Applying the criteria listed immediately after the task, and your consideration of the task may well have prompted others, it is fairly easy to come to the conclusion that the least communicative activities are B and C. While both provide contexts for learner responses (that in C being very contrived – why should someone look at another person's diary and complete *her* conversation *in writing*?), there is no freedom to express one's own ideas and no linguistic freedom either (in B very minimal changes are needed to the notes supplied). D is also controlled linguistically, but involves an exchange of messages and opportunities for learners to make choices concerning the event and (minimally) whether to accept the invitation. In extracts B–D the strict linguistic control is obviously related to the level of learner for whom the materials are intended. But language can also be provided in order to support learners' attempts to express their own ideas. In extract A, the picture context limits the ideas that can be expressed and the imperative form in the example gives a strong hint as to how these ideas should be expressed, but the learner still has to find the words. In E and F, learners are free to express their own ideas, and in F even to choose the task they do at stage 2 (though the talk to the class alternative seems to assume a class of mixed nationalities); however, language support is available (at point 3 in extract E).

TASK 4.7

1. *Language*: this is a focus of adaptation in examples 1 and 4, above, and to a lesser extent in example 5. In example 1, the medium through which the

original activity would have almost certainly been carried out (writing) has been changed to provide practice in a different skill (speaking). Though the indications are less clear in example 4, the adapted version certainly seems to lend itself better to oral practice. In both these examples, the language that learners are expected to produce has also been modified in the direction of more natural language use. In example 1, the decontextualised sentences of the original exercise have been replaced by contextualised and appropriate use of 'these' and 'those'; in example 4, a question prompt and short answers have replaced the complete sentences of the original exercise. In example 5, Student A is given very explicit guidance on what to say, but not the exact words.

2. *Contexts and content*: the content of example 2 (the task rather than the text) has been modified to provide an additional and more realistic focus for listening (to find out who the winner was). Though the content of examples 1 and 4 remains the same, the context-less sterility of example 1 has given way to a contextualised and potentially lively activity. The similarly mechanical exercise in example 4 has been adapted in such a way that students can make their own contributions to the mini-scenarios; picture cue cards such as the one illustrated (which could be drawn by students) also help to contextualise the utterances.

3. *Procedures and classroom management*: the traditional (individual, written) formats of Exercises 1 and 4 have also been adapted to provide opportunities for different forms of interaction (groupwork in example 1 and pairwork, perhaps leading to plenary elicitation, in example 4); in example 1, moreover, individual students, as group leaders, take on the role of teacher, selecting the prompts and directing the activity. The Teacher's Notes for example 2 recommend that the teacher play the tape several times; Grant's suggestion is that the teacher focus students' attention on one category of information (one column in the table) at a time; the same suggestion is made in relation to example 3 by Ur, who feels that a pre-listening stage might also be helpful. One positive effect of the radical change of format in example 5 is to create an information gap. However, while cue cards may be in principle a good way of providing for guided spoken interaction, this particular example is a little unfortunate. Try using the cue cards with a friend or simply imagine what each speaker might say. What your 'conversation' will have revealed is that the incoherence of the original material is replicated in the adaptation. In general, cue cards of the type illustrated in example 5 work best when speakers are guided but not constrained too closely (see the example in Chapter 7).

TASK 5.3

1. On the face of it, extracts A and B may look rather similar; however, there

are important differences. In A, the learner's conscious attention is on choosing a verb which is semantically appropriate for the context, but the real point of the exercise is to raise awareness of the fact that the gerund is used after particular verbs (or to provide low-level drill-like practice designed to create automatic associations). In extract B, the verb to be used is supplied and the focus is clearly on the choice between gerund and infinitive. Both focus on knowledge, but whereas A is probably designed to present knowledge using an inductive approach, B is a testing exercise.

2. Here is a one person's analysis. You might want to disagree with some of these answers. n.a. = not applicable.

Extract	Linguistic focus	Knowledge (K) or Skill (S)	Formal Fluency (Form) or Functional Fluency (Function)	Learning (L) or Testing (T)	Inductive (I) or Deductive (D)	Natural?
A	gerund	K	Form	L	I	Yes
B	gerund vs infinitive	K	Form	T		Yes
C	position of frequency adverbs	K	Form	L	I	Yes
D	position of frequency adverbs	K	Form	T		n.a.
E	giving advice (various language forms)	K	Function	L	I	Yes
F	giving advice using 'should' and 'shouldn't'	S	Function	L		n.a.
G	word order in questions	K	Form	T		Yes

H	word order in questions and embedded questions	K	Form	T		n.a
I.	word order in questions and embedded questions	K	Form	L	I	n.a.
J	reporting verbs	K	Form	T		Yes
K	reported speech	K	Function	T		No
L	use of agent in passive sentences	K	Function	L	I	Yes
M	passive	K	Form	T		Yes
N	active vs passive	K	Function	T		Yes

TASK 5.4

Here is a possible analysis.

Extract	Specific linguistic focus	Type of lexical knowledge	Format
A		collocation	matching
B	language of schools and education	word family	multiple choice
C		lexical set	scale
D		hyponomy	classifying
E	language of law	register	matching
F		style (formal/informal)	gap-fill (options supplied)

Extract	Specific linguistic focus	Type of lexical knowledge	Format
G		affixation (*un-/in-* and *-able/-ible*)	gap-fill
H	language of holiday accommodation	word family	gap-fill (options supplied)
I	language of human anatomy	word family/ hyponomy	classifying
J	phrasal verbs (*put* + particle)	denotation	matching

2. One way of making exercises more interesting is by adjusting the level of challenge. One simple technique in matching exercises is to provide more items than can be matched, so that learners have to discard some items. An alternative is to supply one fewer item than is needed, say, and therefore oblige the learner to produce something appropriate. These techniques could easily be used with extracts A and J above.

   Another possibility is to ask students to extend exercises. In relation to exercise G, for instance, pairs or groups could be asked to think of further items with the same *un/in* + *-able/-ible* structure and prepare definitions for these with which to challenge other pairs/groups. This might also be a dictionary-based activity and extend to negative prefixes beginning with *il-, im-* and *ir-*. B and D could also form the basis of an extension task. For D, the task might be a competitive activity (individual, pairs or groups): for example, 'How many more examples of each category can you find? Allow yourself two minutes per category.' Such tasks lend themselves first to the activation of learners' existing knowledge and then the pooling of this knowledge. If class time is too limited, such tasks can also be set for home-work. A related homework exercise might be to do the same activity in the L1 and to find English equivalents for all the L1 items, using a dictionary as necessary.

   You may have noticed a further limitation in most of the exercises: that they focus on the word-level and/or are essentially receptive in nature. While it is not an absolute necessity to build a 'use' stage into every exer-cise, it seems reasonable to suppose that students are more likely to incor-porate new elements into their linguistic repertoire if they have had an opportunity to practise doing so.

   Two of the exercises deal with the kind of hierarchical relationship between words referred to in semantics as hyponomy. In exercise D, for instance, the supermarket sections can be thought of as superordinates (or categories) within which the more specific items – or hyponyms of that superordinate – can be grouped. In addition to the benefits referred to above, that is, activating existing knowledge at the level of the co-hyponyms and pooling this within a group of learners, exercises of this kind can help learners in three further ways. Brainstorming on a specific lexical field (e.g. types of dwelling) not only activates existing neural connections but also enables new links to be made and new items to be incorporated. Learners become aware of gaps in their lexical knowledge, either at the superordinate level (how many intermediate-level learners know general terms such as *cutlery*, *crockery* or *stationery*?) or at the specific level (e.g. items of clothing, containers) and are helped to fill these. On a more productive level, exercises of this type can form the basis for practice in such communication strategies as these:

Strategy 1: if you can't remember or don't know the specific word, use a more general word to express your approximate meaning ('It's a big *animal* (SUPERORDINATE), it's white, and it lives in the Arctic, or is it the Antarctic?' 'Oh, you mean a polar bear') or another specific word that refers to something similar ('It looks a bit like a *screwdriver* (CO-HYPONYM) but it's broader at the end, and you use it to sort of cut wood.' 'Oh, I know what you mean: a chisel.').

Strategy 2: if you don't know the general word, use two or more specific words ('I'm looking for some *paper*, *envelopes*, things like that.' 'Oh yes, you want the stationery department.').

TASK 6.3

EXTRACT	END (Objective)	MEANS
A	confidence to attempt new things	provide model
B	understand native speakers/writers	expose to samples of authentic language
C	stimulate ideas	provide text containing ideas
D	develop specific receptive skill	consciousness-raising activity or (experiential) task
E	extend linguistic repertoire	draw attention to points of language

Your objectives should be ordered as follows: 2, (4), 1, 5, 3.

TASK 7.2

This task asked two questions. Here are 'the answers', with which you can compare your own.

1. Scott et al. (1984) offer the following description of and rationale for their 'standard exercise':

Question 1: prediction
Question 2: skimming for general overview
Question 3: identification of text purpose (factual exposition vs persuasion/ argument)
Question 4: identification of key words (designed to encourage students to consider relative importance of different vocabulary items, disregard those felt to be insignificant, and try to work out meaning from context before using a dictionary)
Question 5: comprehension of main points ('the ability to distinguish a main point from a minor detail is vital') (p. 117)
Question 6: relating structure of text to main points
Question 7ff: eliciting personal reactions ('reading without some kind of personal involvement is likely to be useless' (ibid.)).
Questions 10–13: eliciting students' reactions to their difficulties and progress (students' answers to Q.13 indicate whether they think they have understood all the details; Question 5 provides evidence on whether they have understood the main points).

In relation to their focus on skimming and main points, they point out that skimming is often adequate in determining what not to read or whether to read more carefully and a grasp of the main points of a text may also be sufficient in many situations.

2. Scott et al.'s colleagues in other universities had predicted that the students would find it boring to use the same exercise repeatedly. The students themselves did not say this; they did, however, complain about the length of the exercise and the time it took to do. They also found questions 3, 5 and 6 'quite tricky'.

Explanations and examples were, of course, necessary, but the writers profess themselves satisfied with the exercise. Students' responses to a questionnaire in which they were asked to rate their ability to read authentic texts at the beginning and end of a semester in which they used the standard exercise at least twenty times (sixteen times on self-selected texts and four times for tests) indicated a self-perception of a clear improvement.

References

Acklam, R. (1994), 'The role of the coursebook', *Practical English Teaching* 14.3: 12–14.

Adaskou, K., Britten, D. and Fahsi, B. (1990), 'Design decisions on the cultural content of a secondary English course for Morocco', *ELT Journal* 44.1: 3–10.

Allan, M. (1985), *Teaching English with Video*, Harlow, Essex: Longman.

Allwright, D. (1981), 'What do we want teaching materials for?' *ELT Journal* 36.1: 5–18 [reprinted in R. Rossner and R. Bolitho (eds) (1990), *Currents of Change in English Language Teaching*, Oxford: Oxford University Press, 131–47].

Allwright, R. (1982), 'Perceiving and pursuing learners' needs', in M. Geddes and G. Sturtridge (eds) (1982), *Individualization*, Oxford: Modern English Publications.

Alptekin, C. (1993), 'Target language culture in EFL materials', *ELT Journal* 47.2: 136–43 [reprinted in T. Hedge and N. Whitney (eds) (1996), *Power, Pedagogy and Practice*, Oxford: Oxford University Press, 53–61].

Alptekin, C. and Alptekin, M. (1984), 'The question of culture: EFL teaching in non-English-speaking countries', *ELT Journal* 38.1: 14–20.

Altan, M. (1995), 'Culture in EFL contexts – classroom and coursebooks', *Modern English Teacher* 4.2: 58–60.

Anderson, A. and Lynch, T. (1988), *Listening*, Oxford: Oxford University Press.

Apple, M. (1986), *Teachers and Texts*, New York: Routledge and Kegan Paul.

Apple, M. and Junck, S. (1991), 'You don't have to be a teacher to teach this unit'. Teaching technology and gender in the classroom, *American Educational Research Journal* 27.2: 227–51.

Ariew, R. (1982), 'The textbook as curriculum', in T. Higgs (ed.) (1982), *Curriculum, Competence, and the Foreign Language Teacher*, The ACTFL Foreign Language Education Series, Hastings-on-Hudson, NY: American Council on the Teaching of Foreign Languages [ERIC document Reproduction Service No. ED 210 908].

Assinder, W. (1991), 'Peer teaching, peer learning: one model', *ELT Journal* 45.3: 218–29.

Aston, G. (1997), 'Enriching the learning environment: corpora in ELT', in A. Wichmann, S. Fligelstone, T. McEnery, G. Knowles and A. McEnery (eds) (1997), *Teaching and Language Corpora*, Harlow, Essex: Longman.

Axbey, S. (1989), 'Standard exercises in self-access learning'. Presentation at British Council course on Self-Access Learning, Cambridge, May 1989.

Balarbar, C. (1995), 'Collaborating with subject specialists', in Hidalgo et al. (eds) (1995), *Getting Started: Material Writers on Material Writing*, Singapore: SEAMEO Regional Language Centre, 149–54.

Barnard, R. and Randall, M. (1995), 'Evaluating course materials: a contrastive study in textbook trialling', *System* 23.3: 337–46.

Batstone, R. (1994), *Grammar*, Oxford: Oxford University Press.

Bautista, M. (1995) 'An early attempt at writing an ESP textbook', in Hidalgo et al. (eds) (1995), *Getting Started: Material Writers on Materials Writing*, Singapore: SEAMEO Regional Language Centre, 157–71.

Benson, P. and Voller, P. (eds) (1997), *Autonomy and Independence in Language Learning*, Harlow, Essex: Addison Wesley Longman.

Bicknell, J. (1999), 'Promoting writing and computer literacy skills through student-authored web pages', *TESOL Journal* 8.1: 20–6.

Block, D. (1991), 'Some thoughts on DIY materials design', *ELT Journal* 45.3: 211–17.

Bolitho, R. and Tomlinson, B. (1995) (new edn), *Discover English*, Oxford: Heinemann.

Boswood, T. (ed.) (1997), *New Ways of Using Computers in Language Teaching*, Alexandria, VA: TESOL.

Breen, M. (1989), 'The evaluation cycle for language learning tasks', in R. K. Johnson (ed.) (1989b), *The Second Language Curriculum*, Cambridge: Cambridge University Press, 187–206.

Breen, M. and Candlin, C. (1980), 'The essentials of a communicative curriculum in language teaching', *Applied Linguistics* 1.2: 89–112.

Breen, M. and Candlin, C. (1987), 'Which materials? A consumer's and designer's guide', in L. Sheldon (ed.) (1987a), *ELT Textbooks and Materials: Problems in Evaluation and Development*, ELT Documents 126, Oxford: Modern English Publications/the British Council, 13–28.

Breen, M., Candlin, C., Dam, L. and Gabrielsen, G. (1989), 'The evolution of a teacher training programme', in R. K. Johnson (ed.) (1989b), *The Second Language Curriculum*, Cambridge: Cambridge University Press, 111–35.

Breen, M., Candlin, C. and Waters, A. (1979), 'Communicative materials design: some basic principles', *RELC Journal* 10.2: 1–13.

Brett, P. and Motteram, G. (eds) (2000), *A Special Interest in Computers*, Whitstable, Kent: IATEFL.

Brindley, G. (1989), 'The role of needs analysis in adult ESL programme design', in R. K. Johnson (ed.) (1989b), *The Second Language Curriculum*, Cambridge: Cambridge University Press, 63–78.

British Council (1980), *Projects in Materials Design*, ELT Documents Special, London: The British Council.

Brown, G. (1990a) (2nd edn), *Listening to Spoken English*, Harlow, Essex: Longman.

Brown, G. (1990b), 'Cultural values: the interpretation of discourse', *ELT Journal* 44.1: 11–17.

Bruder, M. (1978) 'Evaluation of foreign language textbooks: a simplified procedure', Appendix 2, in H. Madsen and J. Bowen (1978), *Adaptation in Language Teaching*, Rowley, MA: Newbury House, 209–17.

Brumfit, C. (1979), 'Seven last slogans', *Modern English Teacher* 7.1: 30–1.

Brumfit, C. (ed.) (1984), *General English Syllabus Design*, Oxford: Pergamon/British Council.

Brumfit, C. and Rossner, R. (1982), 'The "decision pyramid" and teacher training for ELT', *ELT Journal* 36.4: 226–31.

Byrd, P. (1995a), 'Writing and publishing textbooks', in P. Byrd (ed.) (1995b), *Materials Writer's Guide*, Boston, MA: Heinle and Heinle, 3–9.

Byrd, P. (ed.) (1995b), *Materials Writer's Guide*, Boston, MA: Heinle and Heinle.

Campbell, C. and Kryszewska, H. (1992), *Learner-based Teaching*, Oxford: Oxford University Press.

Candlin, C. (1981), *Communicative Teaching of English: Principles and Exercise Typology*, Harlow, Essex: Longman.

Candlin, C. and Breen, M. (1979), *Evaluating and Designing Language Teaching Materials*, Practical Papers in English Language Education, vol. 2, University of Lancaster.

Candlin, C. and Murphy, D. (eds) (1987), *Language Learning Tasks*, Lancaster Practical Papers in English Language Education, vol. 7, London: Prentice Hall.

Candlin, C. and Nunan, D. (1987), *Revised Syllabus Specifications for the Omani School English Language Curriculum*, Muscat: Ministry of Education and Youth.

Carter, R., Hughes, R. and McCarthy, M. (1998), 'Telling tails: grammar, the spoken language and materials development', in B. Tomlinson (ed.) (1998a), *Materials Development in Language Teaching*, Cambridge: Cambridge University Press, 67–86.

Chambers, F. (1997), 'Seeking consensus in coursebook evaluation', *ELT Journal* 51.1: 29–35.

Clark, J. (1987), *Curriculum Renewal in School Foreign Language Learning*, Oxford: Oxford University Press.

Clarke, D. (1989a), 'Communicative theory and its influence on materials production: state-of-the-art article', *Language Teaching* 22.2: 73–86.

Clarke, D. (1989b), 'Materials adaptation: why leave it all to the teacher?' *ELT Journal* 43.2: 133–41.

Clarke, M. (1994), 'The dysfunctions of theory/practice discourse', *TESOL Quarterly* 28.1: 9–26.

Coleman, H. (1985), 'Evaluating teachers' guides: do teachers' guides guide teachers?', in Alderson, J. (ed.) (1985), *Evaluation*, Lancaster Practical Papers in English Language Education, vol. 6, Oxford: Pergamon, 83–96.

Cook, V. (1983), 'What should language teaching be about?' *ELT Journal* 37.3: 229–34.

Crookes, G. and Gass, S. (eds) (1993a), *Tasks and Language Learning*, Clevedon, Avon: Multilingual Matters.

Crookes, G. and Gass, S. (eds) (1993b), *Tasks in a Pedagogical Context: Integrating Theory and Practice*, Clevedon, Avon: Multilingual Matters.

Cunningsworth, A. (1979), 'Evaluating course materials', in S. Holden (ed.) (1979), *Teacher Training*, Oxford: Modern English Publications, 31–3.

Cunningsworth, A. (1984), *Evaluating and Selecting EFL Teaching Materials*, London: Heinemann.

Cunningsworth, A. (1987), 'Coursebooks and conversational skills', in L. Sheldon (ed.) (1987a), 45–54.

Cunningsworth, A. (1995), *Choosing Your Coursebook*, Oxford: Heinemann.

Cunningsworth, A. and Kusel, P. (1991), 'Evaluating teachers' guides', *ELT Journal* 45.2: 128–39.

Daoud, A.-M. and Celce-Murcia, M. (1979), 'Selecting and evaluating a textbook', in Celce-Mucia, M. and McIntosh, L. (eds) (1979), *Teaching English as a Second or Foreign Language*, Rowley, MA: Newbury House, 302–7.

Davison, W. (1976), 'Factors in evaluating and selecting texts for the foreign language classroom', *English Language Teaching* 30.4: 310–14.

Deller, S. (1990), *Lessons from the Learner*, Harlow, Essex: Longman.

Dendrinos, B. (1992), *The EFL Textbook and Ideology*, Athens: N. C. Grivas.

Dickinson, L. (1987), *Self-instruction in Language Learning*, Cambridge: Cambridge University Press.

Donovan, P. (1998), 'Piloting – a publisher's view', in B. Tomlinson (ed.) (1998a), *Materials Development in Language Teaching*, Cambridge: Cambridge University Press, 149–89.

Dougill, J. (1987), 'Not so obvious', in L. Sheldon (ed.) (1987a), *ELT Textbooks and Materials: Problems in Evaluation and Development*, ELT Documents 126, Oxford: Modern English Publications/the British Council, 29–36.

Dubin, F. (1995), 'The craft of materials writing', in P. Byrd (ed.) (1995b), *Materials Writer's Guide*, Boston MA: Heinle and Heinle, 13–22.

Dubin, F. and Olshtain, E. (1986), *Course Design: Developing Programs and Materials for Language Learning*, Cambridge: Cambridge University Press.

Eastment, D. (1999), *The Internet and ELT*, Oxford: Summertown Publishing.

Edge, J. and Wharton, S. (1998), 'Autonomy and development: living in the materials world', in B. Tomlinson (ed.) (1998a), *Materials Development in Language Teaching*, Cambridge: Cambridge University Press, 295–310.

Ellis, M. (1986), 'Choosing and using coursebooks 3', *Practical English Teaching* 64: 47–9.

Ellis, M. and Ellis, P. (1987), 'Learning by design: some design criteria for EFL coursebooks', in L. Sheldon (ed.) (1987a), *ELT Textbooks and Materials: Problems in Evaluation and Development*, ELT Documents 126, Oxford: Modern English Publications/the British Council, 90–9.

Ellis, R. (1986), 'Activities and procedures for teacher training', *ELT Journal* 40, 2: 91–9 [reprinted with slightly modified title in J. Richards and D. Nunan (eds) (1990), *Second Language Teacher Education*, Cambridge: Cambridge University Press, 26–36].

Ellis, R. (1997), 'The empirical evaluation of language teaching materials', *ELT Journal* 51.1: 36–42.

Ellis, R. (1998), 'The evaluation of communicative tasks', in B. Tomlinson (ed.) (1998a), *Materials Development in Language Teaching*, Cambridge: Cambridge University Press, 217–38.

Eltis, K. and Low, B. (1985), 'A Review of the Teaching Process – the Adult Migrant Education Program', report to the Adult Migrant Education Program, Canberra: Department of Immigration and Ethnic Affairs.

Farthing, J. (1981), *Business Mazes*, Oxford: Hart-Davis.

Flores, M. (1995), 'Materials development: a creative process', in Hidalgo et al. (eds) (1995), *Getting Started: Material Writers on Materials Writing*, Singapore: SEAMEO Regional Language Centre, 57–66.

Flowerdew, L. (1994), 'Incorporating aspects of style and tone in self-access CALL courseware', in D. Gardner and L. Miller (eds) (1994), *Directions in Self-access Language Learning*, Hong Kong: Hong Kong University Press, 133–43.

Forman, D. and Ellis, D. (1991), 'Students as a materials producing resource', *Practical English Teaching* 11.3: 49.

Forrester, J. (1994), 'Self-access language learning for secondary school students', in D. Gardner and L. Miller (eds) (1994), *Directions in Self-access Language Learning*, Hong Kong: Hong Kong University Press, 127–32.

Forsyth, I. (1998) (2nd edn), *Teaching and Learning Materials and the Internet*, London: Kogan Page.

Fortune, A. (1992), 'Self-study grammar practice: learners' views and preferences', *ELT Journal* 46.2: 160–71.

Fox, G. (1998), 'Using corpus data in the classroom', in B. Tomlinson (ed.) (1998a), *Materials Development in Language Teaching*, Cambridge: Cambridge University Press, 25–43.

Gadd, N. (1998), 'Towards less humanistic English teaching', *ELT Journal* 52.3: 223–34.

Gairns, R. and Redman, S. (1986), *Working with Words*, Cambridge: Cambridge University Press.

Gardner, D. (1994), 'Creating simple interactive video for self-access', in D. Gardner and L. Miller (eds) (1994), *Directions in Self-access Language Learning*, Hong Kong: Hong Kong University Press, 107–14.

Gardner, D. and Miller, L. (eds) (1994), *Directions in Self-access Language Learning*, Hong Kong: Hong Kong University Press.

Gardner, D. and Miller, L. (1999), *Establishing Self-access: From Theory to Practice*, Cambridge: Cambridge University Press.

Geddes, M. and Sturtridge, G. (1982), *Video in the Language Classroom*, London: Heinemann.

Giles, R. (1996), HTML, editor for the Macintosh. WWW document URL http://www.hwg/org

Graham, A. (1994), 'Working with student-made transcripts', *Modern English Teacher* 3.4: 27–9.

Grant, N. (1987), *Making the Most of Your Textbook*, Harlow, Essex: Longman.

Grellet, F. (1981), *Developing Reading Skills*, Cambridge: Cambridge University Press.

Hadfield, J. (1990), *Intermediate Communication Games*, Walton-on-Thames, Surrey: Nelson.

Hall, D. (1995), 'Materials production: theory and practice', in Hidalgo et al. (eds) (1995), *Getting Started: Materials Writers on Materials Writing*, Singapore: SEAMEO Regional Language Centre, 8–24.

Harmer, J. (1983/1991), 'Appendix: Evaluating Materials', in J. Harmer, *The Practice of English Language Teaching*, Harlow, Essex: Longman, 276–84.

Harmer, J. (1998), *How to Teach English*, Harlow, Essex: Longman.

Haycraft, J. (1978), *An Introduction to English Language Teaching*, Harlow, Essex: Longman.

Head, K. and Taylor, P. (1997), *Readings in Teacher Development*, Oxford: Heinemann.

Heaton, J. (1990), *Classroom Testing*, Harlow, Essex: Longman.

Hedge, T. (1988), *Writing*, Oxford: Oxford University Press.

Hedge, T. (2000), *Teaching and Learning in the Language Classroom*, Oxford: Oxford University Press.

Hedge, T. and Whitney, N. (eds) (1996), *Power, Pedagogy and Practice*, Oxford: Oxford University Press.

Henrichsen, L. (1983), 'Teacher preparation needs in TESOL', *RELC Journal* 14.1: 18–45.

Hewings, M. (1991), 'The interpretation of illustrations in ELT materials', *ELT Journal* 45.3: 237–44.

Hidalgo, A., Hall, D. and Jacobs, G. (eds) (1995), Getting Started: *Materials Writers on Materials Writing*, Singapore: SEAMEO Regional Language Centre.

Hood, S., Solomon, N. and Burns, A. (1995), *Focus on Reading*, Sydney: NCELTR, Macquarie University.

Hubbard, R., Jones, H., Thornton, B. and Wheeler, R. (1983), *A Training Course for TEFL*, Oxford: Oxford University Press.

Hunt, R., Neher, B. and Banton, A. (1993), 'Planning makes perfect', *Practical English Teaching* 14.1: 19–21.

Hutchinson, E. (1996), 'What do teachers and learners actually do with textbooks? Teacher and learner use of a fisheries-based ELT textbook in the Philippines', unpublished PhD thesis, University of Lancaster.

Hutchinson, T. (1987), 'What's underneath?: an interactive view of materials evaluation', in L. Sheldon (ed.) (1987a), *ELT Textbooks and Materials: Problems in Evaluation and Development*, ELT Documents 126, Oxford: Modern English Publications/the British Council, 37–44.

Hutchinson, T. and Torres, E. (1994), 'The textbook as agent of change', *ELT Journal* 48.4: 315–28 [reprinted in T. Hedge and N. Whitney (eds) (1996), *Power, Pedagogy and Practice*, Oxford: Oxford University Press, 307–23].

Hutchinson, T. and Waters, A. (1987), *English for Specific Purposes: a Learning-Centred Approach*, Cambridge: Cambridge University Press.

Johns, T. and King, P. (eds) (1991), 'Classroom concordancing', *ELR Journal*, Birmingham University.

Johnson, F. (1972), 'The design, development and dissemination of instructional materials', *RELC Journal* 3: 1–18.

Johnson, R. (1986), 'Selecting a coursebook: a realistic approach', in S. Holden (ed.) (1986), *Techniques of Teaching: From Theory to Practice*, Papers from the 1985 Bologna conference. Oxford: Modern English Publications/British Council 54–7.

Johnson, R. K. (1989a), 'Overview', in R. K. Johnson (ed.) (1989b), *The Second Language Curriculum*, Cambridge: Cambridge University Press, xi–xxii.

Johnson, R. K. (ed.) (1989b), *The Second Language Curriculum*, Cambridge: Cambridge University Press.

Johnson, S. and Johnson, R. (1970), *Developing Individualized Instructional Materials*, Palo Alto, CA: Westinghouse.

Jolly, D. and Bolitho, R. (1998), 'A framework for materials writing', in B. Tomlinson (ed.) (1998a), *Materials Development in Language Teaching*, Cambridge: Cambridge University Press, 90–115.

Jonassen, D. (2000), *Computers in the Classroom: Mindtools for Critical Thinking*, Englewood Cliffs, NJ: Prentice Hall.

Jones, C. and Trackman, I. (1988), *Choicemaster, Matchmaster*, Computer Authoring Programs, London: Wida Software Ltd.

Jones, C. and Trackman, I. (1992), *Gapmaster 2, Storyboard 2, Testmaster 2*, Computer Authoring Programs, London: Wida Software Ltd.

Jor, G. (1999), 'Web teaching in Hong Kong: a story', in *The Hong Kong-America Center Occasional Paper Series*, no. 13, Fall 1999, Hong Kong: The Hong Kong-America Center: 20–35. Also available at: http://humanum.arts.cuhk.edu.hk/~cmc/eltmatters/e-mail.htm#projects

Jordan, R. (ed.) (1983), *Case Studies in ELT*, Glasgow: Collins.

Katz, A. (1996), 'Teaching style: a way to understand instruction in language classrooms', in K. Bailey and D. Nunan (eds) (1996), *Voices from the Language Classroom*, Cambridge: Cambridge University Press, 57–87.

Kissinger, L. (1990), 'Universal worksheets for using with satellite television'. Poster presentation at TESOL Conference, San Francisco, USA, 6–10 March 1990.

Klippel, F. (1984), *Keep Talking*, Cambridge: Cambridge University Press.

Krashen, S. (1982), *Principles and Practice in Second Language Acquisition*, Oxford: Pergamon.

Lado, R. (1956), 'Patterns of difficulty in vocabulary', *Language Learning* 6: 23–41 [reprinted in H. Allen and R. Campbell (eds) (1972) (2nd edn), *Teaching English as a Second Language: A Book of Readings*, New York: McGraw-Hill: 275–88].

Lake, L. (1997), 'Survey review: learner training in EFL coursebooks', *ELT Journal* 51.2: 169–82.

Lakoff, G. and Johnson, M. (1980), *Metaphors We Live By*, Chicago: University of Chicago Press.

Lee. J. (1975) 'Choosing and using a textbook', *English Teaching Forum* 13: 3/4 (Special Issue Pt 2): 364–5.

Littlejohn, A. (1992), 'Why are ELT materials the way they are?' Unpublished PhD thesis, Lancaster University.

Littlejohn, A. (1997), 'Self-access work and curriculum ideologies', in P. Benson and P. Voller (eds) (1997), *Autonomy and Independence in Language Learning*, Harlow, Essex: Addison Wesley Longman, 181–91.

Littlejohn, A. (1998), 'The analysis of language teaching materials: inside the Trojan horse', in B. Tomlinson (ed.) (1998a), *Materials Development in Language Teaching*, Cambridge: Cambridge University Press, 190–216.

Littlejohn, A. and Windeatt, S. (1989), 'Beyond language learning: perspectives on materials design', in R. K. Johnson (ed.) (1989b), *The Second Language Curriculum*, Cambridge: Cambridge University Press, 155–75.

Littlewood, W. (1981), *Communicative Language Teaching*, Cambridge: Cambridge University Press.

Lonergan, J. (1984), *Video in Language Teaching*, Cambridge: Cambridge University Press.

Low, G. (1987), 'The need for a multi-perspective approach to the evaluation of foreign language teaching materials', *Evaluation and Research in Education* 1.1: 19–29.

Low, G. (1989), 'Appropriate design: the internal organisation of course units', in R. K. Johnson (ed.) (1989b), *The Second Language Curriculum*, Cambridge: Cambridge University Press, 136–54.

Lum, Y. L. and Brown, R. (1994), 'Guidelines for the production of in-house self-access materials', *ELT Journal* 48.2: 150–5.

Lynch, T. (1991), 'On questioning roles in the classroom', *ELT Journal* 45.3: 201–10.

Lynch, T. (1996), 'Influences on course revision: an EAP case study', in M. Hewings and T. Dudley-Evans (eds) (1996), *Course Evaluation and Design in EAP*, Review of ELT 6.1, Hemel Hempstead, Herts: Prentice Hall Macmillan, 26–35.

Madsen, H. and Bowen, J. (1978), *Adaptation in Language Teaching*, Rowley, MA: Newbury House.

Maher, J. (1988), 'Handouts from a Seminar-Workshop on English for Medicine and the Allied Sciences held at De La Salle University, Manila, 25 April–5 May 1988.

Mak, L. (1994), 'From English teacher to producer: how to develop a multimedia computer simulation for teaching ESL', in D. Gardner and L. Miller (eds) (1994), *Directions in Self-access Language Learning*, Hong Kong: Hong Kong University Press, 145–54.

Malamah-Thomas, A. (1987), *Classroom Interaction*, Oxford: Oxford University Press.

Maley, A. (1998), 'Squaring the circle – reconciling materials as constraint with materials as empowerment', in B. Tomlinson (ed.) (1998a), *Materials Development in Language Teaching*, Cambridge: Cambridge University Press, 279–94.

Maley, A. and Duff, A. (1982), *Drama Techniques in Language Learning*, Cambridge: Cambridge University Press.

Masuhara, H. (1998), 'What do teachers really want from coursebooks?', in B. Tomlinson (ed.) (1998a), *Materials Development in Language Teaching*, Cambridge: Cambridge University Press, 239–60.

Matthews, A. (1991), 'Choosing the best available textbook', in A. Matthews, M. Spratt and L. Dangerfield (eds) (1991), *At the Chalkface*, London: Nelson, 202–6.

McDonough, J. and Shaw, C. (1993), *Materials and Methods in ELT*, Oxford: Blackwell.

McGrath, I. (1992), 'The ideas grid', *Practical English Teaching* 12.4: 13–14.

McGrath, I. (1994), 'The open slot', *Practical English Teaching* 14.4: 19–21.

McGrath, I. (1997), 'Evaluating In-service Programmes for Language Teachers'. Unpublished PhD dissertation, University of Edinburgh.

Methold, K. (1972), 'The practical aspects of instructional materials preparation', *RELC Journal* 3.1/2: 88–97.

Mitchell, R., Parkinson, B. and Johnstone, R. (1981), *The Foreign Language Classroom: An Observational Study*, Stirling: University of Stirling Department of Education.

Morrall, A. (1999), 'Teaching English by the Web: strengths, weaknesses, opportunities and threats', in *The Hong Kong-America Center Occasional Paper Series*, no. 13, Fall 1999, Hong Kong: The Hong Kong-America Center: 4–14. Also available at http://elc.polyu.edu.hk/CILL/ICTED99/ICTED99PaperInt–m

Mosback, G. (1984), 'Making a structure-based course more communicative', *ELT Journal* 38.3: 178–86.

Munby, J. (1978), *Communicative Syllabus Design*, Cambridge: Cambridge University Press.

Murphey, T. (1992), *Music and Song*, Oxford: Oxford University Press.

Nathenson, M. and Henderson, E. (1980), *Using Students' Feedback to Improve Learning Materials*, London: Croom Helm.

Naunton, J. (1993), *Think First Certificate*, Harlow: Pearson.

Nunan, D. (1988a), *The Learner-Centred Curriculum*, Cambridge: Cambridge University Press.

Nunan, D. (1988b), 'Principles for designing language teaching materials', *Guidelines* 10.2: 1–24.

Nunan, D. (1988c), *Syllabus Design*, Oxford: Oxford University Press.

Nunan, D. (1989), *Designing Tasks for the Communicative Classroom*, Cambridge: Cambridge University Press.

Nunan, D. (1991), *Language Teaching Methodology*, Hemel Hempstead, Herts: Prentice Hall.

Nunan, D. (1997), 'Designing and adapting materials to encourage learner autonomy', in P. Benson and P. Voller (eds) (1997), *Autonomy and Independence in Language Learning*, Harlow, Essex: Addison Wesley Longman, 192–203.

Nunan, D. (1999), *Second Language Teaching and Learning*, Boston, MA: Heinle and Heinle.

Nuttall, C. (1982/1996) (new edn), *Teaching Reading Skills in a Second Language*, Oxford: Heinemann.

O'Neill, R. (1979), *Kernel One*, London: Longman.

O'Neill, R. (1982), 'Why use textbooks?', *ELT Journal* 36.2: 104–11 [reprinted in R. Rossner and R. Bolitho (eds) (1990), *Currents of Change in English Language Teaching*, Oxford: Oxford University Press, 148–56].

O'Neill, R. (1993), 'Are textbooks symptoms of a disease?', *Practical English Teaching* 14.1: 11–13.

Parkinson, B., Mitchell, R. and McIntyre, D. (1982), *An Independent Evaluation of 'Tour de France'*, Stirling: University of Stirling Department of Education.

Pattison, P. (1987), *Developing Communication Skills*, Cambridge: Cambridge University Press.

Peñaflorida, A. (1995), 'The Process of materials development: a personal experience', in Hidalgo et al. (eds) (1995), *Getting Started: Material Writers on Materials Writing*, Singapore: SEAMEO Regional Language Centre, 172–86.

Porreca, K. (1984), 'Sexism in current ESL textbooks', *TESOL Quarterly* 18.4: 705–24.

Prabhu, N. (1987), *Second Language Pedagogy*, Cambridge: Cambridge University Press.

Prodromou, L. (1990), 'A mixed-ability lesson', *Practical English Teaching* 10.3: 28–9.

Prodromou, L. (1992a), 'What culture? Which culture? Cross-cultural factors in language learning', *ELT Journal* 46.1: 39–50.

Prodromou, L. (1992b), *Mixed Ability Classes,* London: Macmillan.

Prowse, P. (1998), 'How writers write: testimony from authors', in B. Tomlinson (ed.) (1998a), *Materials Development in Language Teaching*, Cambridge: Cambridge University Press, 130–45.

Rajan, B. (1995), 'Developing instructional materials for adult workers', in Hidalgo et al. (eds) (1995), *Getting Started: Materials Writers on Materials Writing*, Singapore: SEAMEO Regional Language Centre, 187–208.

Rea-Dickens, P. (1994), 'Evaluation and English language teaching. State-of-the-art article', *Language Teaching* 27: 71–91.

Rea-Dickens, P. and Germaine, K. (1992), *Evaluation*, Oxford: Oxford University Press.

Richards, J. (1985), *The Context of Language Teaching*, Cambridge: Cambridge University Press.

Richards, J. (1993), 'Beyond the textbook: the role of commercial materials in language teaching', *RELC Journal* 24.1: 1–14.

Richards, J. (1995), 'Easier said than done: an insider's account of a textbook project', in Hidalgo et al. (eds) (1995), *Getting Started: Materials Writers on Materials Writing*, Singapore: SEAMEO Regional Language Centre, 95–135.

Richards, J. (1998), 'Textbooks: help or hindrance in teaching?', Ch. 7, in J. Richards, *Beyond Training: Perspectives on Language Teacher Education*, Cambridge: Cambridge University Press, 125–40.

Richards, J. and Mahoney, D. (1996), 'Teachers and textbooks: a survey of beliefs and practices', *Perspectives* (Working Papers of the Department of English, City University, Hong Kong) 8.1: 40–63.

Richards, J. and Rodgers, T. (1986), *Approaches and Methods in Language Teaching*, Cambridge: Cambridge University Press.

Richards, K. (1995), 'Direction and debate in distance materials for teacher development', in R. Howard and I. McGrath (eds) (1995), *Distance Education for Language Teachers*, Clevedon, Avon: Multilingual Matters, 142–60.

Rinvolucri, M. and Berer, M. (1981), *Mazes*, London: Heinemann.

Risager, K. (1990), 'Cultural references in European textbooks: an evaluation of recent tendencies', in D. Buttjes and M. Byram (eds) (1990), *Mediating Languages and Culture*, Clevedon, Avon: Multilingual Matters.

Rivers, W. (1968), *Teaching Foreign Language Skills*, Chicago: University of Chicago.

Robinson, P. (1991), *ESP Today*, Hemel Hempstead, Herts: Prentice Hall.

Romero, R. (1975), 'What textbook shall we use?', *English Teaching Forum* 13: 3/4 (Special Issue Pt 2): 362–3 [originally printed in *Forum* in 1970].

Rossner, R. (1988), 'Materials for communicative language teaching and learning', in C. Brumfit (ed.) (1988), *Annual Review of Applied Linguistics 8*, Cambridge: Cambridge University Press: 140–63.

Rossner, R. and Bolitho, R. (eds) (1990), *Currents of Change in English Language Teaching*, Oxford: Oxford University Press.

Rost, M. (1990), *Listening in Language Learning*, Harlow, Essex: Longman.

Rozul, R. (1995), 'ESP materials development: the writing process', in Hidalgo et al. (eds) (1995), *Getting Started: Materials Writers on Materials Writing*, Singapore: SEAMEO Regional Language Centre, 209–18.

Rutherford, W. (1987), *Second Language Grammar: Learning and Teaching*, Harlow, Essex: Longman.

Sandholtz, J., Ringstaff, C. and Dwyer, C. (1997), *Teaching with Technology: Creating student-centred classrooms*, New York: Teachers College, Columbia University.

Schmitt, N. (2000), *Vocabulary in Language Teaching*, Cambridge: Cambridge University Press.

Scott, M., Carioni, L., Zanatta, M., Bayer, E. and Quintanilha, T. (1984), 'Using a "standard exercise" in teaching reading comprehension', *ELT Journal* 38.2: 114–20.

Shannon, P. (1987), 'Commercial reading materials: a technological ideology, and the deskilling of teachers', *The Elementary School Journal* 87.3: 307–29.

Sheerin, S. (1989), *Self-access*, Oxford: Oxford University Press.

Sheldon, L. (ed.) (1987a), *ELT Textbooks and Materials: Problems in Evaluation and Development*, ELT Documents 126, Oxford: Modern English Publications/the British Council.

Sheldon, L. (1987b), 'Introduction', in L. Sheldon (ed.) (1987a), *ELT Textbooks and Materials: Problems in Evaluation and Development*, ELT Documents 126, Oxford: Modern English Publications/the British Council, 1–10.

Sheldon, L. (1988), 'Evaluating ELT textbooks and materials', *ELT Journal* 42.4: 237–46.

Shive, G. (1999), 'Collaborative learning across cultures via the Web', in *The Hong Kong-America Center Occasional Paper Series*, no. 13, Fall 1999, Hong Kong: The Hong Kong-America Center, 15–19.

Sinclair, B. and Ellis, G. (1992), 'Survey review: learner training in EFL course books', *ELT Journal* 46.2: 209–25.

Skierso, A. (1991), 'Textbook selection and evaluation', in M. Celce-Murcia, (ed.) (1991) (2nd edn), *Teaching English as a Second or Foreign Language*, Boston: Heinle and Heinle, 432–453.

Slaouti, D. (2000), 'Computers and writing in the classroom', in P. Brett and G. Motteram (eds) (2000), *A Special Interest in Computers*, Whitstable, Kent: IATEFL, 9–30.

Sperling, D. (1997), *The Internet Guide for English Language Teachers*, Upper Saddle River, NJ: Prentice Hall Regents.

Stern, H. (1983), *Fundamental Concepts of Language Teaching*, Oxford: Oxford University Press.

Stevick, E. (1972), 'Evaluating and adapting language materials', in H. Allen, and R. Campbell (eds) (1972), *Teaching English as a Second Language: A Book of Readings*, New York: McGraw Hill, 101–20.

Stevick, E. (1980), *A Way and Ways*, Rowley MA: Newbury House.

Sunderland, J. (1992), 'Gender in the EFL classroom', *ELT Journal* 46.1: 81–91 [reprinted in T. Hedge and N. Whitney (eds) (1996), *Power, Pedagogy and Practice*, Oxford: Oxford University Press, 88–100].

Sunderland, J. (ed.) (1994), *Exploring Gender*, Hemel Hempstead, Herts: Prentice Hall.

Swales, S. (1992), 'Let students make their own worksheets', *Practical English Teaching* 12.4: 58–9.

Tang, L. H. (2001), 'Evaluating Textbooks – a Hong Kong Study'. Unpublished MA ELT dissertation. The Hong Kong Polytechnic University.

Thompson, G. (1995), *Collins Cobuild Concordance Sampler 3, Reporting*, London: HarperCollins.

Thornbury, S. (1997), *About Language*, Cambridge: Cambridge University Press.

Thorne, A. and Thorne, C. (2000), 'Building bridges on the Web: using the Internet for cultural studies', in P. Brett and G. Motteram (eds) (2000), *A Special Interest in Computers*, Whitstable, Kent: IATEFL, 59–72.

Thurstun, J. and Candlin, C. (1997), *Exploring Academic English*, Sydney: NCELTR, Macquarie University.

Tibbetts, J. (1994), 'Materials production for self–access centres in secondary schools', in D. Gardner and L. Miller (eds) (1994), *Directions in Self-access Language Learning*, Hong Kong: Hong Kong University Press, 115–126.

Tice, J. (1991), 'The textbook straitjacket', *Practical English Teaching* 11.3: 23.

Tickoo, M. (1995), 'Materials for a state-level system: a retrospective record', in Hidalgo et al. (eds) (1995), *Getting Started: Materials Writers on Materials Writing*, Singapore: SEAMEO Regional Language Centre, 31–44.

Tomlinson, B. (ed.) (1998a), *Materials Development in Language Teaching*, Cambridge: Cambridge University Press.

Tomlinson, B. (1998b), 'Preface', in B. Tomlinson (ed.) (1998a), *Materials Development in Language Teaching*, Cambridge: Cambridge University Press.

Tomlinson, B. (1998c), 'Introduction', in B. Tomlinson (ed.) (1998a), *Materials Development in Language Teaching*, Cambridge: Cambridge University Press, 1–24.

Tomlinson, B. (1998d), 'Comments on Part B', in B. Tomlinson (ed.) (1998a), *Materials Development in Language Teaching*, Cambridge: Cambridge University Press, 146–8.

Tomlinson, B. (1998e), 'Comments on Part C', in B. Tomlinson (ed.) (1998a), *Materials Development in Language Teaching*, Cambridge: Cambridge University Press, 261–4.

Tomlinson, B. (1998f), 'Access-self materials', in B. Tomlinson (ed.) (1998a), *Materials Development in Language Teaching*, Cambridge: Cambridge University Press, 320–36.

Tomlinson, B. (1999), 'Developing criteria for evaluating L2 materials', *IATEFL Issues*, Feb.–Mar. 1999: 10–13.

Torres, E. (1993), 'A fish's story: insights from investigating use of a fisheries-based ESP textbook in classrooms', in J. Edge and K. Richards (eds) (1993), *Teachers Develop Teachers Research*, Oxford: Heinemann, 173–8.

Tribble, C. (2000), 'Practical uses for language corpora in ELT', in P. Brett and G. Motteram (eds) (2000), *A Special Interest in Computers*, Whitstable, Kent: IATEFL, 31–41.

Tribble, C. and Jones, G. (1990), *Concordances in the Classroom*, Harlow, Essex: Longman.

Tucker, C. A. (1975), 'Evaluating beginning textbooks', *English Teaching Forum* 13: 3/4 (Special Issue Pt 2): 355–61 [originally printed in 1968 in *English Teaching Forum*, 6, 5, pp. 8–15, and subsequently reprinted as Appendix 3 in H. Madsen and J. Bowen (1978), *Adaptation in Language Teaching*, Rowley, MA: Newbury House, 219–37].

Tudor, I. (1993), 'Teacher roles in the learner–centred classroom', *ELT Journal* 47.1: 22–31 [reprinted in T. Hedge and N. Whitney (eds) (1996), *Power, Pedagogy and Practice*, Oxford: Oxford University Press, 271–82].

Tudor, I. (1996), *Learner Centredness as Language Education*, Cambridge: Cambridge University Press.

Underwood, M. (1989), *Teaching Listening*, Harlow, Essex: Longman.

Ur, P. (1981), *Discussions That Work*, Cambridge: Cambridge University Press.

Ur, P. (1984), *Teaching Listening Comprehension*, Cambridge: Cambridge University Press.

Ur, P. (1996), *A Course in Language Teaching*, Cambridge: Cambridge University Press.

Ur, P. and Wright, A. (1992), *Five-minute Activities*, Cambridge: Cambridge University Press.

Vallance, M. (1998), 'The design and use of an Internet resource for business English learners', *ELT Journal* 52.1: 38–42.

Vasilyeva-McGrath, N. (1997), 'Role cards for testing oral Russian', Language Centre, University of Nottingham (mimeo).

Walker, C. (1987), 'Individualizing reading', *ELT Journal* 41.1: 46–56.

Wallace, C. (1992), *Reading*, Oxford: Oxford University Press.

Wallace, M. (1981), *Teaching Vocabulary*, Oxford: Macmillan.

Warschauer, M. (ed.) (1995), *Virtual Connections: Online Activities and Projects for Networking Language Learners*, Hawaii: National Foreign Language Resource Center, University of Hawaii at Manoa.

Warschauer, M. and Kern, R. (eds) (2000), '*Network-based Language Teaching: Concepts and Practice*', Cambridge: Cambridge University Press.

Watcyn-Jones, P. (1981), *Pair work*, London: Penguin.

Weir, C. and Roberts, J. (1994), *Evaluation in ELT*, Oxford: Blackwell.

Wessels, C. (1987), *Drama*, Oxford: Oxford University Press.

Wessels, C. (1991), 'From improvisation to publication on an English through Drama course', *ELT Journal* 45.3: 230–6.

Wessels, C. (1999), *Soap Opera*, London: Pearson.

Whitaker, S. (1983), 'Comprehension questions: about face?', *ELT Journal* 37.4: 329–34.

White, R. (1988), *The ELT Curriculum*, Oxford: Blackwell.

Wichmann, A., Fligelstone, A., Knowles, G. and McEnery, A. (eds) (1997), *Teaching and Language Corpora*, Harlow: Essex: Longman.

Widdowson, H. (1979a), *Explorations in Applied Linguistics*, Oxford: Oxford University Press.

Widdowson, H. (1979b), 'Gradual approximation', in H. Widdowson (1979a), *Explorations in Applied Linguistics*, Oxford: Oxford University Press, 75–85.

Widdowson, H. (1979c), 'Two types of communication exercise', in H. Widdowson (1979), *Explorations in Applied Linguistics*, Oxford: Oxford University Press, 65–74.

Williams, D. (1983), 'Developing criteria for textbook evaluation', *ELT Journal* 37.3: 251–5.

Willis, J. (1996), *A Framework for Task-based Learning*, Harlow, Essex: Longman.

Willis, J. (1998), 'Concordances in the classroom without a computer: assembling and exploiting concordances of common words', in B. Tomlinson (ed.), (1998a), *Materials Development in Language Teaching*, Cambridge: Cambridge University Press, 44–66.

Windeatt, S., Hardisty, D. and Eastment, D. (2000), *The Internet*, Oxford: Oxford University Press.

Wright, A. (1976), *Visual Materials for the Language Teacher*, London: Longman.

Wright, A., Betteridge, D. and Buckby, M. (1984), *Games for Language Learning*, Cambridge: Cambridge University Press.

Wright, T. (1987), *Roles of Teachers and Learners*, Oxford: Oxford University Press.

Wright, T. (1994), *Investigating English*, London: Edward Arnold.

Young, R. (1980), 'Modular course design', in British Council (1980), *Projects in Materials Design*, ELT Documents Special, London: The British Council, 222–31.

Yuen, K. (1997), Review of Allwright's (1981) paper 'Why use textbooks?' BEd assignment. University of Nottingham.

Index